A STORY *of* IRELAND

The people and events that shaped the country

John McCormack

MENTOR BOOKS

First Published in 2002 by

MENTOR BOOKS
43 Furze Road,
Sandyford Industrial Estate,
Dublin 18,
Republic of Ireland.

Tel: + 353 1 295 2112 / 3   Fax: + 353 1 295 2114
e-mail: admin@mentorbooks.ie
www.mentorbooks.ie

ISBN 1-84210-159-5

A catalogue record for this book
is available from the British Library

Cover Photograph courtesy of The Oriel Gallery

Edited by: Una Whelan

Design and layout by: Kathryn McKinney

Illustrations by: Nicola Sedgwick

Printed in Ireland by ColourBooks Ltd.

1 3 5 7 9 10 8 6 4 2

CONTENTS

To my wife
Monica
with love and gratitude

1

◎

FROM PAGAN GODS TO SAINTS AND SCHOLARS

Archaeologists and historians estimate that the earliest inhabitants of Ireland came to the country sometime between 7500 and 6500 BC in the Mesolithic (Middle Stone Age) period. They were mainly fishermen and probably crossed over from the nearest points in Wales and Scotland. Traces of their settlements have been discovered all over the country, from Coleraine in the North, to the Blackwater in the South, in the Shannon basin and in County Louth.

With the coming of Neolithic (New Stone Age) Man about 3200 BC, a more advanced kind of civilisation evolved. The great passage graves at Newgrange and other sites in the Boyne Valley were the work of these people. These marvellous constructions were built about 3000 BC and as such pre-date Stonehenge (ca. 2000 BC) and the pyramids of Egypt (ca. 2500 BC).

In spite of the degree of civilisation displayed by the early settlers in Ireland they do not seem to have left behind any written records. What we know of them has been gleaned from the deductions of archaeologists and the writings of Roman and Greek historians in Europe.

The only 'written' evidence left behind dates from the early centuries AD and consists of marks carved on standing stones, which were often used to indicate important graves. Many examples have been found in Ireland and some in Wales and Scotland. These marks are parts of a primitive alphabet called *ogham*.

The method was extremely crude and limited in scope, being able to record little more than the name of the person buried beneath the stone. (The key to reading these ogham inscriptions was found in the *Book of Ballymote* in the fourteenth century.)

———— ◎ ————

The passage graves at Newgrange and other sites in the Boyne Valley date from 3200 BC or earlier, about 500 years before the pyramids of Egypt were built.

———— ◎ ————

When the portal tomb of Poulnabrone in County Clare was investigated it was found to contain the remains of about twenty adults, male and female, in it. Radiocarbon dating of the bones suggests that burials took place between 3800 and 3200 BC. The skeleton of a newborn baby discovered among them dated from the Bronze Age and had obviously been placed in the tomb much later on. This suggests that the portal tomb was of religious significance for the people at the time.

———— ◎ ————

Various remains from Neolithic times have been found at such places as Ballyglass, County Mayo, Ballynagilly, County Tyrone and especially at Lough Gur, County Limerick where a collection of neolithic houses, cooking utensils, tools and personal items have been discovered.

———— ◎ ————

Irish people with 'Mac' or 'O' in their surnames are all said to be descended from the Milesians.

———— ◎ ————

Various names have been applied to Ireland in literature. It has been called *Éire, Banba, Foðhla* (which are said to be the names of three queens of the *Tuatha Dé Danann*), and also *Inis Fáil* (Island of Destiny) and *Hibernia*.

———— ◎ ————

The Celts were fond of food and drink and great feasts feature largely in their sagas. The greatest warrior present at the feast would be given 'The Hero's Portion' but this could lead to trouble. There was often a fight to the death to decide who would receive the honour.

———— ◎ ————

Traces of the language of these earliest settlers are said to exist in some of the country's place names.

Ogham consisted of twenty-five characters, with notches carved on the edges of standing stones to indicate letters.

Even though no written history survives from the early settlers there exists a rich mythology and store of legends which have been handed on from generation to generation and eventually written down. These legends tell of the incredible exploits of heroes and gods and there is no way of knowing if they have any basis in fact at all. This mythical 'history' relates how Five Invasions of Ancient Ireland occurred. The first invasion brought the *Parthalonians* from Greece who were about one thousand in number. Three hundred years later they had all perished from a plague.

Next came the *Nemedians* who were constantly harassed by a race of fierce sea robbers called the *Fomorians*. So many battles were fought that eventually there were very few left on either side. Some of the remaining *Nemedians* fled back to Greece from whence they returned several hundred years later under the name

———— ◎ ————

The Celts were a warlike people, their main weapons being iron swords and spears. They often rode into battle on light two-wheeled chariots, which carried two men – the warrior and his charioteer. Their favourite form of fighting was single combat where the best warrior from each side settled the issue. According to the historians they sometimes fought completely naked!

———— ◎ ————

An unusual method of cooking was used by the Celts. As metal containers were scarce and too valuable to be used in cooking they filled a pit in the ground with water and heated large stones in a nearby fire. Then by adding the heated stones to the water they could gradually bring it to boiling point. Cooler stones were constantly removed and replaced by new heated ones. Meat was then carefully wrapped in grass and rushes and placed in the boiling water until cooked. (Experiments in more recent times have shown that this method works perfectly well!) A cooking pit like this was called a *fulacht fia* (from the Gaelic *fulacht* meaning a cooking place and *fia* probably coming from *fiáin* meaning wild). Thousands of the cooking pits have been found all over Ireland and excavations in the oldest parts of Dublin in the twentieth century have discovered large stones which may have been used for this very purpose. Another refinement of the same principle was to place the heated stones in the cauldrons filled with water.

———— ◎ ————

Celtic burial customs included cremation and the erection of Ogham stones to mark the graves.

———— ◎ ————

St Patrick spent seven years in Connacht converting the people there and during that time he is said to have spent an entire Lent in fasting and prayer on the summit of Croagh Patrick. This event is commemorated by devout pilgrims to this day.

———— ◎ ————

of *Fir Bolgs*.

The third invasion brought the *Fir Bolgs* who are said to have numbered about 5,000. They divided Ireland into five provinces – Leinster, Connacht, Ulster and East and West Munster and are credited with the erection of the stone forts at Staigue in Kerry and at Dún Aengus on Aran Mór.

The *Tuatha Dé Danann* also came from Greece and were skilful in the art of magic. When they landed in the North of Ireland, under the leadership of Nuada of the Silver Hand, they turned their ships around and, surrounding themselves in a magic fog so that the *Fir Bolgs* could not see them, marched to the west coast. They defeated the *Fir Bolgs* and became the undisputed rulers of the country.

The great burial mounds of the Boyne Valley such as Newgrange, Dowth and Knowth are ascribed to these people. They are also credited with bringing the Stone of Destiny, the *Lia Fáil* (upon which the High King was crowned at Tara) to Ireland. With the coming of the next colonists, the *Milesians*, the *Tuatha Dé Danann* retreated to the hills and *raths* (ring forts) where they remain as the *Sidh* (fairies) of Irish folklore.

The fifth invasion was by the *Milesians* sometime between 1700 BC and 1000 BC. The traditions about these invaders may be based somewhat on real events and even if they still contain incredible stories they may contain some truth. The *Milesians* came from Spain and landed at three points, Wexford Harbour, the River Boyne and the Kenmare River. They took over the country from the *Tuatha Dé Danann* and elected a king whose successors reigned until Rory O'Connor, the last High King.

The Celts first appeared in central and western Europe in about 1200 BC but the date of their arrival in Ireland is unknown. Their arrival is believed to have been a very gradual process and spread over several centuries, culminating with the *Goidels* (Gaels) who brought their Gaelic culture throughout the country. They had a rich oral tradition, which was later to be preserved in the Gaelic writings with the coming of Christianity.

During the early centuries of the first millennium the Romans were extending their control over most of Europe. Christianity was spreading throughout their empire and it is only to be expected that the various raids conducted by Irish Kings into Britain and

———————— ◎ ————————

One of the most famous legends concerning St Patrick is that he banished snakes from Ireland. One legend tells of him standing on a hill and driving the snakes from the country with a wooden staff. Another legend has it that one old serpent refused to go and St Patrick made a wooden box and told the serpent to enter it. The serpent said it was too small for him but the saint insisted it was big enough. To prove his point the snake entered the box, whereupon Patrick banged the lid closed and threw the box in the sea. (It is true that there are no snakes in Ireland but it is most likely that there never were any when the island became separated from the continent of Europe after the Ice Age.)

———————— ◎ ————————

The oldest books of Christian Ireland still in existence are the *Domhnach Airgid* (the *Silver Shrine*), the *Cathach* (the *Battler*) and the *Book of Kells*. The oldest one of the three is the *Silver Shrine*. This is a copy of the Gospels and is enclosed in a shrine of silver, yew and copper. Only a small portion of it now remains. It was thought at first to be written by St Patrick himself but was in fact written some time after him.

The *Battler* was so called because it was carried into battle as a good luck charm by the O'Donnells of Ulster. It is a copy of the Psalms and is supposed to have been secretly copied by Colmcille from a manuscript belonging to St Finian. The King later ordered it to be returned to St Finian on the principle 'To every cow its calf and every book its copy'. The *Silver Shrine* and the *Battler* are now in the National Museum in Dublin.

———————— ◎ ————————

Gaul should bring back Christians to Ireland. In fact there were Christians in the country long before the coming of St Patrick. Some of the Irish saints such as Declan and Ailbe are believed to have been Christians when Patrick arrived and they acknowledged his authority when he organised his church. A chronicle published in AD 433 recorded that Palladius was consecrated by Pope Celestine and sent as 'first Bishop to the Irish believing in Christ'. He is said to have first landed in Wicklow in 430 AD but was repulsed. He retired to Scotland where he died.

Only two years after the failed attempt by Palladius, Patrick, again with the blessing of Pope Celestine, arrived in Ireland as a bishop, with the task of converting the country to Christianity.

Previously, at the age of sixteen, he had been taken captive in an Irish raid in his native Gaul and carried as a slave to County Antrim. There he spent six years tending sheep on the slopes of Slemish Mountain and then – instructed in a vision, the story goes – he escaped and made his way home.

During the next twenty-three years (some experts say forty years) he prepared for the great goal he had set himself – to return to convert the Irish people. And so in 432 AD he came back to Ireland. Like his predecessor he was unwelcome in Wicklow and so made his way north to County Down. Here he was received more favourably and eventually converted the local chief, Dicho, and his family.

Next Patrick decided to carry his gospel to the greatest authority in the land and so he set out for Tara where King Laoghaire resided. Patrick sailed up the Boyne until he reached the hill of Slane. Because it was Easter Saturday he followed the Christian liturgy and lit the Easter fire on top of the hill.

It so happened that King Laoghaire had decreed that no fire should be lit in his kingdom until a great bonfire in his honour was set blazing on the Hill of Tara. There was great anger, therefore, when Patrick's fire on Slane was seen by all. The king demanded that the culprit be brought before him, so Patrick and his followers appeared before the king on Easter Sunday. Patrick set out the leading points of Christian belief in so passionate and persuasive a manner that nearly the whole assembly was converted. The king himself refused to convert but he gave permission to Patrick to preach the gospel throughout his kingdom.

———— ◎ ————

The *Book of Kells* is a copy of the Four Gospels and is the work of a monk in a monastery in Iona during the seventh century. It was brought to Kells in 796 when the monastery in Iona was sacked by the Vikings. It is now in Trinity College, Dublin.

———— ◎ ————

The oldest existing book of Irish literature is the *Book of Armagh*. It was compiled from other manuscripts by a scribe called Feardomhnach in the year 807. It is mainly in Latin but it also has the oldest continuous passages in the Gaelic language existing today. Among its treasures is 'The Confession of St Patrick' which is believed to have been copied from the saint's own writing. It also contains accounts of the lives of St Patrick and St Martin of Tours and a copy of the New Testament. At one time it was believed to have been written by Patrick himself and was given the name 'Patrick's Testament'. It now rests in Trinity College in Dublin and is second only to the *Book of Kells* in the beauty of its illustrations.

———— ◎ ————

Another famous book from these early times is the *Book of the Dun Cow* compiled in the monastery of Clonmacnoise about the year 1105. It contains the *Táin*, an account of the war between the mythical Red Branch Knights and Queen Maeve of Connacht before the coming of Christianity to Ireland.

———— ◎ ————

Writers on the continent of Europe referred to the Irish as Scots up to the fifteenth century.

———— ◎ ————

Later Patrick moved throughout the whole country and in every instance he first approached the local king or chief, because he knew that if he could convert the leader the rest of the people would follow.

Finally, after working tirelessly for thirty-three years, he died in Saul in County Down on 17 March about the year 465 at the age of seventy-eight. He was buried in Downpatrick.

(Note: The dates of many of the events in the life of St Patrick are disputed by scholars. We have given here the most commonly accepted ones.)

The centuries following Patrick's death saw a great outburst of religious zeal and learning throughout Ireland. It was during this period that Ireland earned the title of 'Island of Saints and Scholars'. Monasteries, abbeys and schools of all kinds were established all over the country. The religious zeal was not confined to the island of Ireland but was spread to Britain and the continent by devoted Irish missionaries.

It was also during this period that the great and priceless illuminated manuscripts involving copies of the Gospels and Psalms in Latin were created. Those that have survived to the present day represent only a tiny proportion of the works of the numerous Christian artists during the period. Most of the marvellous works were destroyed during the Norse invasions or during subsequent upheavals.

The oldest Gaelic writings in existence also date from the golden era. They cannot be truly classed as Gaelic literature, however, as they were merely written translations of texts in Latin and other languages. Difficult words and phrases in the originals were explained in Gaelic in the margins or between the lines. These treasures are preserved in libraries throughout Europe.

2

◎

THE 'NORTHERN WOLVES' ATTACK

(Note: The raiders from the Scandinavian countries are variously known as Danes, Norsemen, Ostmen and Vikings. For purposes of convenience the term Viking is used throughout this book.)

For over three hundred years after St Patrick the history of Ireland is mostly concerned with the expansion of religion, art and learning. But before the end of the eighth century the first Viking attack on Irish soil occurred when they plundered St Colmcille's Church on Lambay Island off Dublin in 795 AD. From then on the attacks on monasteries, churches and libraries throughout the country increased. These attacks were generally of the 'hit and run' variety where they attacked suddenly and were gone before any resistance could be mounted but about the middle of the ninth century the Vikings began to remain in the country and established walled towns such as Cork, Bantry, Wexford, Waterford, Limerick and Dublin.

For the most part they came in small individual bands but in 832 a large united fleet arrived. It was under the command of Turgesius who was acknowledged leader by the Vikings already in the country. He set up his headquarters first in Armagh and later in Lough Ree on the Shannon.

The Vikings were defeated in several battles by native kings and chieftains, particularly at Lough Foyle in 866 and Killineer near Drogheda in 869 but they still held on. Generally there was too little unity between the native chieftains to effectively repulse the invaders but things began to change, however, in the late tenth century with the coming to power of Malachy II as King of Meath and Brian Boru as King of Munster.

Malachy defeated the invaders in a great battle at Tara in 979 and then marched on Dublin and freed 2000 captives there. The following year he was elected King of Ireland. The Vikings retook the city some years later, however, but Malachy again captured and plundered it in 995.

Among the treasures he took away on this occasion were two of the greatest possessions of the Vikings – the sword of Carlus the Dane, who had fallen in battle in 869, and the collar of gold which had belonged to the Norwegian prince Tonar. This is referred to in Thomas Moore's poem: 'Malachy wore the collar of gold which he won from her proud invader'.

Irish alphabet: the upper alphabet dates from the seventh century while the lower is from the eleventh century. Two forms of 's' are in each.

All this time Brian Boru and Malachy were quarrelling and fighting but in 998 they agreed to divide Ireland between them. Malachy took control of the country north of a line from Galway to Dublin and Brian took the southern half.

The King of Leinster, Maolmórdha, resented this arrangement and he and the Vikings of Dublin revolted. Brian and Malachy united against this threat and a ferocious battle took place at Glenmama near Dunlavin in County Wicklow in 999. The Vikings and Leinstermen were defeated, with over 4000 of them being killed. Next Brian decided to take over the kingship of the whole country but before taking action he made alliances with his erstwhile enemies. He married Maolmórdha's sister Gormflaith, who was the mother of the King of Dublin, Sitric of the Silken Beard; gave his daughter in marriage to Sitric and formed an alliance with Maolmórdha himself.

———— ◎ ————

The first Viking raid in Ireland is said to be that on the monastery on Lambay Island in 795

———— ◎ ————

The Vikings established a *longphort* (ship harbour) at Annagassen in County Louth in 841 AD. They also established settlements at Drogheda, Waterford and Limerick during the following century.

———— ◎ ————

Legend has it that when Brian Boru became High King of Ireland the country became so peaceful that a beautiful young lady, richly dressed, and bearing a gold ring on her hand, travelled the country from north to south without being molested. Thomas Moore later wrote a song about the event – 'Rich and rare were the gems she wore.'

———— ◎ ————

One fanciful account of the death of Brian Boru describes it thus: 'Brodir could see that King Brian's forces were pursuing the fugitives, and that there were only a few men left to man the wall of shields. He ran from the woods and burst through the wall of shields and hacked at the king. The boy Tadhg threw up an arm to protect Brian, but the sword cut off the arm and the king's head. The king's blood spilled over the stump of the boy's arm, and the wound healed at once. Then Brodir shouted, 'Let the word go round that Brodir has felled King Brian.'

———— ◎ ————

According to legend, when Brodir was captured he was executed by disembowelling. His intestine was tied to a tree around which he was then led until he died. However another account tells how Brian cut off both of Brodir's legs with one blow of his heavy sword before he himself was killed. In all probability there is no truth in either legend.

———— ◎ ————

He then invaded Malachy's territory and he, recognising Brian's superior strength, acknowledged him as King of All Ireland. From Kincora, his palace at Killaloe in County Clare, Brian now set about restoring monasteries and churches which had been destroyed. He founded schools and colleges and built fortresses and bridges throughout the country. By this time Maolmórdha and King Sitric of Dublin were chafing under Brian's rule and determined to overthrow him. Meanwhile Gormflaith had left Brian and returned to Dublin and actively encouraged her son Sitric to organise a Viking army to defeat her ex-husband.

Envoys were sent to Viking strongholds all over Europe and by March 1014 a huge fleet of ships occupied Dublin Bay, while three great battalions of soldiers under the command of Maolmórdha were assembled inside and around Dublin. Brian Boru established his army in the area now known as the Phoenix Park in Dublin. The battle commenced on Good Friday, 23 April 1014, on the north side of the River Liffey.

The Vikings stood with their backs to the sea; the Irish on the land side facing them. By the end of that day, Good Friday, 23 April 1014, about seven thousand on the Viking side had been killed, of whom four thousand are said to have been 'foreigners' that is, they had not been living in Ireland before the battle. Most of the leaders on both sides were killed, including Maolmórdha, the chief inciter of the battle. Brian Boru himself, being too old to take part in the battle, was slain in his tent by Brodir, one of the Danish leaders.

In spite of the fact that the Battle of Clontarf is given a prominent place in romantic Irish history, in reality it was of little real political significance. It is true, however, that it marked the end of the Viking wars. There were some later raids but they had little effect on the internal political struggles which followed the death of Brian Boru. After the death of Brian Boru, Malachy became king of Ireland and reigned for eight years, dying at the age of seventy-two.

Sitric Silkenbeard, the Viking king of Dublin, remained in control until 1036 and far from being the pagan ogre of legend, he was in fact a devout Christian. Coins minted in Dublin during his reign bore his image on one side and the Sign of the Cross on the other.

He also went on pilgrimage to Rome and is credited with the

———— ◎ ————

For many years after the Battle of Clontarf there was constant warfare between various Irish kings. In the 'Battle of Móin Mór' near Emly, County Tipperary between rival members of the O'Brien family of Dal Cais, County Clare over 7000 of the Claremen were killed.

———— ◎ ————

Among the many monasteries raided by the Vikings in the eighth and ninth centuries were those at Scattery Island off the coast of Clare, Bangor in County Down and Clonmacnoise in County Offaly. They are also said to have plundered the famous passage graves in the Boyne Valley.

———— ◎ ————

Even though the Vikings were the first to mint coins in Dublin, it seems that generally they did not have much use for them. They did not carry purses and are supposed to have concealed coins in times of danger by sticking them to armpit hair with beeswax.

———— ◎ ————

foundation of Dublin's Christchurch Cathedral (Originally called the Church of the Holy Trinity). He ended his days as a monk on the island of Iona.

Sitric Silkenbeard's coins were the first ever to be minted in Ireland

Many of the churches of ancient Ireland had round towers close to them. Their primary function was as bell-towers but they also had a defensive role in times of attack. Their chimney-like form left them vulnerable to fire, however, and the *Annals of Ulster* record the burning of one of the earlier towers at Slane, County Meath in 950 and that the tower at Monasterboice was burned 'with its books and treasures' in 1097.

Round Towers had two purposes – to act as belfries and as fortresses in the face of attack

The towers were constructed of stone and were from twenty to fifty metres high and four to seven metres in diameter at the base. The interior was divided into six or seven storeys, which were reached by ladder from one to another. Each storey was lighted by one window, the top storey usually having four windows. The entrance to the tower was placed about three metres from the ground and was reached by a ladder also. Good examples exist at Nendrum, County Down, Devenish, County Fermanagh, Glendalough, County Wicklow and Clondalkin, County Dublin.

———— ◎ ————

During excavations at Copper Alley in Dublin's Temple Bar an extraordinary discovery was made when the archaeologists came across the remains of a 'strange house' which appear to pre-date the arrivals of the Vikings. The house appeared to have measured seven metres by four metres, with a hearth and a side entrance. The walls were of a type not used by the Vikings.

The house was found at the lowest level of the dig, under the Viking buildings and a comb found in it could only have come from Roman Britain. The experts are convinced that the site was occupied by Anglo-Saxons before the arrival of the Vikings in the ninth century.

———— ◎ ————

Vegetables commonly used by the Vikings were onions, cabbages, parsnips, peas, beans and leeks.

———— ◎ ————

With the passing of the years more foreigners intermarried with the native Irish. Both the Vikings and the native Irish practised bigamy. It was considered a status symbol to have more than one wife. When young Viking men were seeking a wife they grew their beards long and used make-up on their eyes.

———— ◎ ————

Not many Norse words entered the Irish language. Most of those that did are connected with sailing, fishing or trading: *pinginn* – penny, *scilling* – shilling, *ancaire* – an anchor, *bád* – a boat, *beor* – beer, *fuinneog* – a window, and *margad* – a market, are some examples.

———— ◎ ————

3

◎

'DERMOT OF THE FOREIGNERS' INVITES THE NORMANS

The century and a half between the death of Malachy and the Norman invasion was a period of great confusion, with the eight provincial kings, each aspiring to be king of Ireland and continually at war with each other. This period is known in Irish history as the time of 'The Kings with Opposition'.

Alliances were constantly being formed, and equally constantly being broken, between leading Irish families. Whenever one leader appeared to be getting too powerful others would combine to bring him down. Towards the middle of the twelfth century two of the main contenders were Rory O'Connor of Connacht and Dermot Mac Murrough of Leinster.

In 1166 O'Connor was formally crowned High King of Ireland in Dublin, the only king of Ireland ever crowned there. The leading families from the rest of the country paid homage and gave him hostages. Among those who submitted was Dermot Mac Murrough, who was actually born in Dublin. In 1152 Mac Murrough had carried off Devorgilla, the wife of Tiernan O'Rourke of Breifne, while O'Rourke was absent from home and she took away all she had brought to her husband as a dowry, including one hundred and forty cows. Some historians say she arranged the whole thing! Mac Murrough was later forced to restore Devorgilla and all her dowry to her husband. (She later retired to Mellifont Abbey in County Louth where she died in 1193 at the age of eighty-five.)

By 1166 Mac Murrough's behaviour had become unbearable and he was banished by O'Connor, O'Rourke and others. He fled to Bristol to seek help from the King of England. On learning that the king, Henry II, was in France at the time, Dermot went there and presented himself before him.

Dermot Mac Murrough who invited the Normans to Ireland was afterwards known as 'Diarmaid na nGall' (Dermot of the foreigners).

Henry was a fierce, determined man, with great energy and ability but so given to violent rages that he was said to be possessed by the devil. He was more French than English; of his thirty-five years as king of England, he only spent thirteen there and never spoke any of the language.

While the Normans (descendants of Vikings who had settled in northern France) had easily conquered England, they got much stiffer resistance from the Welsh chieftains. Henry had placed some of his toughest barons, together with their Flemish mercenaries, on the Welsh 'marches', with the liberty to keep any land they could wrest from the Welsh. It was to these tough barons that Henry sent Mac Murrough with permission to recruit any who would help him.

The chief Norman baron in Wales was Richard de Clare, Earl of Pembroke – better known as Strongbow – who had recently lost back to their rightful owners the lands his father had won. Strongbow was glad of the prospect of new conquest in Ireland. Another group of Norman families, known in Irish history as the 'Geraldines', were also on the Welsh marches. They were closely related and had names like FitzGerald, FitzHenry and de Barri. They were more or less in the same position as Strongbow and so willingly listened to Mac Murrough.

———— ◎ ————

The Vikings in Ireland had meanwhile settled down as citizens of Ireland. They became Christians and took an active part in the life of the country. By the time of the Norman invasion they constituted large proportions of the inhabitants of Dublin, Limerick, Wexford, Larne, Carlingford and Cork.

———— ◎ ————

The love of learning still flourished in the country with famous schools in Clonmacnoise, Monasterboice, Armagh, Lismore and other places. It was in 1123 that the beautiful Cross of Cong was made by order of Turlough O'Conor of Connacht. The cross is 76 cms in height and is covered all over with beautiful Celtic designs in gold, silver, enamel and precious stones. Along its sides are inscriptions in Irish giving its history.

———— ◎ ————

Dermot Mac Murrough's career was extraordinary. He was responsible for the establishment of the Priory of All Hallows on the site of present day Trinity College and also of the Augustinian Convent at nearby Hoggen Green. One of the nuns there was his own ex-wife, the sister of Archbishop Laurence O'Toole. On one occasion he attacked the town of Kildare where he dragged the abbess from her convent and married her off to one of his officers. In 1142 he attacked some of his opponents, killed two of the nobles, gouged out the eyes of another and blinded seventeen lesser chieftains.

———— ◎ ————

What is sometimes called the 'English' invasion of Ireland was, therefore, carried out by the subjects of a French king whose leaders were French-speaking Normans, many of whom were half-Welsh, and many of their followers Flemish mercenaries.

The Normans were famous for their military prowess. Like their ancestors, the Vikings, the Norman barons and knights looked upon fighting as their only profession. Their arms and armour were the best available at the time. The knights fought on horseback, clad completely in armour from head to toe, and carried long lances. Their archers, no less formidable, armed with the famous longbow or the crossbow, supported them on foot. The Normans had perfect discipline in battle, and they never allowed the fierce jealousies which otherwise prevailed among them to interfere with their effectiveness on the field of battle. They were also expert in the building of castles and fortifications.

When Mac Murrough arrived in Bristol he secured the agreement of Strongbow to come to Ireland on condition that Stongbow was given Mac Murrough's daughter, Aoife, in marriage and that he would become king of Leinster on Mac Murrough's death. Mac Murrough also got a number of Geraldines, among them Robert Fitzstephen and his half-brother, Maurice Fitzgerald, to agree to help him, on the promise of the gift of the town of Wexford and surrounding districts. He then returned to Ferns in County Wexford where he spent the winter of 1168 in the monastery founded by himself.

On 1 May 1169 the first party of Normans, in three ships under the command of Robert Fitzstephen and Meiler Fitzhenry, and carrying thirty knights, sixty other horsemen and 300 archers, landed at Bannow Bay in County Wexford. The following day a second body of troops under the command of Maurice de Prendergast and comprising ten men-at-arms and 200 archers arrived. These two armies were joined by Dermot Mac Murrough, with about 500 men and the combined armies proceeded to attack the town of Wexford. The townspeople resisted valiantly, hurling stones and wooden logs down on the attackers. Fitzstephen withdrew his troops for a time and attacked and burned all the ships he found in the area. He led his troops to attack the town again the next day but the local clergy persuaded the townspeople to surrender the town to avoid further bloodshed.

The following is a contemporary description of Strongbow:
    He had reddish hair and freckles, grey eyes, a
    feminine face, a weak voice and a short neck,
    though in almost all other respects he was of a tall
    build. He was a generous and easy-going man.
    What he could not accomplish by deed he settled by
    the persuasiveness of his words . . . When he took
    up his position in the midst of battle, he stood firm
    as an immovable standard round which his men
    could regroup and take refuge. In war he remained
    steadfast and reliable in good fortune and bad alike.
    In adversity no feelings of despair caused him to
    waver, while lack of self-restraint did not make him
    run amok when successful.

The monument to Strongbow and his wife Eva
in Dublin's Christchurch Cathedral.

Mac Murrough then carried out his promise to Fitzstephen and others by making large grants of lands to them – lands that were not his to give away, for they belonged to the people. When the High King O'Connor heard of the invasion he led a large army to Ferns but instead of crushing the invasion he weakly made peace with Mac Murrough on condition that he would bring in no more foreigners and would send home his Norman allies later.

Dermot had no intention of keeping his promise of course and, soon after, welcomed another group of Normans to Wexford. These ten knights, thirty mounted soldiers and 100 archers were under the command of Maurice Fitzgerald. Mac Murrough then marched on Dublin and forced its citizens to submit, while Fitzstephen tried to attack the High King at Limerick but was driven back to Leinster.

In August 1170 Strongbow himself arrived in Waterford Harbour with an army of 3000 men and was immediately joined by Raymond Fitzgerald, better known as Raymond le Gros (the Fat), who had arrived earlier with ten knights and seventy archers. Together with Mac Murrough's army, they then laid siege to Waterford town. There followed a fierce battle in which the local Danish chief, Reginald, and the Decies prince, O'Faoláin, were taken prisoner and locked in the castle known as Reginald's Tower (still standing to this day). The prisoners were about to be executed, when, to his credit Mac Murrough intervened and saved them. At the end of the day Mac Murrough and the Normans were successful and 'while the streets ran red with blood', Strongbow and Aoife were married as promised.

Immediately after the wedding the combined army set out for Dublin. The Vikings of Dublin had a special reason for fearing Mac Murrough, for they had murdered his father and had insultingly buried him with the body of a dog. Accordingly, when Dermot sent messengers demanding their submission, their king, Asculph Mac Torkill, defied him, and at the same time, asked for help from the High King, Rory O'Connor.

O'Connor had a far larger army than the five thousand men who were coming to attack Dublin, while the Wicklow Mountains presented a natural barrier to their progress. When O'Connor arrived at the city he established his main army on a plain on the west of the city and set up defences to the south to block the

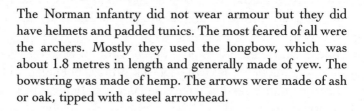

The Norman soldier was a formidable fighting man; fighting was his trade. From the age of thirteen he was specially trained for war. The most important soldiers were the mounted knights who charged the enemy in tight groups. Each knight wore a coat of mail consisting of thousands of rings of steel linked together. The head was protected by a steel helmet, which at first was cone-shaped with a narrow strip to act as a nose guard. Later helmets covered the head completely, with slits for the eyes. Each knight carried a kite-shaped shield, usually bearing his coat of arms. For weapons they used a combination of long lances, swords, battle-axes or maces with fearsome cutting edges.

The Norman infantry did not wear armour but they did have helmets and padded tunics. The most feared of all were the archers. Mostly they used the longbow, which was about 1.8 metres in length and generally made of yew. The bowstring was made of hemp. The arrows were made of ash or oak, tipped with a steel arrowhead.

The Normans had a well-thought-out landing drill. First on shore were the archers who took up advance positions against any attack. Not until a reconnaissance had been carried out and the all-clear given, would the men-at-arms with full equipment go ashore with their horses. They would then ride through the ranks of archers and take up the front line of assault.

The Irish soldiers wore no protective armour at all but only wore linen tunics in battle. For weapons they had the short sword, the sling and the battle-axe.

enemy's advance. But he hadn't reckoned with the local knowledge of Mac Murrough, who simply bypassed the defences and led his forces through thick woods which reached to the very walls of the city.

The defenders were taken by surprise and sent out Archbishop Laurence O'Toole to mediate. But while he listened to the demands of Mac Murrough – for the town to give him hostages and to recognise him as High King – two Normans, Raymond le Gros and Milo de Cogan, led a small party of knights who forced their way into the town. They then commenced slaughtering the townspeople. King Asculph and many of his followers, seeing the town was lost, ran to some ships they had moored on the Liffey for just such an emergency and sailed away. And so, on 21 September 1170 Dublin fell into the hands of the Normans. This date, therefore, marks the start of the 'English' occupation of Ireland. (When Dublin fell to the Normans, O'Connor's army withdrew, each unit going back to its own territory.)

Early the following year Dermot Mac Murrough died at Ferns in County Wexford. On his death Strongbow declared himself King of Leinster, a decision that was bound to annoy King Henry II, among others.

In the meantime, the ex-king of Dublin, Asculph Mac Torkill, had gathered a large force of Viking allies, amounting to about a thousand men, and returned to attempt the recapture of the town. The Norman historian, Giraldus Cambrensis, describes the Vikings thus:

> They were warlike figures, clad in mail in every part of their body after the Danish manner. Some wore long coats of mail, others iron plates skilfully knitted together, and they had round, red shields protected by iron round the edge.

After they landed they attacked the eastern gate of Dublin, armed with that ferocious weapon, the battle-axe. Norman knights on horseback charged out to meet them and after a final fierce fight at Hoggen Green (College Green), the Vikings were routed. Asculph was taken prisoner and tried in the hall of his own palace in Dublin. He was defiant to the end and was beheaded forthwith.

By this time Rory O'Connor had assembled a large army to

———— ◎ ————

When the Normans took over an area, instead of devastating it as the native Irish chieftains would do, they sought to consolidate their position by building a type of castle in the region.

The first fortified castles built by the Normans consisted of earthen and wooden defences called motte-and-baileys. First they built up huge circular mounds of earth over ten metres high with steep sides. On the flat top of this mound they built a wooden tower for living quarters. The whole area was then protected by a wooden palisade around the edges. A sloping ladder-like bridge connected this part, called the motte, to a lower area called the bailey. This was another circular area protected by a palisade inside which soldiers, workers, cattle, horses and provisions were kept in safety. If the castle was attacked, the people in the bailey could retire to the motte and destroy the connecting bridge. The remains of many of these motte-and-baileys can still be seen around the country in the form of grassy mounds, without the wooden buildings of course. There were a huge number of these motte-and-baileys built in Ireland, particularly in east Ulster, Leinster and Munster, in counties such as Antrim, Louth, Dublin, Kildare, Carlow, Waterford, Tipperary and many others.

———— ◎ ————

From about 1200 onwards, because the Normans were more in control in Ireland they started to build more substantial castles of stone. Many of these imposing buildings are still standing to this day in places such as Carlingford, Maynooth, Roscrea, Ferns, Nenagh, Adare and many others.

———— ◎ ————

During Norman times oxen were very important as they were used for ploughing – their tails were tied to the plough. This practice was to last for many more centuries.

———— ◎ ————

retake Dublin. When he reached the town he again set up his camp at the west side and sealed off all approaches in order to force the Normans into surrender by starvation. For two months he cut off all supplies until the Normans were in a desperate state. Not only could they get no assistance from their other Norman strongholds at Wexford and Waterford, but also they had no hope of getting help from King Henry. (He was afraid that Strongbow might set up an independent kingdom in Ireland.)

So the Normans inside the town decided to make one final effort. They assembled three experienced units, each consisting of about forty knights on horseback, sixty bowmen and a hundred foot soldiers. Commanded by Milo de Cogan, Raymond le Gros and Strongbow, who had hurried back from Wexford, they set out to attack O'Connor's main army at Castleknock. The Irish were taken completely by surprise and the king himself, who was in his bath at the time, (other accounts have him bathing in the Liffey), was lucky to escape half-naked from the field. The rest of his army fled in panic, while the Normans returned in triumph to the city with enough provisions for a whole year. After that the Norman presence in Dublin went unchallenged.

By this time King Henry was becoming alarmed at the successes of his knights. First he insisted that the knights return to England to renew their oaths of fealty to him and then in October 1171 he arrived in Ireland with a large well-equipped army to claim the homage of all the kings and chieftains of the country. Henry landed in Waterford Harbour, bringing with him an enormous fleet of 400 ships and a fully equipped army of about 10,000 men. Most of the local chiefs submitted and Henry set out for Dublin where many more chiefs came to give their submission.

Henry and his court spent the winter of 1171 in Dublin. A special palace of polished wickerwork was built beside what is now College Green. Here Henry gave lavish feasts for the local princes and included such delicacies as roast peacock, wild geese and cranes, the latter a food the Irish hated.

Before Henry left Ireland in 1172 he confirmed Strongbow as King of Leinster and appointed William de Burgo as his Viceroy.

———— ◎ ————

The monastery at Clonmacnoise on the Shannon which was founded by St Ciaran in 547 was burned down in 1204 for the twenty-sixth time! It was rebuilt but it was again plundered and desecrated during the Reformation in 1552.

———— ◎ ————

In 1209 one of the greatest tragedies to hit the Normans occurred in Dublin. On Easter Monday of that year a hurling match was played on a pitch located at Cullenswood, in present-day Ranelagh in Dublin. A large number of Dublin citizens were present as spectators at the match when local Irish clans attacked the proceedings. Up to five hundred men were killed. This terrible tragedy, on what was called Black Monday, was commemorated annually in Dublin for six hundred years. Every anniversary the colonists, fully armed and headed by a black banner, would march out to the scene of the tragedy. There they would hold a feast and formally challenge the mountain tribes to combat.

———— ◎ ————

The Christian religion seems by now to have been generally accepted in Ireland. There is only one case of heresy recorded. In 1327 a man named O'Toole was charged with denying the incarnation of Christ and saying the bible was a fairytale. He was found guilty and burned at the stake.

———— ◎ ————

After the Norman Conquest there were constant squabbles, battles and wars between the native Irish chieftains and the new invaders and in 1263 a number of native chieftains offered the crown of Ireland to Haakon IV of Norway. Alas the king died before he could take up the offer, so we will never know what the result might have been had he done so.

———— ◎ ————

Henry II based his right to demand the homage of all the Irish kings and chieftains on a rather curious document known as the papal bull *Laudabiliter*, supposedly given to him in 1155 by Pope Adrian IV, who was an Englishman. This bull granted all of Ireland to Henry, 'to hold by hereditary right'. The authenticity of this document has been debated ever since but, authentic or not, Henry found it a useful reason to proceed to Ireland and so avoid the papal legates on their way to England from Rome to inquire into the murder of Thomas a' Becket, Archbishop of Canterbury. (Thomas a' Becket had at one time been very friendly with Henry who had given him his position as Archbishop of Canterbury but later the two became bitter enemies. The king is said to have eventually given vent to his frustration with Thomas by crying out in anger 'Who will rid me of this turbulent priest?' whereupon four of the king's knights rushed to Canterbury and killed Thomas in the cathedral. Henry was later accused of the murder and was threatened with excommunication.)

In the ancient Celtic world it was taboo to eat the flesh of the crane because they believed that the crane was the form sometimes adopted by hostile goddesses, or by ill-natured and sexually promiscuous women. In one Irish text it was said that to see the three cranes of the god Midir was sufficient to drain away a warrior's entire battle ardour and ability. (Many of the bird superstitions of the ancient Celts still exist in rural parts of Ireland today.)

4

◎

A SCOT IS CROWNED KING
OF IRELAND

S trongbow's office as viceroy was a troublesome one – not only had he to contend with rebellious Irish leaders but the Norman lords frequently quarrelled among themselves. Even so, as time passed the colonists began to be assimilated into the native population, adopting the Irish language, habits and laws.

During the early years of King John's reign (he was King Henry's son) confusion and trouble was widespread throughout Ireland. He decided to visit the country and landed at Crook near Waterford in May 1210 with a strong army. From the very beginning things quietened down and he met with little or no opposition. He then turned his attention to reorganising the administration of government. He divided those parts of Ireland then under English rule into twelve counties. These were Dublin, Kildare, Meath, Louth, Carlow, Wexford, Kilkenny, Waterford, Cork, Kerry, Limerick and Tipperary.

Two months later King John returned to England and things remained quiet in Ireland for the rest of his reign. With his death in 1216, however, trouble again arose throughout the country involving both Irish and Norman chiefs, so that havoc and ruin went unchecked. After constant battles between various claimants to the throne of Connacht, one of the O'Connor clan, Felim, established himself as King of Connacht. In Ulster the O'Donnells of Donegal and the O'Neills of Tyrone were in constant battles against each other, while the MacCarthys and the Geraldines of Munster contended for supremacy.

When the Scottish King, Robert Bruce, had a great victory over King Edward II at Bannockburn in 1314 the Irish chieftains were hopeful that something similar could be accomplished in Ireland.

Some Ulster chieftains sent messengers to Robert Bruce asking him to send his brother, Edward, to be King of Ireland. Edward Bruce was very willing to do so and landed at Larne on 25 May 1315 with an army of 6000 soldiers. Some of the Ulster chiefs immediately joined him and together they moved south, destroying all before them. They burned Dundalk and Ardee in County Louth, setting fire to the Carmelite monastery in the latter town, where a large number of people had taken refuge. They were all burned to death.

From the beginning the campaign was carried on with great cruelty and with reckless disregard for life and property. Everything not required by the army was destroyed, even though famine was widespread and the people were starving.

One of the most powerful Anglo-Irish noblemen of the time was Richard de Burgo, the Red Earl of Ulster and part of Connacht, and he now set out at the head of a large army to attack the invaders. On his march he also destroyed everything in his path because he claimed that all the Irish people supported Bruce. However when his army did eventually meet up with that of Bruce at Connor, near Ballymena, the Scots were completely victorious and De Burgo had to flee for his life back to Connacht.

Bruce then marched into Meath and had a great victory over an army of 15,000 men led by Roger Mortimer at Kells early in 1315. He followed this victory with another over various Leinster nobles at Ardscull in County Kildare and then returned to Dundalk where he had himself crowned as King of Ireland at Faughart on 1 May 1316.

Meanwhile Felim O'Connor, King of Connacht raised a large army and set out to drive out all of the Norman lords from the province but was decisively defeated and killed in a battle with De Burgo and Richard Bermingham at Athenry in 1316. Over 11,000 of his army were slain, including practically all the native nobility of the province.

In 1317 King Robert Bruce joined his brother in Ireland and together they marched on Dublin with an army of 20,000 men, destroying everything in their path. They encamped at Castleknock, just outside Dublin, before attacking the city. The citizens and authorities in Dublin were greatly alarmed. The Scottish army was so close that the citizens on the walls could see

———— ◎ ————

Conditions were pretty grim in Ireland during the first half of the Fourteenth Century, as the *Annals of Connacht* record:

1317   Great famine this year throughout Ireland.
1318   Snow, the like of which has never been seen for many a year.
1322   Great cattle plague throughout Ireland.
1324   The same cattle plague was in Ireland this year.
1325   The cattle plague throughout Ireland still.
1328   Much thunder and lightning this year, whereby much of the fruit and produce of all Ireland was ruined and the corn grew up white and blind. A great and intolerable wind this summer.
1335   Heavy snow in the spring which killed most of the small birds of Ireland.
1338   Nearly all the sheep of Ireland died this year
1363   A great wind this year which wrecked churches and houses and sank many ships and boats

———— ◎ ————

The victor over Edward Bruce at Faughart, Sir John de Bermingham, became so hated by his jealous neighbours that they led him into a trap at Bragganstown near Ardee in County Louth in 1329. Sir John and all his brothers, nephews and servants, numbering 160 in all, were killed.

———— ◎ ————

their campfires. The preceding years in Dublin had been relatively peaceful and the city walls had been largely neglected. Now they were in such a state that they would offer little resistance to a determined army. One of the towers had already collapsed, others were in a poor state. The authorities decided on drastic action – any structure that could hinder the defence of the city was removed. Houses built against the walls were torn down, towers and gaps were repaired and even the bridge over the Liffey was torn down.

The most drastic step of all, however, was the decision of the Mayor to order that the suburbs were to be set on fire. The fire got out of control and four-fifths of the suburbs and a part of Christchurch Cathedral were destroyed by the time it died down. The plans worked, because the Scottish army were so impressed by the determination of the inhabitants to defend their town that they gave up the siege.

The Bruce army then proceeded to Limerick, once more destroying everything in their path but again found that city also too well defended. So they returned northwards again, losing vast numbers from cold, hunger and disease – scourged by the famine for which they, themselves, were largely responsible.

Shortly afterwards Robert Bruce returned to Scotland but Edward remained. He turned south again but was met by a strong army under Sir John de Bermingham at Faughart near Dundalk. Bruce was urged to wait for reinforcements to arrive from Scotland but he was rash and headstrong and said he could defeat an army four times greater than his opponents. The battle took place in October 1318 and the Scots were defeated. An Anglo-Irish knight called Sir John Maupus dashed at Bruce in the middle of his army and killed him. Maupus himself was then attacked by the Scots and cut down. After the battle his body was found to have been pierced in many places and lying on top of the body of his adversary. Bermingham had Bruce's body cut into pieces to be hung up in Dublin and other towns in the colony and brought his head to King Edward II in a salted box. The king immediately made Bermingham Earl of Louth and gave him the manor of Ardee.

Even though Bruce's invasion was a dismal failure the Anglo-Irish government forces grew progressively weaker. The Irish, taking advantage of their condition, attacked them at every turn.

———— ◎ ————

In the fourteenth century one of the Norman bishops, Richard Ledrede of Ossary, tried to ban all secular songs from Ireland and would only allow sacred music to be played.

———— ◎ ————

The oldest harp still in existence in Ireland dates from at least 1300 and is kept in Trinity College in Dublin.

———— ◎ ————

In 1240 the Abbot of the Cistercian Abbey of Knockboy, County Galway was severely censured for allowing a woman to wash his hair.

———— ◎ ————

The whole English colony in Ireland was very badly affected by the Black Death and the Bishop of Armagh calculated that over two-thirds of the colonists died.

———— ◎ ————

All sorts of reasons were advanced for the Black Death, from physiological imbalance to the stars being out of line. One of the cures recommended was to take the flesh of a snake, lizard or toad, roast it, leave for a year and then mash it up and eat it.

———— ◎ ————

Moreover, more and more of the English were becoming absorbed into the native population and culture. They married Irish wives and adopted the Irish language, dress and customs. The government gave an added impetus to the process by favouring the New English over the Old English, putting them into positions of trust over the older colonists. These were so incensed that many of them – Geraldines, Butlers, de Burgos and others, turned against the government.

Almost the only part of the settlement to remain loyal to the English crown was the district in the east of the country, with Dublin as its centre. This area became known as the Pale and though its size varied from time to time it was generally about fifty kilometres long and thirty kilometres wide.

Not only were the inhabitants of the Pale constantly subject to pillage and war but to add to their miseries they were scourged by terrible plagues. It is estimated that between the years 1000 and 1500 up to fifteen epidemics or plagues were suffered by the unfortunate inhabitants of Dublin. The most serious by far was known as the Black Death, which hit the country sometime in 1348. The first places in Ireland to be affected were Dalkey, Howth and Drogheda. It soon spread to areas around busy ports such as Dublin, Waterford, New Ross, Youghal and Cork and later along the trade routes emanating from Dublin throughout Leinster and beyond.

The fleas of the black rat carried the deadly bacilli from person to person, infecting everyone they bit. The plague was given the name 'Black' because the most obvious symptoms of the disease were black inflamed swellings in the armpits and groin of the victim. The swellings are known as buboes, hence the name 'bubonic'. In most instances death occurred within two weeks: first the victim would develop flu-like symptoms, then the buboes would appear, to be followed by vomiting and finally death by pneumonia. The terrible epidemic killed huge numbers of people in the following months although there is no way of verifying the numbers who died. People living in close proximity to each other seemed to be particularly at risk. Consequently, the monasteries were badly affected. After 1348 no new entries were made in the annals of the Priory of the Holy Trinity, which was attached to Christchurch Cathedral, which implies that there was no one left to write the annals.

The plague seems to have had a much greater effect on the colonists in the Pale than on the native Irish, particularly those who lived in the more remote areas. The loss of so many of the colonists greatly alarmed the authorities because the survival of the colony depended on their numbers.

5

◎

THE COLONISTS CAUSE
TROUBLE FOR THE
ENGLISH CROWN

After the Bruce invasion the process of assimilation of the English in Ireland proceeded apace. Two powerful influences helped the process along. Firstly, the colonists found it safer to join the native Irish for protection. They intermarried with them and adopted their language and customs. Secondly, the government began to regard the old colonists as being 'more Irish that the Irish themselves' and consequently was inclined to favour new arrivals over those who had borne the brunt of the struggle against the Irish.

Gradually almost the whole island became independent of England, the only part remaining loyal to the Crown was the area around Dublin which became known as the Pale. Even there the government was unable to protect the inhabitants from the neighbouring Irish chiefs who exacted 'black rents', a form of protection money, in return for being left alone.

When Edward III became aware of the turn of events in Ireland he determined to break the power of the great barons. He sent over three governors to change matters but all three failed and he finally decided to send his own son, Prince Lionel, as Lord Lieutenant. Lionel arrived with a force of 1500 troops in 1361 but his efforts failed and he returned to England. Twice more he came as Lord Lieutenant but was equally unsuccessful. He then decided that the only solution was to try to prevent all contact between the colonists and the native 'Irish enemies'.

At a parliament held in Kilkenny in 1367 the famous 'Statute of Kilkenny' was passed. According to this statute if any Englishman took an Irish name, used the Irish language or dress, rode a horse

———— ◎ ————

At various times the Crown officials passed decrees to regulate the behaviour of their colonists in Ireland. In 1447 it was ordered that every man had to shave his upper lip or 'be treated as an Irish enemy'. In 1465 it was ordered that every Irishman had to shave and dress like an Englishman and to take an English surname, such as the name of a town (e.g. Sutton, Trim) or a colour (Brown, Black) or a trade (Smith, Carpenter).

———— ◎ ————

Because of the swarms of robbers and thieves that beset the inhabitants of the Pale it was decreed lawful to decapitate anyone found robbing 'or going or coming anywhere' unless accompanied by an Englishman. On production of the head to the mayor of the nearest town the bearer would be paid a considerable sum of money. This encouraged any evilly disposed person to kill any Irishman he met, pretend he was a thief, and collect the money.

———— ◎ ————

The Lord of Tyrconnell, Turlough O'Donnell, who died in 1423, was the father of eighteen sons by ten different women. He also had fifty-nine grandsons.

———— ◎ ————

In 1402 the Lord Mayor of Dublin led an army of Dublin militia against the O'Byrnes of Wicklow and killed over five hundred of them in a battle at Bray.

———— ◎ ————

without a saddle or adopted any Irish custom, all his lands were forfeited and he could be put in jail. The Irish themselves were forbidden to use the Irish language and ordered to speak English only – a language they did not have! They were also forbidden to use the ancient Brehon laws under pain of death. No native Irish clergyman was to be given any position in the church within the Pale or to be received into any English religious monastery in Ireland. The colonists were forbidden to entertain Irish bards, pipers or story-tellers, as these were regarded as likely to be spies.

In spite of the high hopes for the new laws they soon became dead letters as it would have required a large army to enforce them, and the governor had no such army. So the laws were generally ignored.

The Irish chieftain who gave most trouble to the authorities based in Dublin Castle towards the end of the fourteenth century was Art Mac Murrough Kavanagh, King of Leinster. After he was crowned king in 1375 he married the daughter of Maurice Fitzgerald, Earl of Kildare. This was in direct contravention of the Statute of Kilkenny so the English authorities immediately confiscated his new wife's vast estates. Shortly afterwards the black rent which he had forced the council in Dublin to pay him was stopped. Mac Murrough responded by devastating large areas of Leinster so that the Dublin council were forced to start paying him black rent again.

The growing threat to the English government by leaders like Mac Murrough Kavanagh and others caused King Richard II to come to Ireland in 1394 with a huge army of 34,000 men to force the whole country to submit to English rule.

Mac Murrough Kavanagh immediately attacked and destroyed the then English town of New Ross and attacked and harassed Richard's army all the way to Dublin. But the Irish chiefs realised that they could not resist such a huge army forever and so about seventy-two of them, including Mac Murrough, offered their submission to the king. They were invited to Dublin where they were feted and feasted by the king for three days in Dublin Castle. Richard then knighted the four provincial kings, O'Neill of Ulster, O'Connor of Connacht, O'Brien of Munster and Mac Murrough of Leinster at a ceremony in St Patrick's Cathedral in Dublin.

After nine months of lavish display, Richard had to return to

———— ◎ ————

When Cormac Láidir (Strong) McCarthy built Blarney
Castle in 1446 it had walls five metres thick and a tower
over thirty-six metres high. A stone tablet in the tower wall
had the inscription *Cormac McCarthy Fortis Me Fieri Fecit AD
1446* (Cormac McCarthy the Strong caused me to be built
AD 1446). Over the years the McCarthys developed the
happy knack of picking the winning side in most political
upheavals and at the time of the Battle of Kinsale in 1601
the then head of the family, also called Cormac, supported
the President of Munster, Lord Carew, on the side of the
English. However, after the battle Elizabeth I requested
him to allow Blarney Castle to be garrisoned with English
troops and this McCarthy was not inclined to allow. Day
after day Carew's officers presented themselves at the castle
only to be met with long fulsome speeches, full of promises
but no delivery date. When Queen Elizabeth was told of
what was going on she is recorded as saying, 'This is all
Blarney; what he says he never means.'

'Blarney' or not, the McCarthy family managed to hold on
to the castle until it was taken by King William's army in
1690 and they left the country at the time of the Wild Geese.

———— ◎ ————

The ritual of kissing the Blarney stone dates from the
eighteenth century when the then owners had the stone
inserted by Cormac Láidir in 1446 removed to a more
accessible position. Even so, to kiss the stone it is necessary
to lie on one's back and lean over a sheer drop while being
held by a pair of strong arms. But then, isn't it worth it for
the 'gift of the Blarney' it confers?

———— ◎ ————

In 1493 the Lord Mayor of Galway hanged his own son,
Walter Lynch, for the crime of murder. The event is still
remembered today in the phrase 'Lynch Law'.

———— ◎ ————

England, leaving his young cousin, Roger Mortimer, Earl of March and heir to the throne of England, as his deputy. No sooner had he gone than the Irish chiefs resumed their old ways and in a battle fought at Kells in County Kilkenny in 1397 between the English and some Leinster clans – among them many of Mac Murrough's soldiers – Mortimer was killed.

When Richard heard the bad news he gathered an army and returned to Ireland, this time landing in Waterford in 1399 with another large army. Again Mac Murrough constantly attacked and harassed the English army as it made its way towards Dublin. The weather was terrible, no provisions could be obtained and progress was extremely slow through moor, bog and hill.

After about eleven days they reached the south coast of Wicklow where three ships from Dublin bearing provisions for the starving army awaited them. The soldiers were so hungry that they rushed into the sea, struggling and fighting for every scrap of food. When they resumed their march along the coast they were once more beset by Mac Murrough and his army.

And so it went on day by day until MacMurrough sent word that he wished to come to terms with Richard. The news was received with great joy by the English army and Richard sent the Earl of Gloucester to parley with Mac Murrough. But the talks came to nothing and Richard resumed the march until he reached Dublin.

Shortly afterwards news reached the king that his throne was under threat in England. He returned there immediately, but his great enemy Henry of Lancaster seized the throne as Henry IV and Richard II was put in prison. There followed the famous War of the Roses, which lasted for thirty years, between the House of York and the House of Lancaster.

When Richard returned to England the English authorities agreed to compensate Mac Murrough for the lands confiscated from his wife and things were fairly quiet for about six years. Then he started attacking the settlers again and plundered and burned Carlow and Castledermot and overran County Wexford. Things did not always go his way, however, and the Lord Deputy totally defeated him near Callan in County Kilkenny in 1407. This kept him quiet for another few years but we find him again attacking, and defeating, the colonists in Wexford in 1413 and 1416.

These were the old warrior's last exploits, for he died in New

———— ◎ ————

When others were accepting Lambert Simnel as the successor to the throne of England the city of Waterford rejected him and remained loyal to the Tudor king. For this reason it got the name *Urbs Intacta*, ('the untarnished city').

———— ◎ ————

Cork's support for the pretender Perkin Warbeck was the reason why it was nicknamed 'The Rebel City' by the followers of Henry VII. The name is still used five hundred years later.

———— ◎ ————

The merchant who was Perkin Warbeck's master, also became a man of some importance in Ireland. He was given Irish citizenship and the right to custom dues at both Drogheda and Dublin ports. He eventually became Governor of Carrickfergus.

———— ◎ ————

The first recorded use of a firearm in Ireland is the shooting dead of an O'Rourke by an O'Donnell 'with a ball from a gun' in a battle in Donegal in 1487. These early guns were called hand-cannons to distinguish them from the more traditional larger type.

———— ◎ ————

Ross in the first days of 1417 at the age of sixty, having been King of Leinster for forty-two years.

During the thirty years of the Wars of the Roses (1455–85) the authorities in England were too occupied to pay much attention to the plight of the settlers in the Pale and the native chiefs continued their attacks on the colonists. The area of the Pale was by now reduced to only County Louth and about half of counties Dublin, Meath and Kildare.

In Ireland the Geraldines sided with the House of York, while the Butlers of Ormond sided with the Lancastrians. When the Yorkists were victorious in 1461 and Edward IV was crowned king the Geraldines were in high favour, while the Butlers were in disgrace.

The accession of Henry VII of Lancaster to the throne in 1485 after the death of Richard III at the Battle of Bosworth, marked an important change in English policy towards Ireland. With the end of the war the Tudors now paid more attention to Irish affairs and succeeded in recovering all that had been lost by neglect and mismanagement. Up to this time all the state offices were in the hands of the Geraldines, supporters of the Yorkist cause. Henry VII wisely decided to allow the Geraldine Earl of Kildare to continue as Lord Deputy as it would cause too much trouble to remove him.

Despite the ascendancy of the Lancastrians, the Anglo-Irish retained their affection for the House of York, so that when a young boy called Lambert Simnel arrived in Ireland in 1486, accompanied by supporters who claimed he was the Yorkist prince Edward, Earl of Warwick, he was warmly received by most of the Anglo-Irish nobles, clergy and people.

Simnel was actually the son of a tradesman at Oxford. He was eleven years old when rumours spread that the two sons of Edward IV, reported to have been murdered in the Tower of London, were still alive. A young Oxford priest first decided to pass Simnel off as one of the sons but later decided he would have a better chance as the Earl of Warwick who was also rumoured to have died in the Tower.

Shortly after Simnel's arrival in Ireland, an army of 2000 Germans came to Ireland to support his claims and he was actually crowned as Edward VI, King of England, in Christchurch Cathedral in Dublin in the presence of the Earl of Kildare. (The

———— ◎ ————

When Garrett Mór was brought before King Henry VII to answer charges that he had committed many crimes, including the burning down of the cathedral in Thurles, his reply was that he would not have done so only he thought the archbishop was inside at the time! Although the archbishop, David Creagh, was present at the trial, the king burst out laughing at the audacious reply.

The king then told Fitzgerald that he could have the benefit of any counsel he wished, to which the earl replied that he would have the best in England, namely, the king himself! This made Henry laugh as heartily as before.

At last, when one of his accusers angrily declared 'All Ireland cannot rule this man!' the king put an end to the trial by saying 'If all Ireland cannot rule him, he shall rule all Ireland!'

———— ◎ ————

The intense rivalry between the Butlers, Earls of Ormond and the Fitzgeralds, Earls of Kildare, led to frequent clashes between the followers of both sides. In 1512 one of the worst disturbances occurred when a fierce row developed between the two factions. The Earl of Ormond was forced to flee from his pursuers and to take refuge in the chapter house of St Patrick's Cathedral in Dublin. He barricaded himself behind a large wooden door and refused to come out until he got assurances from the Geraldines that he would not be harmed. Eventually it was agreed to shake hands on the deal and a hole was chopped in the door through which the two leaders shook hands. The expression 'to chance your arm' is believed to have originated from this event and the hole in the door can still be seen to this day.

———— ◎ ————

crown placed on his head had been taken from the statue of the Virgin of Dublin in the church of Saint Mary del Dam.) Later he was borne through the streets of Dublin on the shoulders of a gigantic Anglo-Irishman named Darcy, to the cheers of the city inhabitants.

On 5 June 1487 a Yorkist army led by Simnel, the so-called Edward VI, and including the Earl of Kildare, landed near Furness in Lancashire and were joined by some English supporters. They were defeated at Stoke on 16 June and Simnel, Kildare, and other leaders were taken prisoner.

Simnel's life was spared when Henry recognised that he had been a tool in hands of the Yorkists. The Earl of Kildare and others humbly asked for pardon from Henry and were forgiven for tactical reasons. The following year they were invited to a banquet in England by the king and no doubt were greatly embarrassed to be served at the table by none other than the 'prince' Lambert Simnel! The king loved a good joke.

In 1492 another pretender named Perkin Warbeck landed in Cork and declared himself to be Richard, Duke of York, the second son of Edward IV, who was supposed to have perished in the Tower. In reality Warbeck was the son of a poor burgess of Tournai in Flanders. He had spent some time in Portugal and finally became a servant of a Breton merchant who brought him to Ireland. The citizens of Cork, seeing him dressed in his master's silks, are supposed to have insisted that he must be Edward, Earl of Warwick, or the illegitimate son of Richard II. He eventually claimed to be the younger of the sons of Edward IV. He was even acknowledged to be Richard IV, the rightful king of England, by the Emperor Maximilian of Vienna. In Ireland he was again supported by the English colonists, including Garrett Mór, the Earl of Kildare. The rest of Warbeck's career belongs more to English history than to Irish but after causing a lot of disturbance in Ireland he ended up being hanged at Tyburn in London along with John Walter, Mayor of Cork, who was his chief supporter in that city.

(Some historians say that it is highly unlikely that the young man who managed to convince the Pope, the King of France, the King of Scotland and others that he was Richard IV, the last Plantagenet king, was really the son of a Tournai boatman and had first learned English at the age of seventeen. Some are convinced that he was in

——————— ◎ ———————

The great Irish families all had their own war-cries. For example, the O'Neills of Ulster had *An Lámh Dearg Abú* (The Red Hand to Victory); the McCarthys and O'Briens of Munster had *An Lámh Láidir Abú* (The Strong Hand to Victory); the Fitzgeralds of Kildare had *Crom Abú*, Crom being the great Geraldine castle in County Limerick.

——————— ◎ ———————

According to legend the Red Hand became the symbol of the O'Neills when the founder of the clan was in a race with a rival to be the first to touch the land – the winner to have first claim on the territory. As O'Neill was losing the race he cut off his left hand and threw it ashore, thereby being the first to 'touch' the land.

——————— ◎ ———————

In 1494 a parliament held in Drogheda by the Lord Deputy Poynings ordered that the area remaining under English control was to be surrounded with a double ditch, two metres high on the part 'which mereth next into Irishmen'. What this meant was that two ditches, with a high bank between them, were to be constructed. It was not meant to be a very formidable defence but was mainly to hinder the theft of cattle from within the area. It seems the double ditch was never entirely completed and large sections of the area were still open to attack. This is the area that became known as 'The Pale'. (The word 'Pale' is from the Latin word for a stake.)

——————— ◎ ———————

A letter falsely reporting the execution of Garret Óg, Silken Thomas' father, was carried, so the story goes, by a priest who lodged in the house of a soldier in Dublin. The priest left the letter for the soldier to find. The soldier used it to block a hole in his shoe but opened it later and spread the news immediately.

——————— ◎ ———————

fact the son of the Duchess of Burgundy, which actually would have made him the cousin of the man he claimed to be.)

By 1494 King Henry VII was becoming increasingly annoyed with the activities of his colonists in Ireland, so he sent Sir Edward Poynings 'to reduce the Lordship of Ireland to whole and perfect submission'. He summoned a parliament in Drogheda which enacted the famous 'Poynings' Law'. The main provisions of that law was as follows:

(i) All laws lately passed in England should apply in Ireland.
(ii) No parliament could be held in Ireland until any acts that it intended to pass, along with a full explanation of why they were required, were submitted to the king and privy council of England for their approval.
(iii) The Statute of Kilkenny was to be revived and implemented, with the exception of the law forbidding the use of the Irish language. (This was too widespread to be stopped.)
(iv) The Anglo-Irish families were forbidden to use Irish war-cries.

The powers of the Lord Deputy were greatly reduced by Poynings, who also diminished the importance of Dublin as the capital of the Anglo-Irish area. No parliament could meet without the express approval of the king. Control of all civic and military administration was also taken over by the Crown.

Even though Garrett Mór Fitzgerald had been pardoned by Henry VII for his support of Lambert Simnel he was later arrested for allegedly conspiring against Lord Deputy Poynings and lodged in the Tower of London.

By this time Ireland had become almost ungovernable and King Henry reluctantly came to the conclusion that perhaps Garrett Mór, with his connections by marriage to many of the great Irish families, might be just the man to be put in charge.

The earl proved to be a loyal servant to the king and governed the country wisely. In 1504 he took part in a savage battle at Knockdoe near Galway which was fought between the O'Kellys and the Burkes and supported on each side by many other Irish chiefs. Fitzgerald supported the victorious O'Kellys and in the battle over 2000 of the Burke alliance were killed. The king considered the Irish to have been so weakened by their losses that he rewarded Fitzgerald by making him a Knight of the Garter.

When Henry VIII came to the throne in 1509 he kept the Great Earl on as his deputy in Ireland. Fitzgerald continued his warlike forays all over the country but in one such expedition, where he attempted to capture the castle of O'Carroll at Leap in County Offaly in 1513 he received a wound from which he died a few days later.

In 1541 Henry VIII assumed the title 'King of Ireland'. Apart from his suppression of the monasteries his treatment of Ireland was generally benign.

Garret Mór was succeeded by his son, Garrett Óg. It was not long before the earl's foes, particularly the Earl of Ormond, accused him of making alliances with the enemies of the king. Henry summoned him to England but the charges against him could not be proven. However the king kept him in England for four years as part of his retinue. He then returned to Dublin where there were riots in the streets between his followers and supporters of his rival, the Earl of Ormond, who had been appointed Lord Deputy in his absence in 1521.

The old hostility between Kildare and Ormond continued as before and the king decided to send over commissioners to investigate the dispute. The result was that Ormond was dismissed and Kildare again was made deputy. Next a kinsman of Kildare, the Earl of Desmond, plotted with the King of France for the invasion of Ireland by the French. Ormond discovered the plot and immediately told the king. Kildare was then ordered to arrest the Earl of Desmond but when he marched into Munster he seemingly allowed Desmond to escape. Ormond again accused Kildare of aiding the king's enemies and once more Kildare was called to London where he was imprisoned in the Tower. In the end, the charges against him were dismissed and he was allowed to return to Ireland. This time, however, he was accompanied by Sir William Skeffington who was appointed Lord Deputy (1530). Because the rule of Skeffington was so disastrous he was recalled in 1532 and Kildare was made deputy once more!

Signature of Garrett Óg, Ninth Earl of Kildare.
'Your most humble subject, G. of Kyldare.'

He immediately returned to his own independent ways and in 1533 a formal complaint was drawn up by his enemies on the council and sent to the king. They said that the citizens of the Pale had no protection from the Irish enemy, that life for the citizens of Dublin was intolerable and the public revenue was ruined.

Henry was greatly angered and immediately summoned Kildare to London to answer these charges. He was allowed to appoint a vice-deputy before he left, so he chose his eldest son, Thomas, just twenty years old. Thomas was dashing and headstrong and so noted for his gorgeous garments that he was known as Silken Thomas. (Another explanation of the name is that he and his followers wore silken fringes on their helmets.)

Soon after the earl arrived in London in February it became known in Ireland that he had been imprisoned in the Tower. Early in June his enemies arranged that a letter, giving the false report that the earl had been executed, should fall into Silken Thomas' hands. Without waiting for confirmation of the report, the headstrong Thomas, saying 'I am none of Henry's deputy but his foe', declared war on all English by birth. (Some historians maintain that Thomas and his father had planned the whole thing in advance and that Thomas was glad of the excuse to act.)

With 140 horsemen Thomas galloped through the streets of Dublin to the Council Chamber in St Mary's Abbey. He flung down the sword of state in front of the assembled council and renounced his allegiance to the king. Archbishop Cromer begged him with tears not to do so but at that moment an Irish harper (Niall O'Kennedy) started chanting the praises of the young leader and his father's wrongs. Thomas would not reconsider. He roughly silenced the archbishop and, before the council could react, he and his followers mounted their horses and rode away.

Thomas now immediately set about gathering support for his cause. The Irish chiefs of Leinster agreed to join him but the Anglo-Irish nobility in the Pale took a neutral stand. In July 1534 Thomas and his army marched on Dublin and the citizens, fearing they were not strong enough to resist him, allowed his troops into the city and lay siege to the Castle. Among those who had taken refuge in the Castle was Archbishop Allen, one of his father's greatest enemies. Before Thomas could get his army into position the archbishop managed to slip out of the Castle and make his escape that night in a ship. Whether by accident or design, the ship became stranded at Clontarf and the archbishop was captured and brought before Thomas. He is supposed to have told his men, '*Beir uaim an bodach*' ('Take the clown away from me') but they, wilfully misunderstanding the order, 'brained and hanged him in gobbets'.

Signature of Silken Thomas, 1536.
'By me Thomas Fitzgerald.'

The murder of the archbishop had a devastating effect on Thomas' cause. It alienated the sympathy of his supporters at home and abroad, and most fatal of all, led to his excommunication by the Pope. All that summer and autumn fighting took place in and around the Pale. Then the citizens of Dublin rose against the besiegers of the Castle and drove them outside the city walls. The Geraldines then besieged the city itself but when the inhabitants found that the attackers were shooting headless arrows at them they rushed out and scattered them.

In October 1534 an English army under Sir William Skeffington, once more appointed deputy by the king, arrived from England, but after several useless marches through the country he took up quarters in Dublin and spent the winter of 1534 there.

The following spring he marched from Dublin to the Fitzgerald castle at Maynooth which was defended by 100 men. This castle was supposed to be too strong to be taken by any method but a lengthy blockade, but Skeffington, using an improved type of cannon gun, battered the castle into submission in nine days. (This was not the first time that cannon had been used in Ireland but it was the first time that its effectiveness was so clearly demonstrated.) When the garrison surrendered there were only thirty-seven defenders left alive but all of them were executed.

Skeffington decided to do no more and in July 1535 a new Marshal of the Forces, Lord Leonard Grey, arrived in Ireland. He immediately marched against the rebels and was so successful that Thomas surrendered in August. He was brought to London and imprisoned in the Tower. His five uncles, some of whom had not taken part in the rebellion, were invited by Grey to a sumptuous banquet in Kilmainham in Dublin. He then treacherously had them arrested when they arrived and they too ended up in the Tower of London. All five, and Silken Thomas, were hanged at Tyburn on 3 February 1537.

6

◎

SHANE THE PROUD

With the execution of Silken Thomas and his five uncles there were only two heirs to the Kildare title and these were the sons of Garrett Óg by Lady Elizabeth Grey, the sister of the Lord Leonard Grey who had arrested Silken Thomas. The eldest of the boys was only twelve years old and he was now smuggled south to Thomond to the protection of the O'Briens. Great efforts were made by Lord Grey, now Lord Justice, to discover the whereabouts of the boy (his own nephew) but all in vain. Because of the relationship between the Kildares and most of the leading Irish families these now formed a league – known as the First Geraldine League – to protect the boy. He was handed on from one safe haven to the next, always one step ahead of his pursuers. Finally, when Lady Grey suspected that her brother was at last about to take him, she had him smuggled on board a ship to France, disguised as a peasant. Even there his adventures continued, being constantly pursued by spies anxious to earn the large reward offered for his capture. Eventually, after a life of adventure and danger he was finally restored to all his possessions and was conferred with the title Earl of Kildare, in 1554 by Queen Mary.

During this period of history the great Shane O'Neill of Tyrone, later known as Shane the Proud, came to prominence. Shane's father, Conn O'Neill, had been made Earl of Tyrone by Henry VIII in 1541 and his son Matthew was given the right of succession. Then in 1551 when Conn approved of Shane as his successor rather than Matthew, he (Conn) was lured to Dublin and made prisoner.

Shane immediately rebelled, both to affirm his right to the title and to avenge his father's arrest. Three different attempts were made by the Lord Deputy, Sir James Croft, in 1551 and 1552 to reduce him to submission. The first attempt was by sea against Shane's then allies, the McDonnells of Rathlin, but Croft's army was so devastated that it is said only one man escaped alive. The next year Croft marched north but even though he was aided by Shane's brother, Matthew, his army was again decisively defeated. The third attempt met a similar fate and all he succeeded in doing was laying waste large areas of Ulster. For the next five or six years Shane was left alone by the authorities.

When his father died in Dublin in 1559, Shane took the title 'The O'Neill' in defiance of English law, and so the government renewed its attempts to bring him to heel but without success. The new Lord Deputy, the Earl of Sussex, having been defeated in battle by Shane, even tried assassination but the man chosen to carry it out got cold feet.

Finally Queen Elizabeth decided to try a more conciliatory approach and invited Shane to London in 1561. The Queen received him graciously and on 6 January 1562 Shane made a formal submission to her.

When he returned to Ireland that same year he had a royal pardon in his pocket, with all his expenses paid and was later allowed to keep the title 'The O'Neill'.

Back in Ireland Shane soon became involved in various tribal wars in Ulster. One of the conditions he had to sign before leaving London was that he would make war on the Scottish settlers in Ulster and accordingly he attacked and heavily defeated his erstwhile friends, the McDonnells of Antrim at Glenshesk near Ballycastle, County Antrim in 1565.

In 1567 Hugh O'Donnell of Donegal invaded Shane's territory and in an ensuing battle Shane's army was wiped out. He and fifty followers then rather foolishly sought refuge with the McDonnells of Antrim whom he had defeated only two years before. They appeared to receive him in friendly fashion but at a feast in his honour they killed Shane and all his companions. On his death, his head was cut off and sent to Dublin where it was placed on the end of a lance on the battlements of Dublin Castle as a warning to others.

Meanwhile the two great Anglo-Irish families the Fitzgeralds and the Butlers were constantly at loggerheads. The head of the Fitzgerald clan, Garret Fitzgerald the Earl of Desmond was a

Shane O'Neill and his followers, dressed in their strange native Irish attire, created a sensation at the English court. He strode through the lines of astonished courtiers, with his band of galloglasses behind him, their heads bare and their long curly hair reaching down to their shoulders. Their wide-sleeved tunics were a bright saffron colour and over them they had a shaggy woollen mantle across their shoulders.

The painted image of a galloglass from a charter of
Queen Elizabeth I in 1582. The name 'galloglass'
comes from the Gaelic *Gall Óglaigh* (foreign warriors).

The poet Edmund Spenser wrote to Queen Elizabeth describing the Irish cloak or mantle as a 'a fit house for an outlaw, a meet bed for a rebel and an apt cloak for a thief.'
The traditional 'shaggy' cloak was associated with rebellion as it was both warm and waterproof and enabled Irish fighting men to remain out in the hills and woods in the worst of weathers. It was called 'shaggy' because the pile of the immensely thick cloth was brushed up on the outside – and often stiffened with honey – in order to help in the waterproofing.

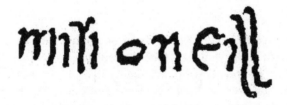

'Misi O'Neill', Myself O'Neill, the signature of Shane O'Neill.
Irish chiefs often used this form of signature.

Catholic, while the Earl of Ormond, head of the Butlers, had become a Protestant and mostly sided with the English authorities.

Their constant quarrelling had laid waste large tracts of the south while squabbles between the Earl of Clanrickard and other chieftains in Connacht had that province in a bad state also.

Finally the Lord Deputy, Sir Henry Sidney set out in 1567 for Connacht and Munster to restore order. He arrested the Earl of Desmond and brought him as prisoner to Dublin Castle, leaving the earl's brother, John, in control behind him. Although John was favourably disposed to the government, he too was arrested at the instigation of the Earl of Ormond and brought to Dublin. Later he and his brother, the Earl of Desmond, were sent to the Tower of London for six years.

James Fitzmaurice Fitzgerald, a cousin of the Earl of Desmond, then got the southern chiefs, Irish and Anglo-Irish, to form a Second Geraldine League in defence of their religion and their lands and thus was started the 'Geraldine Rebellion'.

When Sydney heard this he set out for the south with a large army in 1569. He dealt so severely with any opposition that the league collapsed, the rebellion was considered to be over and the Earl of Desmond and his brother were allowed to go home from the Tower of London.

Fitzmaurice fled to France and six years later returned with eighty Spanish soldiers and three ships he had bought in Spain. The 'invasion' came to nothing and the little force was soon scattered and Fitzmaurice killed. Shortly afterwards, goaded by the extreme harshness of the Lord Justice Pelham, the Earl of Desmond joined the rebellion which had broken out again. Ruthless bands of soldiers from both sides roamed the country for

———— ◎ ————

When the Great Earl of Desmond was on the run from the forces of the Crown in the winter or 1583-84 a spy led his enemies to the hut in which he and his wife were sheltering. The earl heard their approach, however, and the couple rushed out in the darkness and, plunging into a nearby river, remained hidden, with only their heads above water, till the soldiers had left.

The earl finally met his death because some of his soldiers had stolen cattle from the lands Owen Mac Donnel O'Moriarty near Tralee. The owner gathered a force to recover the cattle and in their search discovered a small hut with three people inside. As they attacked the occupants one of them cried out, 'I am the Earl of Desmond. Spare my life', but one of the soldiers smashed the earl's arm with his sword. He then dragged him outside and cut off his head. This was subsequently placed in the Tower of London.

Signature of Garrett Fitzgerald, Earl of Desmond,
leader of the Second Geraldine League

———— ◎ ————

In 1210 King John established the twelve counties of Dublin, Kildare, Meath, Louth, Carlow, Wexford, Kilkenny, Waterford, Cork, Kerry, Limerick and Tipperary. Then during the reign of Queen Mary (1553-1558), Queen's County (Laois) and King's County (Offaly) were formed. About 1565 Sir Henry Sidney formed Longford and the counties of Connacht – Galway, Sligo, Mayo, Roscommon, Leitrim and Clare. Clare was later annexed to Munster to which it had formerly belonged. Around the year 1584 Lord Deputy Sir John Perrot formed the seven counties of Armagh, Monaghan, Tyrone, Donegal, Fermanagh, Cavan and Coleraine (Derry). The two Ulster counties of Antrim and Down already existed. This makes thirty counties. During the reign of Henry VIII Meath was divided into Meath and Westmeath. Dublin at first included the present county of Wicklow but in 1665 Sir Arthur Chichester made it a separate county. This gives the present total of thirty-two.

———— ◎ ————

months, killing and destroying all before them but never meeting in battle.

While Pelham and the Earl of Ormond continued to lay waste to Munster the rebellion suddenly blazed up in Leinster, principally as a result of an extremely harsh tax imposed on the inhabitants of the Pale.

When Pelham was recalled in 1579 Lord Justice Lord Grey was appointed in his place. He immediately set out through the valleys of the Wicklow mountains towards the headquarters of the rebel leader, Fiach Mac Hugh O'Byrne. Grey was a poor tactician and allowed his army to be drawn into the heavily wooded valley of Glenmalure where O'Byrne and Viscount Baltinglass attacked them and almost wiped them out.

Just at this time word came of a landing of a much larger Spanish and Italian force in Smerwick in County Kerry. Grey spent six weeks collecting a new army and set out to besiege the fort at Smerwick where the invaders had taken up headquarters. After battering the fort with cannon, Grey at last forced the garrison to surrender and massacred them all. The event caused horror both in England and the Continent and was said to have greatly displeased Queen Elizabeth herself and she recalled Grey in 1582

Meanwhile the Great Earl of Desmond had become an outlaw and, accompanied by his faithful wife, was hunted from one hiding place to another. He was finally captured in County Kerry in 1583 and killed by some soldiers. This brought an end to the Geraldine Rebellion.

7

◎

'THESE ARE THEY THAT YEAR BY YEAR ROLL BACK THE TIDE OF ENGLAND'S WAR'

Up to the time of Queen Mary (1553–1558) any Irish chieftain who caused the government trouble was deposed or banished, and another leader, usually English or Anglo-Irish, was put in his place. But now a change took place – not only were the chief's lands, but the lands of all his people were also seized by the crown. The first time this happened was in Laois and Offaly. In 1547 the native chiefs, O'Moore and O'Connor, were banished and their lands given to an Englishman, Francis Bryan. He attempted to clear the lands of all its tenants and replace them with English settlers but the attempt did not succeed because of the stubborn resistance of the tenants. During Mary's reign the area was taken directly into the crown's possession and another attempt made to plant it with English settlers but with the same result in the end.

After the death of Shane O'Neill (1567) more than half of Ulster had been confiscated and again an attempt was made to establish a colony of English settlers in the area. It too failed.

Now in 1585 after the collapse of the Geraldine rebellion huge areas of Munster were confiscated by the parliament in Dublin. Englishmen were invited to 'undertake' the plantation of the estates in the province at two or three pence per acre and with no rent to pay for the first five years. Each undertaker who took 12,000 acres also agreed to settle eighty-six English families but no Irish as tenants on his estate. Smaller estates down to 4,000 acres were to settle numbers in proportion. Among the many who accepted the offer were Sir Walter Raleigh who got 42,000 acres in Cork and Waterford and the poet Edmund Spenser, who was given 12,000 acres of Desmond's land near Buttevant in Cork also.

This plantation also failed because the English settlers did not come over in sufficient numbers and the undertakers took on Irish tenants in violation of the conditions.

These plantations and many others caused untold misery and bloodshed to natives and settlers and left a legacy of hatred that was to last for hundreds of years.

In 1587 the Lord Deputy Sir John Perrot, concocted a plan for entrapping young Red Hugh O'Donnell, the son of Sir Hugh O'Donnell of Donegal. At the time the authorities feared an invasion from Spain where the Armada was even then in preparation and Perrot wished to secure hostages from the Irish chieftains to ensure their good behaviour, and in particular from the O'Donnells whom he feared most of all.

In the autumn of that year he sent a merchant ship laden with Spanish wine to Lough Swilly where it anchored near where young Hugh O'Donnell lived with his foster-father, Mac Sweeney. When Mac Sweeney offered to buy some wine he was told there was none left for sale but if he wished to come aboard there was plenty of wine to drink for free. The bait was taken. A party of Mac Sweeneys, and the young Red Hugh, went on board. Then when the visitors were enjoying themselves the ship set sail and Hugh was brought to Dublin and imprisoned in Dublin Castle.

Three years passed and then one dark winter's evening in 1590 Red Hugh and a few companions managed to lower themselves by rope onto the footbridge over the water-filled ditch around the Castle. They were met by one of Hugh's people who gave them two swords, one for Hugh and one for Art Kavanagh, a young Leinster chief who escaped with him. Passing through one of the city's gates, which hadn't been closed for the night, they made their way to Three Rock Mountain in the Dublin hills. They continued until they reached Roundwood in Wicklow where they rested, being too tired to go further. Here they were joined by a local chief, named Phelim O'Toole.

Meanwhile soldiers from Dublin Castle had managed to track them to where they were hiding. Seeing that they were surrounded, O'Toole made a pretence of arresting the fugitives and they were brought back in chains to Dublin Castle. There they were shackled in heavy iron fetters.

A year later Red Hugh and two companions, Henry and Art

———— ◎ ————

The *Book of Common Prayer* was printed in Dublin in 1551, the first book ever to have been printed in Ireland.

———— ◎ ————

The first book to be printed in the Irish language was published in 1571

———— ◎ ————

The conditions of Irish Catholic peasants were extremely poor long before the Penal Laws were imposed in the seventeenth century after the Treaty of Limerick. In 1583 when the Bishop of Meath bequeathed 'his best cooking pot' to the people of Dunboyne they queued up to use it.

———— ◎ ————

Sir Walter Raleigh is credited with planting the first potatoes in Ireland about the year 1590.

———— ◎ ————

O'Neill, sons of the late Shane, escaped again on Christmas night by cutting their chains with a file which had been smuggled in. (It is suggested that the avaricious Lord Deputy Fitzwilliam was bribed by Hugh O'Neill, Earl of Tyrone, to allow the escape.)

Outside the castle they were met by a guide from Fiach Mac Hugh O'Byrne of Glenmalure. They managed to get outside the city walls but lost Henry O'Neill in the darkness. In harsh weather they pressed on, making their way over the Dublin mountains. They continued until at last they could go no further. While they sheltered as best they could behind a large rock, a servant ran on to O'Byrne's headquarters for help. Fiach immediately sent a small party with food and clothing but they were too late to save Art O'Neill, who died of exposure. (A wooden cross in the mountains near the Wicklow Gap marks the area where he died.) Hugh, who was stronger, managed to survive, even though his feet were badly frost-bitten. He was brought to safety in Glenmalure and rested in a secluded cottage to recover from his ordeal until a messenger from the Earl of Tyrone came for him.

Accompanied by Phelim O'Toole, Red Hugh managed to evade all the soldiers on the lookout for him and eventually they made their way to O'Neill's castle in Dungannon. From there Hugh eventually managed to reach his family castle in Donegal. His two big toes had to be amputated and it was a year before he was fully recovered. In May 1592 he was elected 'The O'Donnell', head of his clan.

Meanwhile Hugh O'Neill had been created Earl of Tyrone by the parliament held in Dublin in 1585 but had been given no inheritance of the O'Neill lands, which had been confiscated on the death of Shane O'Neill. Elizabeth now granted the lands to him on condition that he gave up 240 acres of the Blackwater for a fort. This fort of Portmore (in what is now Blackwatertown) was built and garrisoned with English troops because it commanded a very strategic point on the approach to O'Neill's territory. In 1593 O'Neill was made master of all Tyrone but the queen and government were very suspicious of him. He immediately set about drilling his men, small numbers at a time, until he eventually had a large army of trained soldiers. He also imported large quantities of lead, supposedly for the roof of his new house but in reality for the making of bullets.

As Hugh O'Neill was watching the battle of Clontibret and giving his orders, a gigantic knight from the Pale, named Seagrave, charged across the stream with forty troopers and engaged O'Neill in single combat. The two broke their lances in the charge and fell from their horses. They then grappled with each other and, as the huge Seagrave was almost crushing O'Neill to death, one of O'Neill's followers cut off Seagrave's arm with his sword. O'Neill then stabbed his opponent to death.

Hugh O'Neill was born in Dungannon but reared in England in the 'new religion'. He succeeded Shane O'Neill to become the second Earl of Tyrone in 1585.

With Red Hugh O'Donnell in Donegal and Hugh O'Neill in Tyrone, Ulster was more or less united under two chiefs. Munster was relatively quiet but the English settlers ('Undertakers') were greatly resented. Connacht was in a more disturbed state. In 1585 Sir John Perrot had tried to settle the land question by 'The Composition of Connacht' whereby the local chiefs would be left in charge of their lands by paying a rent of ten shillings to the Crown for every 120 acres. Many were willing to accept this arrangement but the head of the commission Sir Richard Bingham treated those who refused with such harshness that soon the whole province was in revolt.

In Leinster an uneasy peace reigned but the two local chiefs, Fiach Mac Hugh O'Byrne and Owney O'Moore were regarded with deep suspicion by the authorities. This then was the situation in Ireland when the great insurrection began.

In 1593 O'Neill had sided with the Lord Deputy Fitzwilliam against O'Rourke of Breifne who had been goaded into rebellion by the sheriff of Fermanagh. The following year Fitzwilliam took Hugh Maguire's castle at Enniskillen. Maguire and O'Donnell immediately besieged the castle and when the Lord Deputy sent reinforcements they were intercepted at a ford on the River Erne near Enniskillen. The government forces were utterly routed and left the provisions intended for the castle behind. The place consequently got the name *Áth na mBriosca* (The Ford of the Biscuits). The castle garrison immediately surrendered.

The authorities suspected that Hugh O'Neill had been involved but he travelled to Dublin Castle and managed to convince the council of his 'innocence'. Finally back in Tyrone, in 1595 he came out into the open and sent his brother Art to attack and capture the English garrison at Portmore. This was the start of the Nine Years' War.

O'Neill then plundered the English settlements in Cavan and the following year he laid siege to Monaghan. A force under the command of Sir John Norris, President of Munster, and his brother Thomas, managed to relieve the town with little opposition. On their return march to Newry, however, O'Neill ambushed them at Clontibret, ten kilometres from Monaghan town on 13 June 1595 and severely defeated them, the Norris brothers being badly wounded in the battle. Shortly afterwards the town of Monaghan surrendered to O'Neill.

That winter O'Neill, O'Donnell and some other chiefs met the English commissioners in a field near Dundalk. The Irish side demanded complete religious freedom, that no English officials should come into the lands of the chiefs and no English garrisons should be set up in Ulster except at Carrickfergus and Newry. The English side completely rejected these terms and the war went on.

Some time later a new Lord Deputy, Thomas Borough, was appointed and he made plans for an attack on Ulster from three different points in 1597 – Sir Conyers Clifford would attack from Galway, Barnewell, son of Lord Trimblestone, would proceed from Mullingar, while Borough himself would march from Dublin to attack the fort at Portmore. The plans ended in failure, however, as O'Neill harassed the Lord Deputy's army all the way and eventually defeated him at Drumfliuch on the Blackwater near Benburb. Sir Conyers Clifford was driven back to Connacht by O'Donnell, while Barnewell was defeated by Captain Tyrrell near Mullingar at a place now known as Tyrrell's Pass. Barnewell himself was captured and sent as prisoner to O'Neill.

The Lord Deputy, Thomas Borough, did manage to recover the fort of Portmore however and installed a garrison of 300 men under the command of a very capable officer called Captain Williams. As soon as Borough returned to Dublin O'Neill again laid siege to the fort but no matter what stratagem he used the vigilant Williams was equal to it. Once when O'Neill's men used scaling ladders they proved to be too short and William's garrison killed thirty four of the attackers. Next O'Neill settled down to starve the fort into surrender but Williams managed to capture a number of O'Neill's horses and these provided food for a further period.

The council in Dublin was first inclined to tell Williams to surrender but was persuaded by Marshal Bagenal to allow him to march north to relieve the fort. Bagenal set out for Armagh with an army of 5,000 soldiers and 350 cavalry. The eight kilometres of passageway between the town and Portmore was a narrow strip of land with bogs and woods on each side and O'Neill had set up his army to bar the way at the Yellow Ford on the River Callan, three kilometres north of Armagh. O'Neill's army was slightly more numerous than Bagenal's and was well trained and disciplined. It was not as well equipped however, and unlike the English, had no body armour. One thing O'Neill did have, which was critically important, was an excellent position, chosen by himself. At intervals along the pass he had dug holes and trenches and had placed felled trees across the path. Right in front of the main body of his troops he had a trench almost two kilometres long and over a metre deep with a thick thorn hedge all along the top of it.

On the morning of 14 August 1598 Bagenal began his march with fife and drum. He had three divisions with two regiments in each, each regiment following the one in front at about 600 paces. He also had a regiment of horse on each wing.

O'Neill was well prepared. The night before he had hidden 500 lightly armed soldiers along the way and these opened fire on the advancing troops and continued to fire on them as they attempted to pass. Still Bagenal's army advanced till the head of the army reached the long trench. After some fierce fighting the attackers managed to cross the trench but were then completely overwhelmed by fresh Irish troops who attacked en masse. A fatal flaw in Bagenal's tactics now manifested itself – the gap between his regiments was too wide. The forward regiment could be wiped out before the next one could come up. O'Neill waited for Bagenal himself to advance so that he could engage him personally in combat but it was not to be. The brave marshal had fought in the thick of battle but, when he paused to raise his visor to survey the situation and take a breath, a carefully aimed musket ball pierced his brain and he fell dead.

Meanwhile the other regiments were facing similar disaster. O'Neill sent O'Donnell and other leaders to attack the last two regiments and after some ferocious fighting the remains of the English regiments fled in disorder back to Armagh. Portmore then surrendered, with the garrison being allowed to depart without their arms and munitions.

The defeat at the Yellow Ford was the greatest defeat suffered by the English in Ireland since the coming of the Normans. When the chiefs in Munster heard of O'Neill's victory the Munster rebellion broke out. The Geraldines won back all their lands and Thomas Norris, President of Munster, left the province in the hands of the rebels.

When Queen Elizabeth I heard of the disastrous defeat at the Yellow Ford she was extremely angry and the following year sent a huge army of 20,000 to Ireland under her great favourite, Robert Devereux, Earl of Essex. He was given the title of Lord Lieutenant of Ireland (a higher one than 'Lord Deputy') and almost as much power as if he had been made king of Ireland. He had been clearly ordered by the queen to attack O'Neill in the North but now he weakened his forces by sending detachments of troops to various positions throughout the country and then set out for the South of Ireland! (It seems some influential persons who had lost their lands in Munster had persuaded him to try to get them back). By this time the army directly under his control numbered only about 7000.

His progress was marred by disaster after disaster. Near Maryborough (Portlaoise) Owney O'Moore's soldiers killed 500 of his men at the 'Pass of the Plumes', so called because of the many helmet plumes of Essex's soldiers strewn on the ground after the battle.

He then led his weary army through the midland counties to Cahir in Tipperary where he had the only success of his whole expedition when he captured the castle of Thomas Butler after a siege of ten days. Next he moved to Limerick and from there to Fermoy, Lismore, Waterford, Wicklow and on to Dublin. They were harassed and attacked every step of the way so that the soldiers were 'weary, sick and incredibly diminished in numbers'.

Naturally enough the queen was extremely angry when she heard the news of his futile march but relented enough to send him a further 2,000 men and again ordered him to proceed at once against O'Neill. But still Essex remained in Dublin allowing his army to be affected by illness and desertion. Two months later, Essex ordered Sir Conyers Clifford in Connacht to cross the Curlew Mountains to relieve the garrison of Collooney Castle in Sligo which was being attacked by O'Donnell's troops.

Clifford assembled an army of about 3,000 men, including some bands of soldiers, under a few Irish chieftains but Hugh O'Donnell was waiting for them at a pass in the Curlew Mountains called Ballaghbuy (Yellow Pass) which was narrow at its entrance and wider further back. On the sunny morning of 15 August 1599 Clifford and his army set out from Boyle, County Roscommon. After a long weary journey they reached the pass which they had been told was unguarded. As the British troops entered the pass they encountered a barrier of some felled trees which was lightly defended by some of Red Hugh's men. These had been instructed to offer only token resistance and to fall back to where the main body of Irish troops was waiting. The British troops fell into the trap. They rushed after the fleeing enemy and came up against the fresh, well-prepared Irish troops. Clifford's weary, hungry army fought valiantly for over an hour, with their leader showing incredible courage. At last, when he saw that the day was lost, he resolved to die fighting and rushed into the battle where 'he was stroke through the body with a pike and died'. The remains of his army then fled, leaving behind them over 1,400 dead. The victorious Irish soldiers then moved through the battlefield, killing and beheading the wounded. Clifford's head was cut off too and brought to O'Donnell but his body was later buried with honour in Boyle.

When Essex heard of the defeat of Clifford he decided he had to face O'Neill at last. He marched north with an army less than a third of its original strength. O'Neill moved to meet him and the two armies faced each other at the little River Lagan about halfway between Carrickmacross and Ardee. Essex now willingly agreed to a conference suggested by O'Neill. The Ulster chief rode his horse into the middle of the river until the water reached his stirrups while Essex spoke from the bank.

A truce was agreed but nothing tangible came from it as Elizabeth rejected all of O'Neill's terms. Essex retired to Dublin and later sailed for England where he made a foolish attempt at revolt and ended on the executioner's block in 1601.

Essex was replaced by a man of much greater ability – Charles Blount, Lord Mountjoy. He arrived in Dublin in 1600 accompanied by Sir George Carew, who was bent on revenge for the death of his brother at Glenmalure in 1580. Carew proceeded against the Munster rebels and set out on a deliberate policy of laying waste the countryside through which his army passed.

Mountjoy meanwhile ordered Sir Henry Dowcra to take a force into Lough Foyle to plant garrisons on the shore. At the same time Mountjoy marched north as if to invade Tyrone. The plan worked, O'Neill and O'Donnell moved to oppose Mountjoy while Dowcra was relatively unopposed at Derry and succeeded in establishing a fort at Culmore at the mouth of the Foyle and another further up the river. Mountjoy then returned to Dublin. Later that year he set out for the southern Leinster counties and continued Carew's 'scorched earth' policy, leaving devastation, hunger and famine behind. Next he moved north again carrying out the same devastation.

By now, 1601, the rebellion was almost crushed in Leinster, Munster and Connacht and even in Ulster O'Neill and O'Donnell were greatly under pressure. Bit by bit their enemies were making progress all over the province. And then at last the aid they had sought from Spain, at war with Elizabeth at that time, arrived. But it was at the other end of the country!

A Spanish fleet with about 4,000 men on board under the command of Don Juan Del Aquila sailed into Kinsale, County Cork, on 23 September 1601 and immediately took over the town. The Spaniards were all trained soldiers and were to prove their mettle in the following months.

When Mountjoy and Carew heard this news they gathered their forces and accompanied by troops commanded by O'Brien, Earl of Thomond, Burke, Earl of Clanrickard and others, immediately marched south to besiege the town of Kinsale.

The northern chiefs heard of the Spanish arrival by 20 October (about three days after Mountjoy began his siege) and O'Neill immediately sent an acknowledgement, but no firm commitment, which reached Del Aquila at the end of the same month. The messengers took back an urgent message from the Spaniard urging O'Neill to come at once. It was only then that O'Neill made any serious preparations to march south.

He sent Hugh O'Donnell ahead of him first and the latter brought his army as far as Roscrea in County Tipperary where they waited for O'Neill to join them. Carew moved to cut them off at Cashel and a powerful force from the Pale under Lord St Lawrence was approaching from the east. To the west of O'Donnell's army lay the Slieve Felim Mountains which were sodden and impassable in the constant November rain.

Then on the night of 23 November 1601 there came a sudden and most intense frost, which made the ground bone hard. O'Donnell immediately set out for Limerick over the hardened ground and reached Croom after a journey of about sixty kilometres in one day. His enemy, Carew himself, declared that 'It was the greatest march with baggage that hath been heard of'.

By this time Mountjoy had received artillery and reinforcements by sea which brought his army strength up to 12,000 men. He commenced a heavy bombardment of Kinsale town and on 28 November demanded Del Aquila's surrender. Del Aquila replied that he held the town firstly for Christ and secondly for the King of Spain and was prepared to defend it to the bitter end. The siege went on but the Spaniards resisted every attempt to take the town. They engaged in bitter hand-to-hand fighting with the besiegers and on the night of 2 December a large party of 2,000 men sallied out and wreaked fearful damage on Mountjoy's troops. By 5 December, Mountjoy's position was very bad – O'Neill was only a few days' march away, O'Donnell was only about eighty kilometres away, and now he got news that six more Spanish ships and a further 700 men with guns and munitions were off the coast at Castlehaven.

Some time later O'Neill's forces joined O'Donnell's and the combined armies settled into a blockade of the English who now found themselves cut off from the interior by the Irish and from the sea by the Spaniards. O'Neill knew that all they had to do was wait but at a council of war the other chieftains, led by O'Donnell, voted for immediate action. And so, the ever-cautious O'Neill made the fatal decision to agree to their urgings – it was one of the most momentous decisions in Irish history.

It is thought that the English learned of the plans from a traitor in O'Neill's camp and waited anxiously for the expected attack. The weather on the night of 21 December was so terrible that after some initial skirmishes O'Neill withdrew. The night of the 22 December was equally bad and O'Donnell had a furious row with O'Neill for still not launching the attack. It was then decided that 'come what may' the attack would begin on 23 December.

All was confusion during the night. The English troops were on the alert, while many of the Irish guides lost their way and led the troops in aimless marches. By daybreak O'Neill found himself close to the English lines, which he saw were already prepared, while his own men were weary. He thought he was facing an English army of about 3,000 men and was not aware that Mountjoy's army had shrunk to only about 1,500 through death and desertion. Nevertheless these troops immediately launched an attack against his position but O'Neill repulsed these initial assaults. Mountjoy quickly sized up the situation and launched an attack with all the cavalry at his command. The light Irish cavalry, using no stirrups because they regarded them as unmanly, were no match for the fully equipped heavy English horse. The Irish foot soldiers then fled in panic, while Del Aquila, for some unexplained reason, remained inside the walls of Kinsale. The Spanish soldiers later made a futile sally that came to nothing. The Battle of Kinsale, which had lasted about three hours, was lost.

The next day the Irish chieftains retired with their broken armies to Innishannon. It was then decided that O'Donnell would go to Spain to ask for another expedition. Leaving his brother Rory in command of his army, Red Hugh set out for Spain where he was received with great honour. (He never saw Ireland again, however, for he was suddenly taken ill there and died on 10 September 1602, aged only twenty-nine years.)

Mountjoy allowed Del Aquila to leave Kinsale on condition that he handed over various castles which had been entrusted to him by local chiefs. After doing so Del Aquila returned to Spain where he was blamed for the disaster and put under arrest.

The abbreviated signature of Red Hugh O'Donnell in Irish.

Hugh O'Neill's signature on a document in 1601.

In the years after 1601 Mountjoy and Carew continued the work of destroying crops, castle and homesteads in Munster, Leinster and Ulster. Mountjoy himself said, 'We have seen no one man in all Tyrone of late but dead carcasses merely hunger starved, of which we found divers as we passed. Between Tullaghoge and Toome (twenty-seven kilometres) there lay unburied 1,000 dead and . . . there were about 3,000 starved in Tyrone.' Then he wrote 'Tomorrow by the grace of God I am going into the field as near as I can utterly to waste the County Tyrone.' His secretary Moryson wrote 'And no spectacle was more frequent in the ditches of towns than to see multitudes of these poor people dead with their mouth all coloured green by eating nettles, docks and all things they could rend up above ground.'

Among the many destructive acts carried out by Mountjoy was the smashing to pieces of the coronation stone of the O'Neills at Tullaghoge – there would be no more 'The O'Neills'.

With the death of Red Hugh O'Donnell most of the chiefs submitted and at length on 30 March 1603 O'Neill and Mountjoy met at Mellifont near Drogheda. When O'Neill reached the threshold of the room where Mountjoy awaited him he went down on his knees and humbly submitted. When Mountjoy told him to approach he again knelt at his feet and once more offered his repentance and loyalty. The next day he put his submission in writing, begged Queen Elizabeth's forgiveness, surrendered everything he had to her and promised to serve her loyally if he was pardoned. (In fact Queen Elizabeth had died on 24 March but this fact was kept from O'Neill who could possibly have hoped for a deal under the new king.)

On 3 April Mountjoy and O'Neill rode to Drogheda and the next day they reached Dublin. On the 5 April letters arrived from England announcing the queen's death and that James I was now king. O'Neill wept when he heard the news and while some of his enemies said they were tears of rage at being tricked, others say that he was genuinely distressed at her death.

The following June, O'Neill and Rory O'Donnell (Red Hugh's successor) went to England with Mountjoy to renew their submission. The new king, James I, received them kindly. He confirmed O'Neill as Earl of Tyrone and made O'Donnell Earl of Donegal and restored them to their possessions and privileges. But

─────── ◎ ───────

With the 'flight of the earls' and the departure of local
chieftains such as O'Sullivan, Carew was free to remove all
opposition and in his own words 'caused all the county of
Kerry and Desmond, Beare, Bantry, and Carbery to be left
absolutely wasted, constrayning all the Inhabitants thereof
to withdraw their Cattle into the East and Northern parts of
the County of Corke.'

─────── ◎ ───────

When Del Aquila surrendered Kinsale he also agreed to
give up the castles which were garrisoned by Spanish troops
at Castlehaven, Baltimore and Dunboy.

Dunboy was an extremely strong castle on the mainland
opposite Beare Island and was thought to be impregnable.
The rightful owner of Dunboy, Donall O'Sullivan, the lord
of Beare and Bantry, was determined to hold on to the castle
as he expected Red Hugh O'Donnell would return with
help from Spain. He therefore sent away the Spanish
garrison and in their place installed his own troops,
numbering 143 men under the command of Richard
McGeoghegan and an Englishman named Thomas Taylor.

George Carew, President of Munster, immediately
assembled an army of 3000, while another army of 1000
under Sir Charles Wilmot soon joined him. The combined
armies with supplies and guns were then brought by sea to
Great Beare Island and laid siege to Dunboy castle.

The attacking guns wreaked terrible damage on the castle
walls and by 17 June conditions inside the castle were so
bad that McGeoghegan offered to surrender if he was
allowed to withdraw at the head of his men. Carew's answer
was to hang the messenger and renew the siege.

The defenders fought bravely but the overwhelming
attacking forces eventually managed to breach the castle
walls in the front and the rear. By the end of the day there
were only seventy-seven defenders left alive, and these took
refuge in the cellars which were the only parts of the castle
left intact. Taylor now took command as McGeoghegan was
dying from a wound received.

Because the situation was so desperate, twenty-three
defenders were allowed to surrender but the rest of the
garrison agreed to fight on to the end. Carew's cannon were

even though O'Neill and O'Donnell were graciously received by the king they still had many enemies in Ireland. They were constantly subjected to annoyance and harassment from their enemies in the administration.

Things came to a head in 1607 when an anonymous letter was deliberately dropped outside the Council Chamber in Dublin. The letter contained a report that a new rebellion was planned, that Dublin Castle was to be seized and the Lord Deputy murdered. No names were mentioned but the Government claimed they knew O'Neill was involved. (The writer of the letter later proved to be Christopher St Lawrence, Baron of Howth near Dublin).

All this time O'Neill had been so harassed and insulted that he was near despair and then he got word that his son Henry had sent a ship to Lough Swilly to take him away to Europe. O'Neill was at the time on a visit to Slane, County Meath in the company of the Lord Deputy Chichester when he heard of the news. Saying nothing to Chichester he took his leave and went to visit his old friend Sir Garrett Moore at Mellifont. Moore was struck by an unusual display of emotion from his visitor but O'Neill never revealed the cause and rode away on a Sunday afternoon after saying goodbye to every member of the household. From there he made his way to Rathmullan on Lough Swilly where the ship, captained by John Rath of Drogheda, was waiting.

Ninety-nine men, women and children, including Hugh O'Neill and Rory O'Donnell and their families, crowded on board, 'leaving their horses on the shore with no one to hold their bridles' and set sail for Spain on 4 September 1607 an exodus forever known as the 'flight of the earls'. Storms and gales forced the ship to land in the Seine estuary in France, however, but there they were well received by the French king. Later they made their way to Rome where they took up residence with the help of a pension from the Pope and the King of Spain. Rory O'Donnell died the following year (1608) while O'Neill lived on, blind and feeble until 1616 when he died, aged about seventy years. He is buried in St Peters where a simple slab marks his grave.

now directed down on the cellars and so devastating was the damage that the remainder were then forced to surrender also. When a party of English soldiers descended into the cellars to take out the captives, McGeoghegan who was lying on the floor made one last desperate effort. He grabbed a lighted candle and attempted to thrust it into some barrels of gunpowder but he was seized by one of Carew's officers, who held him while other soldiers killed him with their swords. Carew then killed fifty-eight of the men who had surrendered but spared Taylor and fourteen others in the hope that they would give him information concerning their lord, Donall O'Sullivan. When they refused everyone was hanged and Carew set off a huge explosion in the cellars that completely destroyed Dunboy.

By this time O'Sullivan had no home, for his other castles had also been taken but he still commanded a formidable small army among the glens of South Munster. Towards the end of the year (1602) he got the bad news that Red Hugh O'Donnell was dead, and that King Philip, on hearing of the fall of Dunboy, had cancelled the planned expedition of help.

O'Sullivan Beare then resolved to seek a refuge in Ulster where the Gaelic chiefs were still strong. On 31 December 1602 he set out from Glengarriff with his small army of 400 fighting men, and 600 women, children and servants.

The march was one unbroken story of conflict and hardship, with not a day going by without a battle to be fought or evasive action to be taken. As the small band was unable to take much provisions with them they tried to buy their requirements along the way. Very often they found that the people were too terrified of Carew's vengeance to help them, so they had to use force to obtain enough to keep them on the march. And day by day they lost some of their party through illness, hunger or attack.

After the first day's march they reached Ballyvourney after a journey of some twenty-four miles. Having rested there for the night they then pressed on through Duhallow, Liscarroll and round by the Ballahoura mountains to the Hill of Ardpatrick. The following night found them in the Glen of Aherlow in the Galtee Mountains. They then pushed on through the Golden Vale and all the time they had to fight off their enemies who beset them at every turn. By the ninth night they had reached Portland in North

O'Sullivan Beare

Tipperary, near the Shannon. To cross the great river they made currachs from the hides of twelve of their horses and even then they had to fight a rearguard action against Donagh MacEgan, the sheriff of Tipperary. He attacked them and tried to throw some of the women into the Shannon but O'Sullivan resisted and MacEgan was killed in the battle.

They then pushed on west of the Shannon and were still harassed at every turn. Most of the horses had broken down by this time and as there was no other means of carrying the sick and wounded many of them had to be abandoned to their fate. The dwindling band of travellers continued on with the anguished cries of their abandoned comrades ringing in their ears.

When they reached Aughrim they found their way blocked by a much larger force than their own, under the command of Captain Henry Malbie. O'Sullivan carefully placed his men so that the enemy could only attack over boggy ground. As Malbie fought at the head of his men he was killed in the first attack so that O'Sullivan and his companions were able to force their way through with little loss.

Onwards they pressed through the territory of Mac David Burke who attacked them all the way. When they reached Ballinlough in County Roscommon they intended to rest for the night in a forest there but they got word that Burke was setting an ambush for them for the following morning, so on they went till they found a safer wood in which to stay.

The next day they crossed the Curlew mountains to where the River Boyle enters Lough Key and rested there for some time. Their ultimate destination all along had been the territory of O'Rourke of Breifne, and after another day's march they reached O'Rourke's castle where at long last they received a warm and friendly welcome.

O'Sullivan and his small force had numbered one thousand when they had set out from Dunboy a fortnight earlier but only eighteen armed men, sixteen servants, and one woman, an aunt of O'Sullivan, had survived the journey. During the following days a few stragglers arrived in twos and threes but all the rest had either perished or had attempted to make a new life somewhere along the way. (The unfortunate O'Sullivan Beare was later murdered in Spain by agents of the Crown in 1618.)

8

◎

THE CURSE OF CROMWELL

With the 'flight of the earls' the way was clear for King James I to carry out a favourite project of his – to colonise a large part of Ireland with English and Scottish settlers. A large part of Ulster, the six counties of Donegal, Derry, Tyrone, Armagh, Cavan and Fermanagh, were confiscated and allotted to settlers. The man entrusted with the task was Sir Arthur Chichester, the Lord Deputy.

The area was divided into lots of 2000, 1500 and 1000 acres. Those who got the 2000 acre lots were called 'undertakers'. They were required to have only English or Scottish tenants and no Irish. The 1500 acre lots were given to 'servitors' – Protestants who had served the Crown in Ireland during the recent wars. They could take English, Scottish or Irish tenants but no Catholics. The last group getting the 1000 acre lots could be English, Scottish or Irish, Protestant or Catholic.

Only about 286 of the old owners of the land got any share – about one ninth of the lands all told. All the rest of the inhabitants were 'to depart with their goods and chattels on or before the first of May next (1609) into whatever part of the realm they pleased'. This was an empty gesture – no other 'part of the realm' would accept them and anyway a great number of them remained where they were.

Chichester made a special offer of land to the London City Guilds. They were given the cities of Derry and Coleraine. The name of the city on the Foyle was consequently changed to Londonderry. (Trinity College in Dublin also got nearly 10,000 acres.)

Many other smaller plantations took place throughout the country during the reign of James I and later in the early years of Charles I parts of Wexford, Longford, Laois, Offaly, Cork and Leitrim were involved.

———— ◎ ————

James Ussher, Church of Ireland Archbishop, was born in Dublin in 1581. During his life he became a famous scholar and established a huge library containing 10,000 volumes, including very valuable early Irish and Oriental manuscripts.

Ussher believed that the Bible was literally true and from it he calculated that creation occurred exactly at noon on 23 October 4004 BC and that the world would end on 23 October 1997. Although we know now that his calculations were completely wrong they were widely accepted at the time and were even inserted as addenda to editions of the authorised Bible in1701. Five years after his death in1656 the library was donated to Trinity College in Dublin by Charles II.

———— ◎ ————

On 29 March 1613 Derry became Londonderry by royal charter.

———— ◎ ————

During the seventeenth century Catholics and Nonconformists were not allowed into the walled town of Bandon in County Cork. The following notice is said to have been written on one of the entrance gates:
>   Jew, Turk and Atheist,
>   May enter here
>   But not a Papist.
Later this reply was posted:
>   Whoever wrote this,
>   Wrote it well,
>   For same is writ,
>   On the gates of Hell.

———— ◎ ————

King Charles I, who had previously given his word that he would not allow Wentworth to be injured 'in life, freedom or fortune', signed his death warrant without protest.

———— ◎ ————

Charles I, who succeeded James in 1625, was always short of funds so the Irish Catholics hoped that if they gave him money he would relax the laws against them. Many Protestants were also feeling insecure in their estates because the country swarmed with people called 'discoverers' who made it their business to find any defect in the titles of estates. In return they got the estates themselves or were given money by the owners to be left alone.

In 1628 both Catholic and Protestant gentry, encouraged by the Lord Deputy, Viscount Falkland, offered the then enormous sum of £120,000 in instalments to King Charles for certain concessions or 'Graces'. Two of the most important of these were that land owners should be reasonably secure in their holdings and that Catholics should not be harassed because of their religion. The king promised that a parliament would be summoned to enact the changes but although the first instalment of £5,000 was given to the king the parliament was never summoned.

In 1633 the king sent over one of the most efficient deputies ever to hold power in Ireland – Thomas Wentworth. He had two objectives: to make the king absolute master in Ireland and to raise as much money as he could for him. He immediately got the gentry to give another £20,000 to the king on the promise that penal statutes would not be enforced against them and that he (Wentworth) would summon a parliament in Dublin to have the Graces confirmed.

In 1634 Wentworth duly assembled the parliament in Dublin Castle and got it to vote £240,000 to the king. But once again Charles avoided granting the Graces.

In the following years Wentworth proceeded to break land titles all over Connacht, Clare and Tipperary. Out of every transaction he made money for the king. He also destroyed the flourishing Irish wool trade lest it compete with that of England, but on the other hand he set up the linen trade which was to turn out so successful in Ulster.

In 1639 he called another Dublin parliament and again secured money for the king. He was now made Earl of Strafford and Lord Lieutenant, a more honourable title than Lord Deputy, and he raised a well-trained army of 9,000 men in Ireland to serve the king in England. But his career was drawing to a close. In 1640 he was recalled to England and in the following year was impeached by the House of Commons. (The most damaging charges against him came from Ireland.) He was sentenced to death and beheaded.

Thomas Wentworth constantly raised money for Charles I
and insultingly abused the hospitality of nobles,
'casting himself in his riding boots upon very rich beds'.

When Wentworth was summoned to England the arrangements to transport his Irish troops to England went to pieces. There was no money to pay or feed them, so they readily took to the traditional practice of plundering the civil population. Finally when they were disbanded, many joined continental armies and those who didn't, proved to be a well-trained nucleus for the regiments of the Confederates in the civil wars which followed shortly in Ireland.

The many plantations, the ruthless behaviour of Wentworth and the refusal of the king to grant the Graces, eventually led to a determination by some Irish chiefs to obtain their rights by insurrection. A rising throughout the country was set to take place on 23 October 1641. Dublin Castle and other fortresses throughout the country were to be seized and their stores of arms taken. On the evening of October 22, when all the plans were in place in Dublin, a man named Owen Connolly went to one of the Lords Justices, Sir William Parsons, and told him of the plot. Connolly had been drinking with two of the leaders, Hugh Óg MacMahon and Lord Maguire, and had been told the secret. At first Parsons didn't believe the story, for Connolly was drunk. But when Parsons consulted the other Lord Justice, Sir John Borlase, they decided to arrest the two leaders, MacMahon and Maguire, on the morning of the twenty-third. (The two of them were subsequently hanged in London.) Another leader, Rory O'More, escaped by rowing up the Liffey to Islandbridge to his daughter's house, where he was able to hide until it was safe to go further.

Although the rising failed in Dublin it broke out elsewhere in Ireland. The government was totally unprepared and its army was undisciplined, poorly paid and managed. Soon the rebels in Ulster under Sir Phelim O'Neill had overrun the province, taking Newry, Dungannon, Castleblayney and other smaller towns. He now had an army of 30,000, largely undisciplined, men. They were poorly armed, mostly with knives, scythes and pitchforks. They roamed throughout the province attacking settlers' homes. One historian estimated that 4,000 were murdered and a further 8,000 died of starvation and exposure. Soon a flood of refugees, men, women and children, were making their way to Dublin for shelter.

In Cavan the settlers were attacked by a force led by the local O'Reillys. After they were robbed and stripped naked the settlers were released and 'turned naked, without respect to age or sex, upon the wild barren mountains, in the cold air, exposed to all the severity of the winter from whence they . . . wandered towards Dublin'.

Of course the cruelty was two-sided. The Scottish garrison of Carrickfergus slaughtered hundreds in Island Magee. The two Lords Justices in Dublin, Parsons and Borlase, treated the Anglo-Irish nobles and gentry of the Pale with such unbelievable cruelty that it finally drove them to join the rebels. Parsons and Borlase also sent out military parties from the city to wreak terrible vengeance throughout the country. Their general, Sir Charles Coote, caused havoc in Wicklow, killing men, women and children. Munster saw similar atrocities by Sir William St Leger, to avenge, as he said, the outrages in Ulster.

This period of Irish history is extremely confused and confusing. The following is an attempt to unravel it. At the beginning of 1642 there were four distinct parties in Ireland, each with its own army.

First: the Old Irish whose leader was Rory O'More of Laois. They had suffered most from persecution and wanted complete independence from England. Their army was mostly confined to Ulster under the command of Sir Phelim O'Neill. The Old Irish

———— ◎ ————

A version of the bible was printed in 1631 by Robert Barker and Martin Lucas, the king's printers. It contained several mistakes, but one in particular caused great trouble. The Ten Commandments were printed with the word 'not' omitted from the Sixth Commandment and thus ordered its readers, on the highest authority, to commit adultery! King Charles I was so incensed by this that he recalled all 1,000 copies and fined the printers the then huge sum of £3,000.

———— ◎ ————

When Sir Phelim O'Neill assembled his Ulster army he produced a forged commission giving him the authority from King Charles himself! He even had the royal seal attached, which he had found in one of the castles he had taken.

———— ◎ ————

General Robert Monro, commander of the Parliamentarians, escaped after the battle of Benburb by throwing away his topcoat, hat and wig and mingling with the rest of the fleeing soldiers.

———— ◎ ————

party hoped to get aid from Irish exiles who had risen to positions of influence on the continent, particularly Owen Roe O'Neill, who had distinguished himself in the service of the King of Spain and who was a nephew of the great Hugh O'Neill.

Second: the Old Anglo-Irish Catholics, who were chiefly based in central and southern Ireland. These too had suffered because of their religion and from plantations. They wanted religion and civil liberty but not separation from England.

Neither of these parties really trusted the other.

Third: the Parliamentarians, who included the Presbyterians and the Scots of Ulster under General Robert Monro. The English Parliament in its war with King Charles had sent a Scottish army to Ulster, where it had joined English troops already there.

Fourth: the Royalist party, which held Dublin. These were mostly Protestants of the Established Church who opposed the Parliamentarians. They were the party of the king and they wished to make it appear that the Catholics were the king's enemies. Their leader was the Lord Lieutenant and Duke of Ormond, James Butler.

The war went on in 1642 – sometimes the rebels had victories, sometimes the government side. Things were not going too well with the Ulster rebels – Sir Phelim O'Neill was a poor leader while the Scottish army of 20,000 men under General Monro ravaged the province unchecked.

Owen Roe O'Neill defeated a Scottish army led by General Monro
in the Battle of Benburb, June 1646.

When Owen Roe O'Neill landed in Donegal in July 1642 with a hundred officers he immediately set about imposing discipline and putting an end to attacks on Protestant settlers.

Soon afterwards Colonel Preston, who also had a distinguished career on the continent, landed in Wexford with 500 officers and stores, and now took charge of the Anglo-Irish Catholic army.

By mid 1642 the rebels held most of Ireland except a few large towns. The only counties not in their control were Dublin, Louth, Antrim, Down, Derry and parts of Cork

The two branches on the Catholic side had acted mostly independently of each other from the beginning but the bishops now made a great effort to get them to act together. A general assembly, known as the Confederation of Kilkenny, first met on 24 October 1642 consisting of eleven bishops, fourteen lords and 226 commoners. The Royalist party of Dublin accused them as being in rebellion but the Confederate leaders denied this and said they were loyal subjects of the king. After their declaration of loyalty they appointed O'Neill in command of the Ulster army and put Preston in charge in Leinster.

The king was very willing to have the Confederation on his side against the English and Scottish Parliamentarians and he removed Borlase from office. He then appointed James Butler, Duke of Ormond as Lord Lieutenant to offer terms to the Confederation. Butler was very half-hearted in his efforts and anyway the king was a double-dealer. When the English parliament accused him of dealing with the Catholics he vehemently denied it.

The Pope, Innocent X, sent his personal nuncio, John Baptist Rinuccini, to the Confederation in October 1645 to unite the two Catholic parties in defence of their religion and to aid the king against his enemies in parliament. But the divisions in the Confederation were too great. The Old Irish side, led by O'Neill, and the nuncio wanted to carry on the war as vigorously as possible, while the Anglo-Irish section was for seeking agreement with the Royalists.

O'Neill managed to gather an army of 5,000 men and 500 cavalry which he positioned on the Cavan borders. Meanwhile, when Monro in Carrickfergus heard that Preston had taken his army to Connacht, leaving the Confederation undefended, he decided to attack Kilkenny and end the Confederation. Monro had 6,000 foot soldiers and 800 cavalry. O'Neill then marched from Cavan to intercept Monro on his way to Kilkenny. When Monro reached Armagh he heard of O'Neill's move and called on his brother, George, in Coleraine, to come with his cavalry to Glaslough in Monaghan and together they would crush O'Neill.

But O'Neill was too quick for him. He arrived in Glaslough before Monro and crossed into Tyrone and pitched his tents at Benburb. The next morning he sent two regiments to intercept George Monro and prepared his army for the arrival of the enemy. He selected an excellent position between two small hills with a wooded area to the rear. He divided his army into seven sections, placing four at the front with wide spaces between each section; the other three sections he placed at the rear, ready to move into the spaces provided as required. When Monro arrived at the battle site he arranged his army into nine sections, with five in front and four behind but he allowed no spaces between the forward troops. Consequently those at the rear were unable to advance to the front when needed. O'Neill then allowed the Scottish army no rest after their long march by constant light skirmishes until the afternoon when the sun was shining straight into their eyes.

Late in the day the arrival of a large body of troops from the north was at first taken by Monro to be his brother's army arriving but in fact they were O'Neill's two regiments arriving back from a successful demolition of George Monro's troops. The Scottish general was on the point of ordering a retreat when O'Neill gave the order to attack. His whole army surged forward with pike and sword and wreaked such awful damage on the Scots that they broke and ran. Monro himself barely escaped with his life. Over 2,000 of his men lay dead on the field while O'Neill had only about 200 men killed and wounded.

In the south of the country the Confederate army was also successful, with a force under Lord Muskerry capturing the Castle of Bunratty in County Clare.

The victory at Benburb greatly increased the influence of the Old Irish party in the Confederation. Then it became known that Ormond, head of the Royalist party, was in negotiations with the Parliamentarians to surrender Dublin to them. O'Neill and Preston were then ordered to proceed to Dublin to take over the city.

The two armies arrived within a few kilometres of Dublin and

Owen Roe O'Neill died on 6 November 1649 at Cloughoughter Castle in County Cavan at the age of about 65. It has always been maintained that he was poisoned but there is no evidence that this was so.

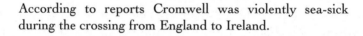

Signature of Owen Roe O'Neill shortly before his death.

Oliver Cromwell was a gentleman farmer from the east of England, who had no military training but emerged as the greatest general of the English Civil War. He believed everything he had heard about the massacre of Protestants during the rising of 1641 and perhaps this explains the appalling harshness with which he treated Irish Catholics later.

According to reports Cromwell was violently sea-sick during the crossing from England to Ireland.

Among Cromwell's supplies when he came to Ireland were thousands of bibles, which were to be distributed among his soldiers and to the native Irish (who would not understand a word of their contents!).

When Drogheda surrendered to Cromwell's forces his soldiers killed Aston, the garrison commander, by beating him to death with his own wooden leg.

O'Neill was so close that the city's anxious inhabitants could see hundreds of fires started by his army, raging from the Liffey round to Howth. But instead of attacking the city at once there was a delay, mainly due to Preston wishing to make a deal with Butler, Duke of Ormond. When Owen Roe heard of Preston's duplicity he withdrew his army in disgust. Ormond then surrendered the city to the Parliamentarians under General Jones, and fled to France.

Soon afterwards Jones inflicted a heavy defeat on Preston near Summerhill in County Meath and another Parliamentarian army under Lord Inchiquin, once a Royalist, who is remembered as 'Murrough of the Burnings' for his depredations in Munster, defeated a Confederate army near Mallow in County Cork.

A year later Ormond returned from France and managed to broker a peace between the Confederates and the Royalists but it was all too late – Charles I was beheaded that same year, Dublin was firmly in the hands of the Parliamentarians and the papal nuncio went back to Rome.

The execution of the king caused such a revulsion in Ireland that nearly all the Irish parties, including Ormond, the Confederates and the Scots and Presbyterians of Ulster, declared for the Royalist cause against the Parliamentarians and proclaimed the Prince of Wales as King Charles II. The Parliamentarians under Jones still held Dublin but Inchiquin – once more a Royalist – captured Drogheda, Dundalk, Newry and Trim from the Parliamentarians. Now Ormond marched with an army from Kilkenny to recover the city of Dublin which he had surrendered so tamely two years earlier. He reached the outskirts of the city on 21 June and the next day he made some half-hearted attacks on the north side of the city.

Jones had about 4,500 men to defend Dublin while Ormond had roughly the same amount. The city itself was in a very poor state to defend itself against attack. It had no proper fortifications and was low on provisions.

Ormond seems not to have known the poor state the city was in, for he delayed his attack for so long that the defenders were able to get new supplies from England and were able to strengthen the fortifications. Ormond did very little until the end of July when he decided to march around to the south of the city but a surprise attack on his army on the night of 2 August 1649 caused his men to flee in utter panic.

———— ◎ ————

After Cromwell's forces captured Drogheda many of the leading ladies of the town were found hiding in the church's crypt, but they too were killed without mercy. One officer wrote later of finding 'the flower and choicest of the women and ladies of the town' among whom was 'a handsome virgin, arrayed in costly and gorgeous apparel, who knelt before him with tears and prayers to save her life'. He took pity on her and raised her up but another soldier thrust his sword through her body. Whereupon her erstwhile rescuer threw her down, having first taken all her money and jewellery.

———— ◎ ————

During the siege of Clonmel one attack was led by a Colonel Charles Langley but as he tried to climb over the defences his hand was cut off by a scythe. He survived however and was granted lands at Ballingarry, County Tipperary. He later had a steel replacement hand made and the hand is said to have remained in the family until the early twentieth century.

———— ◎ ————

Cromwell's attack on Clonmel was going very badly at one stage and he was on the point of withdrawing but legend has it that he found a rough silver bullet that had been fired by the defenders. From this he surmised that Hugh Dubh O'Neill was reduced to using every available metal in the town as ammunition and this encouraged Cromwell to continue the siege.

———— ◎ ————

By this time the Parliamentarians in England under Oliver Cromwell were triumphant. He now turned his attention to Ireland with the intention of crushing any Royalists still active there. On 14 August 1649, accompanied by his son-in-law, Sir Henry Ireton, as second-in-command, Cromwell landed at Ringsend at the mouth of the Liffey. He was accompanied by 9,000 foot soldiers, 4,000 cavalry and a large supply of war materials and money. When his army arrived in the city he stabled his horses in St Patrick's Cathedral, which was in a bad state of disrepair at the time. His forces quickly captured the castles at Rathfarnham, Kimmage and Tallaght.

Oliver Cromwell, forever associated with the massacre of Drogheda in 1649, issued a proclamation to his troops against plunder of any kind.

Later Cromwell addressed a large crowd in Dublin and told them that, by God's providence, he would 'restore them all to their just liberties and properties'. On 23 August he made an order forbidding the citizens from 'profaning, swearing, drinking and cursing, which were said to be the daily practice of the place'.

On 31 August he left Dublin and proceeded against Drogheda and encamped outside the town on 2 September. Ormond had put a garrison of 3,000 of his best troops in the town, many of whom were Englishmen, commanded by Sir Arthur Aston. Cromwell had a much larger army but the town's defenders hoped that 'Colonel Hunger and Major Sickness' would soon help to reduce the besieging army. To help the process along Aston sent out raiding parties to harass Cromwell's forces – with limited success it must be said, for on one occasion 200 men in a raiding party were captured. When Cromwell had his guns in position on the hills overlooking the town on the south side, and with the harbour blocked off against relief by sea, he sent a message to Aston calling on him to surrender the town. Aston immediately refused and the bombardment of the walls began at eight o'clock on the morning of 9 September 1649. When two breaches were made by 10 September Cromwell sent in his troops at 5 o'clock in the evening.

The defenders had meantime built earthworks behind the breaches and met the attackers with stern resistance but at last they were forced to yield with the promise that their lives would be spared. Aston had retired with his men to an old mill but when they surrendered the Cromwellians killed them all. There followed five days of appalling slaughter. Men, women and children were killed without mercy. A number of the people had taken refuge in the Protestant church, St Peters, at the top of Magdalene Street. The soldiers proceeded to kill every one of them and when they discovered that others had climbed up into the church's wooden steeple they set it on fire and everyone perished.

Cromwell later wrote that,

> It hath pleased God to bless our endeavours at Drogheda . . . The enemy were about 3,000 strong in the town . . . I believe we put to the sword the whole number of defendants. I do not think that thirty of the whole number escaped with their lives. Those that did are in safe custody for shipment to the Barbadoes.

The ferocity of Cromwell's treatment of Drogheda had its effect and other towns in the area such as Dundalk, Carlingford, Trim and Newry quickly surrendered.

Next Cromwell returned to Dublin and from there proceeded to Wexford where there was a garrison of 3,000 men under a Captain Synnot. He refused to open the gates and the Cromwellian guns opened fire on 11 October 1649. After they had managed to breach the walls Synnot agreed to parley. The talks were still going on when Captain Stafford, the commander of the castle just outside the walls, opened the gates to Cromwell's army. This enabled them

to enter the town and once more they proceeded to slaughter all
before them.

After a two-day siege, the town of New Ross surrendered to
Cromwell on 18 October 1649. On 24 November he began to
attack Waterford but, as his troops were being ravaged by sickness
and fever, he was forced to abandon the siege, and retire to winter
quarters.

During those winter months many towns all over Ireland
accepted the authority of the English Parliament, so that only a few
towns still remained loyal to the king.

At the end of January in the new year Cromwell again led his
army south through Munster. Most towns surrendered without a
fight but his army was to meet stiff resistance at Clonmel in
Tipperary. The town was defended by Hugh Dubh O'Neill, a
nephew of the famous Owen Roe, in whose service he had spent
sixteen years on the Continent. (Hugh Dubh, 'Black Hugh', was so
called because of his dark complexion.)

In the winter of 1649 he had been appointed governor of
Clonmel by the Lord Lieutenant, Ormond, and had a garrison of
1500 men and 100 horse soldiers. O'Neill stubbornly held out
against every assault and even made frequent raids on the
besieging army outside the walls, killing 200 to 500 of the attackers
with little loss to himself. Cromwell's army was becoming
increasingly weakened by disease and these attacks but there were
still about 14,000 men attacking the town.

Even though his guns could not force a surrender they were still
able to breach the walls sufficiently in one place to warrant an
assault by his troops. But O'Neill had guessed that an assault would
take place at that point and had organised soldiers and
townspeople to construct a makeshift cul-de-sac of stones, wood
and mud, stretching back from the breach in the wall. At the end
of the lane he had dug a deep trench and then concealed two
cannon guns overlooking the trench and cul-de-sac. The guns were
loaded with chain-shot and aimed at waist level. O'Neill had
organised his men, armed with muskets, swords, pikes, scythes and
every type of weapon available, and lined them up behind the walls
of the lane.

Cromwell knew nothing of these preparations as they were
carried out at night and were concealed from view by the town's

walls. At eight o'clock in the morning he ordered the assault. His troops poured in through the breach in great numbers and met no resistance until they came up against the barrier at the end of the cul-de-sac. Their shouts of 'Halt! Halt!' to their companions behind were taken by them as being addressed to fleeing Royalists and they pressed forward in increasing numbers. Soon there were about 1000 of them, hemmed in and at the mercy of O'Neill's men who quickly blocked off the breach in the wall to prevent reinforcements entering, Then O'Neill gave the order to attack. The two concealed cannon opened up and cut down swathes of the invaders, while the swords, pikes and muskets of the defenders caused horrific damage. Soon there was not a single Cromwellian soldier alive.

Cromwell was meanwhile on horseback outside the main gate waiting for it to open and when he realised what was happening he tried to organise another assault on the breach. His foot soldiers were so terrified that they refused to advance, so he called on his cavalry to do so. Led by a Colonel Langley, the horsemen dismounted and charged the breach again but with very limited success. Even though Cromwell threw more and more troops into the assault he was forced eventually to withdraw his troops to a safe distance from the town and settle down for a long siege. Later a delegation from the town led by the mayor went out to discuss surrender terms with Cromwell who, having lost up to 2,500 men, was very willing to accept any terms which would yield the town to him. Only when the surrender terms were agreed and signed did he learn that Hugh Dubh was not in the town but had slipped away under cover of darkness and was far away by then. Cromwell was said to be furious at being thwarted but, honourably enough, stood by the agreement.

By May the Parliamentarians were in control of most of the country and the Parliament in England made pressing demands for Cromwell to return to sort out problems there. He sailed from Youghal on 20 May 1650 after a stay of nine months in Ireland, leaving Major General Ireton in command.

Ireton now turned his attention to Limerick, the most important town left in the hands of the Royalists. Hugh Dubh O'Neill, the hero of Clonmel, had been put in command of the town by Ormond in June 1650. By this time a plague was raging among the city's citizens and also among the Cromwellian soldiers. Eventually the town was betrayed by a Colonel Fennell who opened St John's Gate in the walls. Among those executed by the victors was the same Fennell but O'Neill's army were allowed to depart after laying down their arms. (O'Neill eventually made his way to Spain.)

Ireton did not live to enjoy his success – he caught the plague and died a fortnight later. When he died the command of the army passed to Lieutenant General Ludlow who now marched on Galway. After a nine month siege the town surrendered in 1652 and the 'Cromwellian Wars' were over.

Cromwell's soldiers were due a lot of money in wages but it was felt that it would be cheaper if they were paid in land. Consequently the English Parliament passed an act dispossessing the Irish of their lands in Ulster, Munster and Leinster and told them to depart for Connacht by 1 May 1654. Anyone ordered away who was later found in any of the other three provinces after this date might be killed by whoever met them. This later became known as the 'To Hell or to Connacht' decree.

Many of the dispossessed disobeyed the order and formed themselves in roving bands of outlaws who became known as 'rapparees' and 'tories'. They roamed the country plundering, killing and being killed. They were mercilessly hunted down by the settlers – no quarter was given or asked by either side.

Many of the younger Irishmen chose to leave the country altogether and about 34,000 of them entered the armies of France, Spain, Austria and Venice.

Generally, however, the aftermath of the Cromwellian plantation was similar to that of Munster and the Ulster plantations. The English, especially the soldiers, ignored the prohibition against intermarrying with the native Irish. They adopted the Irish language, customs and religion. In a census of 1659 it was found that the proportions of Irish to English were as follows: Leinster 13 to 2, Munster 10 to 1, Ulster 5 to 2 and Connacht 11 to 1. Even though the census is not regarded as very accurate it does give a general overall picture. In one respect, however, the Cromwellian settlement was very successful in that the land of Ireland was now largely in the hands of the occupiers.

9

◎

'CHANGE LEADERS AND WE'LL FIGHT YOU ALL OVER AGAIN'

The restoration of Charles II to the English throne in 1660 was greeted with great joy by Irish Catholics. They now expected some redress for their sufferings at the hands of the Cromwellians but they were to be bitterly disappointed.

In 1661 the Dublin Parliament passed an Act of Settlement, giving the new settlers a title to their holdings. The Catholics strongly objected to this and after several years wrangling the matter was finally settled by allowing the Protestants two-thirds of the lands and the Catholics one-third. (This was a complete reversal of the situation before the Act of Settlement.)

While the king, Charles II, was suspected of being secretly a Catholic, it was known that his brother James, Duke of York (later James II) was indeed one. In 1678 a 'Popish Plot' to restore the Catholic monarchy in England was 'discovered'. An Englishman of low character called Titus Oates (a disgraced Anglican clergyman and for a brief time a Catholic seminarian) pretended to have discovered a plot to kill the king and install James on the throne with the help of a French invasion. While his evidence was extremely flimsy the Privy Council appeared to believe him. A veritable frenzy of persecution of Catholics ensued, leading to the execution of many leading (and innocent) Catholic gentlemen. The fury soon spread to Ireland and Archbishop Talbot of Dublin was selected as the first victim. Although he was extremely ill in his bed at the time he was arrested and taken to Dublin Castle. He died there two years later. Two other 'conspirators' were also named: Lord Mountgarrett and a Colonel Peppard. Mountgarrett was in his eighties, confined to bed and senile, while no trace could ever by found of a 'Colonel Peppard' for the simple reason that he didn't exist.

James II, the first English king to attend the opening of an Irish parliament, wore a crown specially made for him in Dublin.

One of the very few who had escaped the Cromwellian massacre at Drogheda in 1649 was a young lieutenant called Richard Talbot. Cromwell later arrested and jailed him in London but he managed to get his jailers drunk one night and escaped over the prison walls by means of a home-made rope. He made his way to a boat on the Thames and subsequently reached the Low Countries where he joined the future King James.

When James II succeeded his brother Charles II in 1685 he set about restoring the Catholic religion in England and Ireland in such a heavy-handed, harsh and illegal fashion that he deeply offended the Protestant population. Shortly afterwards he rewarded the faithful Talbot by giving him the title Earl of Tyrconnell and sending him to Ireland as commander of the forces in 1687.

One of Talbot's first acts was to disband thousands of Protestant soldiers and officers and put Catholics in their place. Many of the officers went to Holland where they went into the service of William, Prince of Orange. Next Tyrconnell was appointed Lord Lieutenant by James and this caused even more dismay among the Protestants.

Meanwhile in England the reign of King James was bitterly resented by the people but they could console themselves that at least an end was in sight of Catholic rule. James was then fifty-five years old and as his second wife, Queen Mary of Modena, had no surviving children, the successor to the throne would be Mary, his eldest daughter of his first marriage. Mary was a Protestant and was married to William of Orange of Holland, who was also a Protestant.

King William of Orange arrived in Carrickfergus in June 1690 and defeated James II at the River Boyne in July.

Then in 1688, to the horror of the Protestant population of England, the queen gave birth to a son who would, of course, be brought up as a Catholic and would inherit the throne. With the prospect of a succession of Catholic monarchs before them, the English people offered the throne to William of Orange. He readily accepted and landed with his army in England in November 1688.

When William landed at Torbay in the South of England James mustered an army to resist William's march on London. The Lord Deputy in Dublin, Tyrconnell, immediately dispatched three Irish regiments to England to help James and also set about securing Ireland for him. He raised a large, irregular, untrained and undisciplined army of Catholics and took possession of the most important places throughout the country. He also ordered Colonel Mountjoy and Lieutenant Colonel Robert Lundy, the officers commanding the regiment based in Derry, which was then a completely walled city situated on the Donegal side of the River Foyle, to march south to Dublin on 20 November 1688 to replace the regiments sent to England.

At the same time, Lord MacDonnell, Third Earl of Antrim, was ordered to raise a regiment of Catholic Irish and Scots to march to Derry to garrison that city. Lord MacDonnell, at the age of seventy-six, was quite willing to obey but he took his time. He wanted only fine physical specimens, over six feet tall, in his army, so recruitment went slowly. Consequently the regiment was not ready to take over Derry on 20 November. Colonel Mountjoy could not wait, so he marched his regiment out of the city three days later, leaving it without a garrison.

By December 1688 Antrim had got his regiment of 'Redshanks', as the bare-legged Highlanders were called, and got ready to march to Derry. Then in that same week the strange affair of the 'Comber Letter' occurred. This semi-illiterate letter was found on a street in the village of Comber, County Down. The letter was addressed to the Protestant Earl Mount-Alexander of County Down, warning him that there was a plan for the Irish to murder every Protestant man, woman and child they could find.

To this day, no one knows whether the letter was genuine or a hoax but it had the effect of galvanising Protestant resistance all over the North. In Derry it further added to the fears of the citizens as they awaited the arrival of Antrim's Redshanks. This twelve-hundred strong army had by now arrived in Limavady, twenty-seven kilometres from Derry and messengers were sent to the city by local officials to warn the citizens to close the gates and resist any attempt of the army to enter.

The city council was in a dilemma – if they admitted the Redshanks they might all be slaughtered but at the same time the troops were acting under orders of Tyrconnell, the Lord Deputy of the lawful king, James. While the leaders dithered and debated thirteen apprentice boys took the law into their own hands. They rushed down to the Ferryquay Gate in the south wall and closed it almost in the faces of the Jacobite soldiers. When the soldiers hung around outside undecided on what to do, a citizen inside the walls shouted loudly to an imaginary colleague 'to bring the great gun over here'. At this the soldiers took to their heels and retreated over the river Foyle to the Waterside. Lord Antrim himself arrived

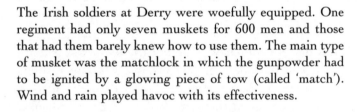

Many innocent people were arrested and imprisoned because of the 'Popish Plot', the most famous of whom was the Archbishop of Armagh, Oliver Plunkett. He was arrested and charged with planning a French invasion. A first trial in Dundalk collapsed when his accusers – some priests he had earlier dismissed for various misdemeanours – withdrew from the trial. He was then brought to London where he was tried again and convicted. Even though the evidence against him was totally discredited, King Charles refused to jeopardise his position by granting him a pardon. Oliver Plunkett was 'hanged, drawn and quartered' in 1681. He was also beheaded and his head was thrown into the fire but it was rescued before being incinerated. It is now on display in St Peter's Church in Drogheda. In 1920 he was beatified and in 1975 he was canonised.

The Irish soldiers at Derry were woefully equipped. One regiment had only seven muskets for 600 men and those that had them barely knew how to use them. The main type of musket was the matchlock in which the gunpowder had to be ignited by a glowing piece of tow (called 'match'). Wind and rain played havoc with its effectiveness.

Derry's walls were constructed between 1613 and 1618 and had an outer stone section two metres thick. The earth in front of the walls was dug out to form a ditch about three metres deep and nine metres wide. This ditch ran along the whole length of the wall except for the part overlooking the Bogside on the northern side (where the ground was very steep) and at the part of the wall along the river where the Guildhall is at present. The earth removed was used to form an earthen rampart three and a half metres thick behind the wall.

Derry was the last walled city to be built in western Europe and is the only town in Ireland where the complete surrounding stone wall survives.

just in time to witness his Redshanks running headlong away from the walls. Many of them had removed their boots because they found it easier to run without them. Some shots had indeed been fired from the walls and they had fled in panic, not knowing that the shots were blanks.

The closing of the gates also instilled in the citizens a strong determination to defend the city at all costs. But the city was in no condition for a long siege. There were only about three hundred men fit to bear arms, while the arms themselves were in poor condition. There were less than six barrels of gun-powder and hardly any provisions. Later, when news of the parlous state of the defences spread, reinforcements began streaming in from the country all around and from Donegal. Among the volunteers was a Derry lawyer, David Cairns, who rode in on his horse from his country house in Tyrone. He was the uncle of one of the apprentice boys and he now helped to organise the defenders into military-style companies and regiments with officers to command them. There were now about 7000 men to man the defences. A gun was placed at every gate and two were positioned on the roof of the Protestant cathedral. These were to prove very troublesome to the besieging army later on. Later Cairns travelled to England seeking help from the Irish Society (the company set up in London to manage the Plantation of Ulster).

The Lord Deputy Tyrconnell meanwhile ordered Mountjoy, whose army had only reached Dublin three days before, to return to Derry to take over the city.

When Mountjoy and his army reached Omagh a group from the Derry Corporation met him and told him that although the corporation and people were still loyal to James there was no way they would allow Catholic soldiers to take over. They eventually agreed to let two of his companies under the command of Lieutenant-Colonel Robert Lundy into the city, provided that every soldier was a Protestant. In the meantime all Catholics in the city were told to leave and Lundy was then appointed governor. Soon afterwards the Protestants of Derry renounced their allegiance to James and publicly declared that they were holding the city for William and Mary.

James now fled from England to France and William sent a ship, the *Deliverance*, to Derry with supplies for the garrison and

———— ◎ ————

The largest gun on Derry's walls was 'Roaring Meg', so-called because of the tremendous sound it made. It was a gift from the Fishmongers of London in 1642. It is 3·3 metres long and 1·4 metres wide at its thickest part. It still stands silently on guard facing the Guildhall today.

———— ◎ ————

During his escape from Derry Lieutenant-Colonel Robert Lundy, governor of Derry, disguised himself as a private soldier or camp follower and is said to have escaped over the east wall by climbing a pear tree growing against it. He was carrying a 'load of match' on his back to aid his disguise. 'Match' was the name given to the pieces of hemp or cotton rope which were specially prepared so that when lighted it was hard to extinguish them. Match was used to ignite the powder to fire the muskets or cannon guns at the time. Later Lundy's 'load of match' was mistakenly confused with matchwood and this is why his effigy is burned every year with bundles of firewood tied to it.

———— ◎ ————

Lundy, after he escaped, made his way to Culmore and then to Scotland where he was arrested. He was sent to the Tower of London and tried for treason but was later released on bail and allowed to join the English army. He helped to defend Gibraltar in 1707 in the War of the Spanish Succession. Taken prisoner by the Spanish he was later released in exchange for twenty Spanish soldiers and returned to England. He died in 1717.

———— ◎ ————

citizens. The ship's captain, William Hamilton, also carried with him a commission for Lundy but was instructed that he was not to hand over any arms, ammunition, money or commission until Lundy swore his allegiance to William. Lundy opted to take the oath in private in the captain's cabin aboard the *Deliverance*. (Controversy has persisted ever since as to whether he ever did swear allegiance but since the ship's captain, Hamilton, was intensely loyal to William it is very likely that Lundy did take the oath.)

When James heard of all that Tyrconnell was doing on his behalf he mustered up the courage to return and landed in Kinsale in Cork on 12 March 1690, the first English king to come to Ireland since Richard II in 1399. He was accompanied by a small number of French officers and some Irish troops, among whom was one officer called Patrick Sarsfield, who was six feet tall, well built and thirty-eight years old. The overall commander of the forces was a French general, Marshal Rosen.

Just one day after his arrival in Dublin, James summoned a parliament in the city to meet on 7 May 1690. James himself attended the opening ceremony, wearing his robes and a crown specially made for him in Dublin. Never before had an English king attended the opening of an Irish parliament.

Meanwhile the attempts to capture Derry were getting no further but when James was told that he only had to appear at the gates of that city and they would be thrown open to him, he set out for the North. His journey was very miserable, as the country was completely desolate, but he eventually joined his commander, James Hamilton, and his army a few kilometres south of Derry. Hamilton had about 7,000 soldiers at his command and together with another force under the French general, Rosen, they set up camp at a crossing on the Foyle twenty-four kilometres south of the city near Lifford and Clady.

Showing great bravery, Rosen led his army across the swollen river and routed the Protestant army under Lundy which had attempted to halt their progress. The Irish cavalry chased the fleeing enemy and killed up to four hundred of them. The rest of them took refuge in the bogs into which the cavalry could not follow. Those that escaped made their way back to Derry which was already filling up with refugees from the countryside all

———— ◎ ————

During the hungry days of the siege of Derry 'a certain fat
gentleman conceived himself in great danger and, fancying
several of the garrison looked at him with a greedy eye,
thought fit to hide himself for three days.'

———— ◎ ————

A Captain Holmes said that during the Derry siege 'one
bomb slew seventeen persons. I was in the next room one
night at my supper and seven men were thrown out of the
third room next to that we were in, all killed and some in
pieces.'

———— ◎ ————

The fiery Reverend George Walker who became governor
of Derry gave a price list for food within the city:
'Horseflesh 1s 8d lb; quarter of dog (fattened by eating the
bodies of the slain Irish) 5s 6d lb; a dog's head 2s 6d; a cat
4s 6d; a rat 1s; a mouse 6d; a small flook (flounder) taken in
the river – not to be bought for money.'

———— ◎ ————

The Jacobite leader Rosen was a soldier of fortune from
what is present-day Estonia. He joined the French army as
a private and eventually reached the rank of colonel-
general. It was said of him that his temper was savage, his
manners were coarse and his language was a strange jargon
compounded of various dialects of French and German.

———— ◎ ————

around. This battle led to suspicions that Lundy had somehow aided the Jacobites in their routing of the Protestant forces. Be that as it may, he certainly was among the first to reach the safety of the city walls where he ordered that the gates be closed. By doing so he shut out thousands of his own men, among whom was the Reverend George Walker (of later fame). Then at the darkest hour for the defenders of Derry came the wonderful news that three ships had entered Lough Foyle bringing relief to the beleaguered city.

The leader of this expedition was Colonel Cunningham and some time later he and some of his officers disembarked and made their way in to the city. They immediately went to Governor Lundy's house and then adjourned to the Council Chamber where a very select few, including Lundy and Cunningham but not George Walker (who had managed to enter the city in the meantime) held a secret meeting. When Walker tried to gain entrance he was forcibly ejected.

What exactly happened at that meeting has been debated ever since but the upshot of it was that Cunningham and his men sailed back to England bringing with them most of the leading men of the city, together with many of the garrison's officers. Seemingly Lundy had convinced the meeting that Derry could not be defended.

The meeting also began to draft an 'instrument of surrender' in the hope that King James would pardon them for their actions. Lundy got everyone to declare 'on their honour' that they would not divulge what they had decided but he forgot to include the silent secretary taking the minutes. It was a grave mistake, for very soon the news of what the council had done was common knowledge throughout the city. The populace was enraged – so much so that Lundy was forced to flee the city. The new governors, Reverend George Walker and Major Henry Baker (a professional soldier from County Louth) allowed Lundy to escape, due to the respect for his person and former office.

The two governors now set about reorganising the city's defence. The city was divided into eight sectors and each sector had a 'home-guard' regiment to defend it. They certainly needed to be ready quickly because the Irish army under King James was now nearing the city.

When the king and his army approached Bishop's Gate he

stopped about 200 metres from it. Immediately a terrific barrage of cannon and musket fire was directed at them from the walls and the famous cry 'No Surrender' rang out for the first time.

An officer at the king's side was killed and the rest of the soldiers took to their heels, although many were killed. James himself retired out of shooting range and sat on his horse all day watching the city in the pouring rain.

Even at that stage there was the possibility that the city would surrender, for Walker and Baker sent an abject apology to James, saying that a rabble had seized the cannon and fired on the king's army. The king accepted the apology and sent a messenger, 'a lord with a trumpet', to ask for twenty men to be sent to the king to arrange the surrender. Again the city council gave in and appointed the twenty representatives that would discuss terms but when they approached the city gates the men on guard threatened them that any man who left would be treated as a traitor. Mindful of the fact that one of the city's officers had previously been shot for trying to escape, the representatives decided to stay put. From that point on, all thought of surrender ceased.

A message was sent to James to the effect that the city was determined to hold out for King William, and realising that no further purpose would be served by remaining at Derry, James, accompanied by Rosen, returned to Dublin.

The commander of the Jacobite army at Derry now was the French general, Maumont. His army settled in on the hills surrounding the city, stretching from the south right round to Culmore Fort, which was six kilometres north of the city on Lough Foyle. The fort itself had been in the hands of a Protestant garrison but they surrendered without a fight.

The Jacobite soldiers were very poorly equipped for a long siege. One French officer said that 'most of the soldiers in front of Derry have still only pointed sticks, without iron tips'. When King James had inspected one regiment he found that only one gun in a hundred could be fired. A number of guns were then put in place on the east bank of the river, particularly opposite the Shipquay Gate.

Two days earlier the Protestants had a victory at Pennyburn, just north of the city. The small village was in their hands and as the Jacobite army moved in to occupy it they were ambushed by some

Protestants who lay behind the hedges. This group was later strengthened by a further 500 musketeers from Derry. Hamilton, the leader of the Jacobites, immediately sent for reinforcements and when the commander-in-chief, Maumont, rode to his aid at the head of a small cavalry troop, Maumont himself was killed. The Protestants were driven back to Derry, however, but the Irish cavalry riding in pursuit were almost wiped out by the musketeers lying in ambush.

The siege continued, with the Jacobites bombarding the city and small bands of defenders rushing out to repel any Irish who approached the walls. By the end of six weeks up to 3,000 of the besiegers had died of disease or been killed.

At the end of May the Jacobites decided to build a floating boom across the river mouth to prevent relief of the city from the sea and by 4 June it was completed. The boom was made of oak planks at first but when that sank they replaced it with one made of pine. It was bound with chains and cables and attached to each side of the river but the whole assembly could float up and down with the tide.

In the meantime the Jacobites made several determined efforts to attack the city outposts but were beaten back each time. The Derry women-folk took an active part in the proceedings 'carrying ammunition, match, bread and drink to our men . . . and beating off with stones the grenadiers who came next to our lines'.

Then on 31 May a fleet of thirty ships under the command of Major-General Percy Kirke, carrying 5,000 soldiers and a cargo of food, set sail from Liverpool to raise the siege of Derry. On 7 June the delighted Derry garrison saw the masts of three shallow draught ships, the *Greyhound*, the *Fisher* and the *Edward* approaching. After some brisk exchange of fire with the Jacobite land guns the three ships were extremely lucky to escape back to safer waters. Four days later, on 11 June, Kirke's full fleet sailed into view to the intense joy of the garrison who fired off celebratory cannon and rang the cathedral bells. And then, to the rage of the besieged and the puzzlement of the besiegers, Kirke proceeded to do absolutely nothing!

There was no means of communication between city and fleet and all efforts at signalling failed. When a large banner was waved four times from the steeple of the cathedral to show that the people were in desperate straits the fleet took it to mean that they were

———————— ◎ ————————

During the siege of Derry great efforts were made by Major-General Kirke to establish communications between the fleet and the city's defenders. Two volunteers a Scot, James Cromie, and an Irishman, James Roche, stepped forward. Cromie couldn't swim but Roche was a powerful swimmer. A small boat landed the two brave volunteers at Faughan on the eastern bank of the Foyle about eight kilometres from the city. The two men managed to make their way through Irish lines for about three kilometres and then Roche stripped off at a deserted fish house and entered the river to swim the remaining distance. He staggered ashore, nearly dead from cold and exhaustion. When he recovered enough to be aware of his circumstances he found he was in the hands of the city's citizens and that they were about to hang him as a spy.

He managed to convince them that he was a genuine messenger from Kirke by predicting accurately what Kirke's reply would be to a signal from the cathedral steeple. After that he was warmly welcomed by the garrison and he gave them a letter from Kirke and details about the relieving fleet. He told them that there were great supplies on board the ships for them but also gave them the sobering message from Kirke that they should carefully ration their food as their deliverance would take some time.

Roche then set about the arduous return trip with the message that there was only enough food left in the city for four more days. He swam all the way back to the fish house to retrieve his clothes at midnight only to find that Jacobite dragoons were in hiding waiting for him. He managed to evade them and fled totally naked through the woods for five kilometres with the dragoons in hot pursuit. Just as they closed in on him and broke his jaw and a collarbone with a blow from a musket he jumped from a nine-metre cliff into the Foyle. Even then he was not safe, for they fired hundreds of shots and wounded him in the chest, hand and shoulder.

Miraculously he managed to swim back to Derry city where he lay unconscious for an hour. He later made a full recovery from his wounds and was rewarded with a captain's commission in the army of King William and later some lands in County Waterford.

———————— ◎ ————————

proudly showing off captured enemy colours! Various valiant attempts to send messages by hand between the fleet and city all failed and another six weeks of ever-increasing starvation was to be endured by the desperate inhabitants before they got any relief.

In the middle of all this trouble the city got more bad news – the ruthless French General Rosen returned from Dublin on 17 June to take command of the besieging army again. He very soon lived up to his reputation for cruelty by sending word to the city that unless they surrendered he would round up every Protestant he could find and send them into the city. His purpose was to further increase the appalling starvation the citizens were suffering. Not receiving an immediate response to his ultimatum he drove over a thousand Protestant men, women and children to the city's walls in the hope that the garrison would be forced to admit them. But the brave refugees called on their friends inside the walls not to give in, telling them that if they surrendered they would all be killed.

The garrison then neatly met threat with counter-threat. They erected a large gallows in full view of the enemy and announced that unless the Protestants in front of the walls were allowed to depart they would hang every Jacobite prisoner they had.

Shortly afterwards the attackers relented, gave the Protestant refugees food and money and allowed them to return to their homes. In response the garrison dismantled the gallows. Later when King James heard what Rosen had done he was furious and said that 'only a barbarous Muscovite' could have thought up such a scheme.

In letters to King James at this time Rosen complained that the reinforcements from Dublin were useless – one regiment had only seven muskets among them, the rest had only sticks! Hamilton's soldiers at Derry were even worse off – more than two thirds of them had 'no swords, belts or bandoliers' and they were dying faster from disease than from battle. One regiment given the task of guarding the chest that contained the money to pay the troops had not been issued with a single round of ammunition! Two or three weeks later Rosen left for France to the great satisfaction of both Jacobites and Williamites.

On 10 July Hamilton again called on the city to surrender by firing a hollow cannon ball containing the surrender terms into the grounds of the cathedral. (That cannon ball is still on show in

———— ◎ ————

The Scotsman Cromie, the second volunteer, had his own story to tell. After Roche set out to swim to Derry he remained in hiding in the woods but was captured by the Jacobite soldiers. He was brought to the French officer in command, the Chevalier de Vaundry, who questioned him closely and frightened him sufficiently to bring a false message supposedly from Kirke to the Derry garrison. The Jacobites also invited the city to send out a deputation to parley. This they did and Cromie told them that there was no hope of relief from Kirke. When they asked Cromie why his story was so different from Roche's he pointed out that he was a prisoner of the Jacobites. This hint confirmed their belief that Roche was the genuine messenger.

It had been prearranged that the boat which had landed Roche and Cromie should return to pick them up on 26 June. When it arrived at Faughan, however, the Jacobites, informed by Cromie, were waiting for them. They called on the crew to come ashore but when asked for the password the Jacobites didn't know it. The small boat immediately pulled away and in spite of heavy fire managed to get back to the fleet. It was assumed then that both Cromie and Roche had been captured.

On that same night of 26 June another brave man called McGimpsey volunteered to swim from the city to the fleet. He entered the river at Ship Quay with messages for Kirke in a bladder which was tied to his neck. He never reached the fleet, however, but drowned in the river. His body was later pulled out of the water by the Jacobites who found the letters. These greatly encouraged the besieging army for the letters stated that 'if you do not send relief we must surrender the garrison in six or seven days'. (In fact the siege was to last another six weeks.)

———— ◎ ————

St Columb's Cathedral today.) The temptation was great to accept, as the population was on the point of starvation. Even more disheartening was the disappearance of most of the fleet from Lough Foyle on 12 July. On 13 July a deputation was sent to the besieging army carrying a list of terms which would allow an honourable surrender. Deadlock followed and the delegation was allowed to go back to the city to get the council to agree to surrender by 15 July instead of the proposed 26 July. Hamilton was convinced the council was playing for time in the hope that Kirke would relieve the siege before then.

The council would not yield on the date and then they found out that Kirke had only withdrawn most of his fleet in an attempt to cut off the Jacobites' supply of food from Inch Island in Lough Swilly and also to give the soldiers a break from aboard ship. Messages now passed back and forth between city and Kirke by the ingenious use of small boys. (Some of them carried messages concealed in their rectums.)

On 26 July at 3 a.m. 200 men left by Bishop's Gate and another 200 by Butcher's Gate with the intention of capturing some of the Jacobites' cattle. The plan was a failure and the plight of the city's inhabitants was so desperate that men could hardly stand or walk, never mind fight. The besieging army was almost in as bad a state and knew that they had no hope of storming the city and their only hope was to starve it into surrender.

Meanwhile, King William's Marshal Schomberg had written to Kirke to tell him he must try to relieve the city. Kirke selected three small ships, the 50-ton *Phoenix*, the *Jerusalem* of about the same size, and the 150-ton *Mountjoy* to attempt to break the boom. The warship, the *Dartmouth*, commanded by Captain Leake, was sent as escort.

The plan was that the *Mountjoy* and *Phoenix* would attempt to break the boom, while the *Dartmouth* would engage the enemy guns on each side of the river. The *Jerusalem* was to be kept in reserve and only to sail when the boom was broken. A longboat crewed by nine seamen from the *Swallow*, (which was too big to navigate the river) was to help in the task of breaking the boom.

At 7 o'clock on the calm Sunday evening of 28 July the *Dartmouth* led the way, followed by the three smaller ships and the longboat. While the *Dartmouth* exchanged gunfire with the

———— ◎ ————

Walker said that the army besieging Derry lobbed mortar bombs weighing 270 lbs each into the city. These 'contained several pounds of powder in the shell; they plowed up our streets and broke down our houses, so there was no passing the streets or staying within doors.'

———— ◎ ————

Schomberg issued an order to his troops at Derry forbidding 'the Horrid and Detestable Crimes of Prophane Cursing, Swearing and taking God's Holy Name in vain'.

———— ◎ ————

During the Williamite war the men of Enniskillen kept the town well supplied with food by frequent raids into the countryside. They are said to have brought into the town 3,000 cattle, 2,000 sheep and tons of grain from one raid that went as far south as Kells in County Meath.

———— ◎ ————

Because its walls have never been breached Derry earned the name the 'Maiden City'.

———— ◎ ————

It was estimated that during the Derry siege 15,000 men, women and children died, many from hunger but most from the fever that raged through the city. 'People died so fast at length as scarce could be found room to inter them, even backsides and gardens were filled with graves, and some thrown in cellars; some whole families were entirely extinct.'

———— ◎ ————

Jacobite guns at Culmore, the two small ships slipped by and made for the boom. By now the air was so calm that their sails were useless and the ships had to rely on the incoming tide to carry them onwards. The heavier *Mountjoy* sailed into the boom and broke part of it. The sailors in the longboat then used axes to make a gap in the boom.

The *Mountjoy* meanwhile had rebounded from the boom and got stuck fast in the mud. Two regiments of Jacobite cavalry immediately rode into the shallow water to capture the boat whose crew prepared to resist all attempts at boarding. The *Mountjoy* fired off three of her cannon at the approaching cavalry and not only did this cause considerable damage but fortuitously enough, the recoil drove the ship back out into the deeper water. Then, towed by the longboat, she followed the *Phoenix* through the gap that had been made, right up to the city. The joyful citizens rushed to the Ship Quay and started unloading their precious cargo.

In the midst of all this the brave Captain Brown lay dead upon the deck of his ship, the *Mountjoy*. He had been shot in the head when the ship had been stuck in the mudbank. (He was later buried in Derry Cathedral.)

Three days after the boom was breached and 105 days from the start of the siege the Jacobite army withdrew. When they reached Strabane they received the further bad news that their other army at Enniskillen had been utterly defeated. That town's garrison had marched out to meet the approaching army at Newtownbutler and had inflicted such terrible casualties that the Jacobites fled from the battlefield.

The days following the relief of Derry were ones of great rejoicing and Kirke and some officers were given a hero's welcome as they marched in on 4 August. Two days later Kirke led the rest of his men from Inch Island to the city but did not allow his men to enter because of the plague that was raging through its garrison.

Kirke's hero status did not last very long among the citizens of Derry, however. His brutish disregard for the heroic resistance of the garrison and his high-handed dealings with the refugees who had taken shelter in the city – he made them all go back to their own homes, leaving practically everything behind them in the city – meant that the citizens of Derry were relieved when he returned to England.

———— ◎ ————

When William of Orange landed in Carrickfergus his army brought with them more than forty pieces of artillery: six and twelve-pounder demi-culverins, nineteen and twenty-four-pounder cannons and mortars. Some of the guns were so big that each one needed sixteen horses to pull it. William had more than 1,000 horses for this purpose.

———— ◎ ————

William had a superstition against doing anything important on a Monday and it was on a Monday that he was nearly killed while surveying the Jacobite positions at the Boyne.

———— ◎ ————

One account says that the shot that killed Schomberg at the Boyne was accidentally fired by one of his own Huguenot troops.

———— ◎ ————

One of the English regiments which fought at the Boyne was the Hastings Regiment. It numbered about six hundred men in ten companies. They consisted of musketeers armed with flintlocks, and grenadiers carrying grenades, axes and muskets. The soldiers wore red coats, yellow breeches and a sash around their shoulders on which they hung their cartridges. Their hats were turned up at one side rather like the present day hat of Australian soldiers.

———— ◎ ————

By the time of the battle of the Boyne the use of pikemen in the English army had almost ended. Muskets had become much lighter and the use of the bayonet was more widespread. The earlier bayonets were stuck down the muzzle of the muskets, which meant that the guns could not be fired when the bayonets were in use. The ring and socket type was soon introduced but there were very few of them at the Boyne.

———— ◎ ————

The siege of Derry was only the beginning of the Williamite war. King William was now able to pay more attention to what was happening in Ireland. He sent over the Duke of Schomberg (then over seventy years old) with an army of 15,000 men in August 1689 and they landed at Bangor, County Down to a rapturous reception from the local Protestants. The Jacobite army withdrew without a fight and Schomberg led his army to besiege Carrickfergus and after a five-day siege the garrison surrendered. As they marched out the Jacobites were lucky that they were not all killed, so great was the hostility towards them. The local people 'stript most of the women and forced a great many arms from the men.' In fact the duke had great difficulty in preventing his troops from killing them all.

With the arrival of reinforcements Schomberg's troops now numbered 20,000 men, including two Dutch infantry battalions and four Huguenot regiments. He then moved to Dundalk where he set up camp near a marsh. His army soon became ravaged by fever, so that he lost nearly half his men.

William himself now decided that he had to come to Ireland and landed with his army at Carrickfergus on 14 June 1690 and was immediately joined by Schomberg. The two then proceeded to the camp at Dundalk where their combined army consisted of 36,000 English, French, Danish, Swedish, Dutch and Russian soldiers – all trained and well equipped.

James first advanced with his army towards Dundalk but then fell back to the south bank of the Boyne, just west of Drogheda, making his headquarters at the village of Oldbridge. William and his army arrived on Monday 30 June and that evening he set out with a small party of horse to survey the scene. Some of the Jacobite soldiers on the opposite bank recognised him and began to shoot. One musket ball went so close it hit him on the right shoulder where it tore away parts of his topcoat, waistcoat and the shirt underneath and 'all to draw near half a spoonful of blood'.

The calm assurance of William was in sharp contrast with the behaviour of James. The latter was nervous and undecided – at one time contemplating a full retreat and the next moment determined to risk a battle.

On the morning of 1 July 1690 William gave the order to move. The weather was dry at the time and because the tide was out the

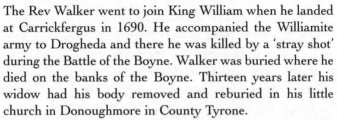

The Rev Walker went to join King William when he landed at Carrickfergus in 1690. He accompanied the Williamite army to Drogheda and there he was killed by a 'stray shot' during the Battle of the Boyne. Walker was buried where he died on the banks of the Boyne. Thirteen years later his widow had his body removed and reburied in his little church in Donoughmore in County Tyrone.

In 1938 it was discovered that the casket supposedly containing his bones contained thigh bones from two different males. It was suspected that Walker's widow had been swindled and indeed the remains of George Walker may still rest 'on the green grassy slopes of the Boyne'.

Many of William's soldiers had more modern flintlocks. These could fire sixteen balls per pound of lead as against twelve for the matchlocks and their rate of fire was double the old ones.

William wore his Star and Garter during the battle of the Boyne but so confused was the battle that he was almost shot by one of his own Inniskilling soldiers who aimed a cocked musket at him till he called out, 'What, are you angry with your friends?'

Before the battle of the Boyne every Williamite soldier was told to wear a sprig of green foliage in his cap to distinguish them in battle from the Jacobites who wore little pieces of white paper.

river was fordable in several places. One division of the Williamites moved upriver to Slane where there was a bridge which James unwisely had left unguarded. On their march there they found a ford that they could cross at Rossnaree, three kilometres from Slane. Several regiments crossed at that point after some hard fighting with a small Jacobite force which rushed to oppose them. The rest of the Williamite force continued on to Slane and crossed the open bridge there. Their objective was to get behind the Irish army and so cut off the pass at Duleek which would be their retreat route to Dublin. The Williamite progress was slow, however, as the terrain proved extremely difficult.

When William heard news that a successful crossing of the Boyne had been made he ordered his men to cross the river at several other fords between Drogheda and Oldbridge. His artillery opened fire on the Jacobites without reply, as their six cannon had been rushed to repel the crossing at Slane. At a quarter past ten William's men, ten abreast, entered the water at Oldbridge opposite the Jacobite centre. They were fiercely opposed by the Irish and French troops but, in spite of everything, succeeded in getting across. It was at this time that the old marshal Schomberg was killed by a musket bullet which struck him in the neck. The hero of Derry, the Reverend George Walker, was also killed at this time.

Meanwhile the rest of William's army began to cross and when he was satisfied that they were all committed, he, himself, crossed at a ford near Oldbridge. Once on the south side of the river he led his men to the scene of the fighting but the ground was so soft that his horse got bogged down and he had to dismount until the horse was lifted clear. He then led his Dutch and Enniskillen troops towards the Jacobite troops and though repulsed at first, charged forward again.

All day the battles raged along the south bank of the Boyne until, towards evening, the Irish side began to yield. When the battle was lost, the main body of the Irish army was able to retreat to Dublin in good order through the still open pass of Duleek. The town of Drogheda, which had a garrison of Jacobite troops, now surrendered on the honourable terms offered by William. Other towns throughout the country, such as Kilkenny, Duncannon and Waterford quickly surrendered shortly after.

———— ◎ ————

Dutch soldiers of the time carried a kind of wooden *chevaux de frise* which was extremely effective against cavalry. It was a portable fence with sharpened wooden stakes sticking out at all angles to provide a fearsome obstacle. The Dutch troops at the Boyne did not have such a fence with them and the Irish cavalry inflicted heavy losses on them.

———— ◎ ————

Schomberg said that his men at the Boyne were so untrained that only one in four could even fire their muskets and 'those that did thought they had done a feat if the gun fired, never minding what they shot at'!

———— ◎ ————

During the Williamite war both sides used bundles of brushwood and hurdles to spread on soft boggy ground to allow them to cross. William's army even crossed rivers by building bridges on tin pontoons much like armies do today.

———— ◎ ————

When William's army made their way to Dublin after the Battle of the Boyne they brought with them the body of the great old soldier, Duke Schomberg, who had been killed in the battle. His body was later interred in St Patrick's Cathedral. The inscription on the stone later erected to his memory was composed by Dean Swift in 1730.

———— ◎ ————

During the battle of the Boyne the gates of Dublin were closed and the citizens were not allowed out of the city, while Protestants were ordered to stay indoors for the day. After the battle many of the defeated soldiers made their way back to Dublin and by nightfall the city was filled with weary, exhausted soldiers.

James meanwhile had taken no part in the battle at the Boyne and when he saw how things were going that evening, he fled with a bodyguard of 200 horse to Dublin. The next morning he left for Wexford and, eventually, France. He had carefully provided for his own safety by placing two troops of horses at Bray in County Wicklow to make sure the road to Wexford was kept open.

The victorious Williamite army made its way to Dublin after the battle and camped on the common in Crumlin. On 16 July William rode into the city to a rapturous reception from the Protestant population, who showered the soldiers with flowers and gifts and even hugged their horses. One account describes how 'they ran about shouting and embracing one another and blessing God for His wonderful deliverance. The poor Roman Catholics [were] now lying in the same terror as we had done some days before.'

Although Patrick Sarsfield was present at the Boyne he was not given an active part in the battle. According to some accounts his principal duty was to command the 200 horse that escorted James in his flight to Dublin.

With the departure of James, Lord Talbot (Tyrconnell) was again in charge, with Sarsfield as the leading Jacobite officer. The Irish then decided to make the River Shannon their line of defence, concentrating their forces at Athlone and Limerick. When 12,000 of William's army under General Douglas arrived at Athlone they found the only bridge across the Shannon had been destroyed. Douglas sent a messenger to the governor of Athlone, Colonel Grace, demanding surrender but the colonel fired a pistol over the messenger's head and sent him back. Douglas then settled in to a siege of the town, which mostly lay on the western side of the river. When Douglas got news that Sarsfield was approaching he gave up the siege and marched southwards to join King William who was leading the rest of the army towards Limerick.

The Williamite army arrived before the walls of Limerick on 9 August 1690 but delayed attacking as they were awaiting the arrival of their artillery, which was following behind from Dublin. When

————— ◎ —————

After the Battle of the Boyne Patrick Sarsfield is supposed
to have said to one Williamite officer 'Change leaders and
we will fight you all over again.'

————— ◎ —————

When one spot in Limerick's wall showed signs of
crumbling under the Williamite bombardment Captain
Boileau ordered huge sacks of wool to be hung over the spot
to deaden the effect of the cannon balls. It did not seem to
work, however, as the gunners managed to breach the wall.

————— ◎ —————

All during the siege of Limerick King William personally
directed proceedings with great coolness in face of danger.
On one occasion a twenty-four pound cannon ball struck
the very spot he had moved from an instant before but he
took little notice of it and calmly went on with his work.

————— ◎ —————

Patrick Sarsfield was informed of the impending gun convoy he decided to intercept it. On Sunday 10 August he quietly crossed Thomond Bridge to County Clare with 500 horsemen. Guided by the famous rapparee, 'Galloping' O'Hogan, he made his way to Killaloe where he forded the Shannon. Meanwhile the siege train had reached Ballyneety about twenty kilometres from William's camp. The troops were relatively relaxed as no danger was expected, although sentries were posted. By a strange quirk of fate the password for the night was 'Sarsfield'.

The relatively unprepared state of the siege train was reported to Sarsfield by his scouts and he immediately set out for Ballyneety. By a lucky accident the password was discovered and it allowed Sarsfield and his troops to pass through the outlying checkpoints. When they reached the camp itself they were challenged for the password and answered with the famous reply 'Sarsfield is the word and Sarsfield is the man!'

Patrick Sarsfield was over six feet tall and was a descendant of one of the Normans who had come to Ireland with Henry II in the twelfth century.

The camp was quickly overrun and the Williamite soldiers either fled or were killed. Since Sarsfield could not take the heavy guns with him he ordered that they should be packed with explosives, their muzzles buried in the ground and the lot blown up in one tremendous explosion. Sarsfield and his party then safely made their way back to Limerick where the news of their success greatly encouraged the garrison.

Meanwhile King William and his generals were busy preparing for the siege. They were within cannon shot of the walls, with their lines extended in a curve south and east of the city. The Limerick defences were in such a poor state that the French General Lauzun was appalled, declaring that 'the walls could be taken with roasted apples'. The elderly Tyrconnell agreed with him and they both recommended surrendering the city. Sarsfield would not hear of it and, together with a Frenchman, Captain Boileau, organised the soldiers and the remaining citizens in repairing the walls, towers and forts. Later Tyrconnell and Lauzun withdrew from the city to Galway, taking the French troops with them.

The badly armed defenders numbered about 25,000 men while William's well-equipped army numbered about 26,000. While at first the attackers were heartened by the departure of the French, they were dismayed some time later when news of the disaster at Ballyneety reached them. Still, after a delay of about a week, William started the attacks. He had got two large guns from Waterford and two of the great cannons at Ballyneety were found not to have been destroyed in the explosion.

The action started with the attackers digging trenches towards the walls while the defenders did everything to hinder them by shooting at the sappers from a number of towers on the walls. When William's big guns were in position they opened up and soon levelled the towers. They then concentrated on a spot near St John's Gate to make a breach.

Cromwell's Fort, just outside the walls between St John's Gate and William's army, still remained in Sarsfield's hands, however, and provided strong resistance. Eventually the fort was stormed by the attackers and the garrison was forced to retreat within the city, leaving the fort to the Williamites. Eventually a wide breach was made in the city walls and the attacking army poured through, only to be met with ferocious resistance by the defenders.

One of William's foreign regiments, the Prussian Brandenburghs, forced their way right up to one of the main defending batteries, when suddenly the gunpowder in the vaults beneath them exploded with a roar and blew men, battery, and everything above it to fragments.

The battle went on for four hours, with more and more troops pouring forward only to be hemmed in between the houses within. The defenders fought until their ammunition was exhausted, and then they resorted to showering stones upon the attackers. The citizens of the city joined the defence, and women, following the example of the women of Derry, joined the fray, throwing bottles, stones and anything that came to hand at the attacking soldiers.

Finally the attackers gave way before the tremendous resistance and rushed back through the breach, so that not a foreign soldier remained within the walls within a short time. William lost over 2,000 men in the attack, while the defenders suffered comparatively few losses.

Because the chance of future success was doubtful and the rains of autumn and winter were approaching William decided to raise the siege. He went back to England, leaving General Ginkel in charge and on the last day of August 1690 the Williamite army marched away from the city.

In September Cork surrendered to John Churchill (later to be Duke of Marlborough) and this was followed by the capture of Kinsale. These two successes ended the campaign of 1690 on a better note for the Williamites.

In January 1691 Talbot (Tyrconnell) returned from France with some money and material for the Jacobite cause. As he was still the Lord Lieutenant appointed by the exiled James, he again assumed control. The following May a French expedition entered the Shannon with provisions and military stores and also on board was a French officer, Lieutenant-General St Ruth. He had orders from James to take over control of the Irish army even though Sarsfield was a far more competent soldier and had a greater knowledge of the country.

The next phase of the war began when Ginkel laid siege to Athlone on 19 June 1691 with an army of 18,000 men. That town lay on both sides of the Shannon with the Irish Town in the western side and English Town on the eastern side and the Irish army now occupied both parts.

After a tremendous bombardment the Williamites succeeded in occupying English Town and the resisting Irish troops withdrew across the bridge over the river to Irish Town. They then defended the bridge so fiercely against Ginkel's attacks that he sent a part of

———— ◎ ————

As Ginkel marched through the country to Aughrim he complained that the rapparees were burning all before him and they were so numerous that 'we can neither find forage nor cover, which hinders much our march'.

———— ◎ ————

Around 1678 a new type of soldier was introduced in the English army, the grenadiers. Their name came from the fact that they actually threw grenades. These were hollow metal spheres filled with gunpowder and plugged with a wooden stopper through which a length of match was inserted. The grenadier would light this 'fuse' and hurl the grenade at the enemy positions. The grenadiers took a prominent part at both sieges of Limerick.

———— ◎ ————

For years after the triumphs at the Boyne (1 July 1690) and Aughrim (12 July 1691) the Protestants of the North celebrated both victories on their anniversaries. Later they took to celebrating both on the Twelfth. This was also greatly influenced by the change from the Julian calendar to the Gregorian in the eighteenth century when eleven days were added to the old dates.

———— ◎ ————

Less than two years after the surrender at Limerick Patrick Sarsfield was fatally wounded at the Battle of Landen in the Netherlands. As he lay on the ground, seeing his hands covered with blood from his wounds, he is said to have exclaimed, 'Would that this were shed for Ireland.'

———— ◎ ————

his army northwards along the river in the hope that they could cross at Lanesboro and come back down to attack Irish Town from the west. The ploy was foiled, however, when the Irish defenders resisted any crossing of the river and the party had to return to the main army.

Ginkel now renewed his efforts to cross the bridge. His army was only able to advance inch by inch, suffering heavy casualties in the process. Eventually the defenders yielded and retired to the western shore but not before tearing down the last arch of the bridge on the Connacht side. Ginkel then directed a terrific fusillade onto the farther bank and, under cover of this bombardment, his soldiers managed to place a number of wooden planks over the gap to allow his army access to the western bank. But just as his advance party was about to cross, a body of eleven Irish troops wearing whatever armour they could find as protection rushed forward to throw the planks in the river. Volleys of shots from Ginkel's army soon killed every one of the party but their places were immediately taken by others willing to attempt the suicide mission. Nine of this eleven were also killed but they succeeded in tearing down all the planks remaining. Next Ginkel's men constructed a makeshift wooden shed which they managed to get in place over the gap but the defenders managed to set it on fire and its brave occupants had to run for their lives.

The heroic and stubborn resistance encountered by his army made Ginkel contemplate abandoning the siege altogether but his officers persuaded him to try a different plan. Because the summer had been unusually dry, the water level in the Shannon had dropped and it was felt that the river could be forded about sixty metres below the bridge. Ginkel decided to make the attempt.

A deserter from the Williamite army informed St Ruth of the plan but he scoffed at the idea and decided that no attempt would be made to cross at the ford. As a concession to the doubters he placed a small party of untrained soldiers to guard the crossing. Ginkel became aware of this lackadaisical approach and called for volunteers to make the attempt. A small party of grenadiers plunged into the rapidly flowing river on 30 June 1691, reached the other bank with little resistance and made their way to the bridge. Some of them quickly placed planks across the gap and others made a bridge of small boats they had brought with them. In less

———— ◎ ————

The battle of Aughrim was one of the bloodiest ever fought in Ireland. Among the dead after the battle were one general, three major-generals, twenty-two colonels, seventeen lieutenants, and seven thousand rank and file.

———— ◎ ————

It is estimated that nearly half a million Irishmen died in the French forces between 1691 and 1745. The total population of Ireland in 1700 was estimated to be two million.

———— ◎ ————

When Ginkel advanced with his army across Thomond Bridge, fighting hand to hand with the Irish troops, a French officer, fearing that Ginkel's grenadiers might enter the city in the confusion, ordered the drawbridge to be raised, leaving the Irish troops to their fate. The drawbridge was raised and one hundred and fifty men were pushed into the river by the weight of the numbers behind them and were swept away by the tide and drowned. Six hundred more were cooped up at the end of the bridge and so wedged together that they were not able to defend themselves and were easily cut down by Ginkel's men.

———— ◎ ————

than half an hour Ginkel's army had crossed and taken command of the town. The Irish army under St Ruth was camped only a short distance away but Athlone had been taken before they could do anything about it.

St Ruth was blamed by the Irish officers for the debacle and now he determined to risk all in a single battle. He brought his army to a small village called Aughrim, six kilometres from Ballinasloe, County Galway. He set his army in a carefully chosen position on top of a hill with a river and bog to the front, while at each end of his main body there was a narrow pass. The pass on the left was beside the ruined castle of Aughrim, while that on his right was near a ford over a small stream. Any attack on his troops would have to be up across the hill where he had lines of marksmen hidden behind the fences across the face of it.

Ginkel's army of about 20,000 English, Scottish, Danish, French and Dutch soldiers arrived at the battle area at midday of 12 July 1691. St Ruth's army was of equal strength but consisted entirely of Irishmen.

The battle began around noon. Wave after wave of Ginkel's army attempted to take the hill but were repulsed every time with dreadful slaughter. Ginkel conferred with his officers and was about to draw back for the day and start again in the morning when he saw what he took to be some disorder in the Irish camp. This encouraged him to make one more attack.

He made as if to make another attempt to cross at the ford on St Ruth's right with the hope of drawing off some of the Irish forces at the pass at Aughrim Castle. The plan succeeded. St Ruth withdrew some of his army from the pass on his left to resist the perceived threat on the right. Ginkel then sent one part of his troops to attack the weakened defences at the castle pass, while his main army attacked up the hill. This main thrust up the centre was repulsed time and again and in fact the battle was going so well for the Irish side that St Ruth is said to have waved his hat in the air and shouted 'The day is ours, my boys! We shall now drive them back to the gates of Dublin.' Then as he rode down the hill to direct further operations, a gunner in Ginkel's army loosed a lucky cannon ball shot that swept his head from his body.

The Irish army was now leaderless for St Ruth had deliberately kept Sarsfield so far to the rear that it was some time before he

———— ◎ ————

Many of the Jacobites went into exile to various countries on the Continent after the Treaty of Limerick. These exiles became known as the Wild Geese. Many others became outlaws known as rapparees or tories. One, Patrick Connelly, lived in a cave near Monaghan and terrorised the inhabitants of the surrounding countryside. He was eventually captured and hanged in 1711. Another called Seán Bearnach (Gap-toothed John) lived where the borders of Monaghan, Tyrone and Fermanagh meet. He rustled cattle, ambushed stage-coaches and robbed the rich until he was caught and beheaded. He was said to be able to test gold and silver coins by biting them with his gums!

———— ◎ ————

After the Treaty of Limerick one of the regiments which went abroad to France was Lord Clare's own regiment, known as the 'Clares'. When the Clares fought at the Battle of Fontenoy in 1745 – fifty-four years later – their officers led them into battle shouting *'Cuimhnigidh ar Luimnach agus feall na Sasanach'* (Remember Limerick and the perfidy of the Saxon).

———— ◎ ————

Rapparees got their name from their use of a half-pike called a *rapaire* in Irish. The name 'tory' comes from *toraidhe*, a raider or robber.

———— ◎ ————

The best known rapparee in the Carrickmacross area was a man called Patrick Fleming. He and his gang were eventually captured as they were drinking in a shebeen. The woman owner summoned the authorities after she had neutralised the outlaws' pistols by pouring water into them. They were all beheaded on a local rock and their heads were sent in creels to Dundalk. Their blood seeping out of the baskets is said to have caused one driver to die with fright.

———— ◎ ————

heard of the disaster. Even though the fighting continued for a while, the Irish side finally retreated from the field and withdrew once more to Limerick. The garrisons at Galway and Sligo soon surrendered but were allowed to retire to Limerick also.

Now Ginkel marched on Limerick to make a second attempt to take it. Talbot, Lord Tyrconnell, tried to marshal the city's defences but he died suddenly of a stroke on 24 August and was buried in the Cathedral there. Sarsfield then took over command.

Ginkel began the second siege on 4 September 1691 by bombarding the city with sixty cannons and nineteen mortars and soon had many parts of the city in flames. Part of his army then managed to cross the Shannon north of the city and attack it from the Clare side. A fort at the western end of Thomond Bridge was stoutly defended by its garrison for a time but they were eventually forced back across the bridge into the city. The troops in charge of the drawbridge were commanded by a French major and he now gave the order to raise the bridge, leaving about 600 Irish soldiers with no means of escape. Even though these troops now threw down their arms and raised white flags in surrender, they were massacred to a man.

There was then a short truce for by this time both sides were weary of war and extremely short of supplies. The possibility of fresh supplies from France for the Irish side convinced Ginkel that this was the best time to end it. Accordingly on 13 October 1691 the Treaty of Limerick was signed, with Ginkel representing King William and Sarsfield representing the Irish side.

A few days later a French fleet with large supplies of men and munitions sailed up the Shannon but Sarsfield refused to deal with them, as he felt bound by his agreement with Ginkel. The fleet turned around and sailed back to France, carrying with them nearly 5,000 officers and men of the Irish army as well as hundreds of women and children.

Thus ended the 'War of the Revolution' and William and Mary officially became sovereigns of Ireland.

10

◎

THE BROKEN TREATY

The terms of the Treaty of Limerick were quite fair. King William often declared that he 'had come to delivery Protestants but not to persecute Catholics'. The main provisions were as follows:

(i) Roman Catholics were to have the same freedom of religion as they had enjoyed during the reign of Charles II.

(ii) Those in arms for King James were to keep any estates they possessed in the time of Charles II and to be free to exercise their callings and professions without hindrance.

(iii) The Irish garrison in Limerick was free to march out of the city with colours flying and drums beating, with weapons and baggage. The soldiers were to be permitted to go to any foreign country or join William's army. (More than 20,000, including Patrick Sarsfield, entered the French army, 1,000 joined William and over 2,000 returned home.)

King William was well disposed towards the Irish; he restored many of them to their estates and granted numerous pardons. Of course he also rewarded his own troops as well – Ginkel was made Earl of Athlone with an estate of 26,000 acres and other officers were given large grants of land.

In October 1692 Lord Sidney, the Lord Lieutenant, summoned a parliament in Dublin, exactly a year after the Treaty of Limerick. The parliament was exclusively Protestant, for the very good reason that every member had to take an oath that the chief doctrines of the Catholic Church were false and of course no Catholic could take such an oath. (According to the Treaty of Limerick they were only obliged to take an oath of allegiance, so this represented the first breach of the treaty.) Sydney, representing the king, opposed the measure but was outvoted. All the Catholics immediately walked out.

One of the first things this parliament did was to declare that it was independent of the English Parliament. A money bill sent from England was rejected on the grounds that it had not originated in the Irish House of Commons. The Lord Lieutenant was so angry at this snub to the English Parliament that he twice suspended the Dublin parliament and in November 1693 he finally dissolved it.

By 1695 a new Lord Lieutenant, Lord Capel, was appointed and he at once summoned a new parliament which sat for several sessions, during which some of the 'Penal Laws' were passed. (There had been many Penal Laws against Catholics in the years before this but they were passed only at long intervals and, often enough, not carried out. But now they came in quick succession, growing more and more severe as time went on.) These laws were for the most part enacted by the Irish parliament which, as already stated, was entirely Protestant. (The Code of Penal Laws was to remain in force until the passing of the Catholic Emancipation Act of 1829 put an end to the disabilities of Irish Catholics.)

The first action of the 1695 parliament was to confirm all the minor provisions of the Treaty of Limerick and to omit all the important ones. The bill passed easily through the Commons but some peers, seven Protestant bishops and seven laymen, vigorously condemned this breach of faith.

Once this bill was passed the parliament passed a whole series of penal laws in 1695 and 1697. The number of these laws is too large for them all to be listed here but some of the most important were as follows:

(i)   Catholic schoolteachers were forbidden to teach.

(ii) Catholic parents were forbidden to send their children abroad for education.

(iii) Catholics had to hand in their arms, and magistrates could forcibly enter homes to search for arms.

(iv) If a Catholic had a valuable horse any Protestant who offered £5 for it had to be given it.

(v)   All existing parish priests had to be registered and were not allowed to have curates.

(vi) All other clergy – bishops, priests, members of religious orders, etc. – had to leave the kingdom by 1 May 1698. These last two laws meant that after the existing Catholic clergy died out there would be none to take their place.

(vii)   Any Catholic priest who came into the country could be hanged.

(viii) Catholics were forbidden to travel more than eight kilometres from home, to keep arms, to take cases to court, or to be guardians or executors of wills.

(ix)   Catholics were forbidden to wear swords.

These are only a few of the Penal Laws but they were only the first instalment; worse was to follow. When the Duke of Ormonde (grandson of Ormond of Cromwell's time who, from 1662 onwards, spelled his name with an 'e') became Lord Lieutenant he passed further penal regulations.

(i)   If the eldest son of a Catholic declared himself a Protestant he became owner of all his father's land.

(ii)   On the death of a Catholic landowner all his property had to be divided equally between his sons.

(iii)   If any other son declared he was a Protestant he was placed in the care of a Protestant guardian and his father had to pay all the expenses of his upkeep.

(iv)   No Catholic could become guardian of a child, so that often the dying hours of a Catholic parent were tormented by the knowledge that the orphaned children would be brought up as Protestants.

(v)   No Catholic was allowed to vote without first taking an oath that the Catholic religion was false. Later on they were not allowed to vote under any circumstances.

In court a Catholic would come before a Protestant judge and jury and be represented by a Protestant lawyer. The Lord Chief Justice Robinson declared, 'The law does not suppose any such person to exist as an Irish Roman Catholic.'

(It must be remembered that elsewhere in Europe similar penal laws were passed by Catholics against Protestants and by Protestants against Catholics but only in Ireland was there an attempt by a small minority to suppress the religion of a whole nation among whom they lived.)

The Penal Laws had the effect of eroding respect the Irish had for all law. They ignored and forgot about it and developed a practice which has lasted even to the present day of seeking their remedies in secret societies.

It must also be remembered that ordinary Protestants had no

responsibility for the enactment of the Penal Laws and in many instances actively circumvented them. Friendly Protestant neighbours would often go through the charade of taking over a Catholic's estate or becoming guardian of his orphaned children but restoring the lands to his heirs later or having the children secretly educated as Catholics.

The Penal Laws did not only affect Catholics. The Presbyterians, who were particularly plentiful in Ulster, were also discriminated against. Even though they were recognised by the Crown they were forbidden to celebrate the Lord's Supper, Presbyterian marriages were declared invalid and subsequent children branded as illegitimate. Presbyterians could not even be buried according to their Church's rites. But the northern Presbyterians were a tough hardy race. They built their meeting houses, attended their services, openly defied the restrictive laws and worked hard. They prospered in trade and industry, particularly the linen industry in places like Belfast and Derry

11

◎

PARLIAMENTARY ACTIVITY
AND SECRET SOCIETIES

E fforts to develop alternative industries during the early
eighteenth century were constantly hindered by vested
interests in Britain. The linen industry which had been
started to compensate for the suppression of the woollen industry
during Penal times now found itself excluded from the British
market. Similarly the Irish brewing industry was destroyed when
the importation of hops from any country but Britain was
forbidden and at the same time the duty on hops was greatly
increased. In 1746 an act totally forbidding the export of glass soon
put a stop to the budding glass industry.

In spite of these draconian measures a wealthy Catholic middle
class, which engaged in trade, slowly developed and in many cases
became more wealthy than their Protestant masters in the Irish
Parliament. So successful were the new middle classes that by 1751
the Irish government found itself with a surplus of taxation income
and parliament decided that the money should go to reducing the
national debt. The British Privy Council, however, decided that the
money should go to England to be spent as they wished. The same
thing happened again in 1753 but this time the Irish parliament
defeated the bill. The outcome was celebrated all over the country
as a great victory.

Public life in Ireland in the eighteenth century, especially that of
the Protestant minority, centred on the parliament. It was always
held in Dublin and from 1731 onwards was based in the building
in College Green now occupied by the Bank of Ireland.

From 1715 to 1783 the parliament met for only one session of six
months every second year. In the House of Commons there were
200 members and all had to be members of the Established
Church. (In fact Catholics were allowed absolutely no part in the

proceedings of parliament until the arrival of Daniel O'Connell and his successful campaign for Catholic Emancipation in the early part of the nineteenth century.) The higher government officials were nearly all Englishmen, always willing to carry out the wishes of the king and English council. By fair means or foul they were always able to command a majority in their favour. These officials formed what may be called the 'Court Party'.

The power of these English officials, and the unjust laws that had wreaked such havoc on Irish trade, provoked feelings of resentment towards the English Parliament among a certain section of Irish Protestants and evoked a growing sense of patriotism. They were only a small group and they became known as the 'Patriot Party'. They had two main objectives: to remove restrictions on trade and to make the Irish Parliament independent of that of England. Among their leaders were Jonathan Swift, Charles Lucas, Henry Flood, William Molyneux, Edmund Burke and Henry Grattan. The Patriot Party worked solely for Protestants – the plight of the Catholics never concerned them. Even such great leaders as Swift, Flood, Lucas and Molyneux were against the easing of any political restrictions on Catholics. Henry Grattan and Edmund Burke stood almost alone in accepting that Catholics should have equal rights with Protestants.

Gradually as the years went by the small Patriot Party grew in strength and ultimately they succeeded in their main objectives but it was to be a long drawn-out struggle. The conflict between the Patriot Party and the Court Party was to be the main feature of the political history of Ireland for most of the eighteenth century.

As early as 1698 William Molyneux, MP for Dublin University, had published a pamphlet claiming that the Irish Parliament had the right to make its own laws and that it should be independent of the English Parliament. The pamphlet, which was called *The Case of Ireland's Being Bound By Acts Of Parliament In England Stated*, caused great indignation in England and the parliament there ordered that it be burned by the public hangman. The very same year that Molyneux published his book the Irish wool trade was destroyed by acts of the parliament in London at the behest of English merchants: the export of woollen goods to any country but England was prohibited by these acts.

The outrage in Ireland at these actions was greatly exacerbated

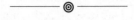

During the debate in the Irish Parliament demanding Free Trade, Hussy Burgh used a sentence which has become famous. To the claim that Ireland was at peace he said 'Talk not to me of peace. Ireland is not at peace; it is smothered war. England has sown her laws as dragons' teeth; they have sprung up in armed men.'

Ireland's oldest surviving newspaper, *The Belfast Newsletter*, was first published in 1737.

Between 1727 and 1730 famine hit Ireland hard. So many of the poor died from starvation that their bodies often lay unburied outside their hovels. It was during this time (1729) that Jonathan Swift wrote his final pamphlet *A Modest Proposal*. In it he attacked the neglected state of the country and mocked the fears of the upper classes of being overrun by the children of the poor. Calculating that there were one hundred and twenty thousand children born to the poor every year he put forward his own solution to the problem – they should be sold as food! 'I have been assured that a young healthy child well nursed is at a year old a most delicious, nourishing and wholesome food, whether stewed, roasted, baked or boiled . . . A child will make two dishes at an entertainment for friends, and when the family dines alone, the fore or hind quarter will make a reasonable dish, and seasoned with a little pepper or salt will be very good boiled on the fourth day, especially in winter.'

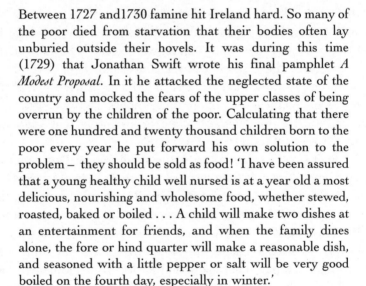

During the eighteenth century capital punishment by hanging was an extremely common occurrence. Pirates on the Irish Sea were especially savagely treated and many were left hanging in chains on cliffs and rocks around Dublin Bay as a warning to others.

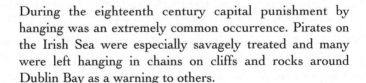

by the strange court case known as the 'Annesley Case' which occurred early in the eighteenth century. A dispute over some property arose in 1719 between two Irishmen named Hector Sherlock and Maurice Annesley and when the case was brought to the Dublin court it decided in favour of Annesley. On appeal to the Irish House of Lords the judgement was reversed in Sherlock's favour. Next Annesley appealed to the English House of Lords, which reversed the decision once more in his favour and they also fined the sheriff of Kildare for not obeying their ruling. In turn the Irish House of Lords cancelled the fine, declared the appeal to the English House of Lords illegal, praised the sheriff for his action and arrested the three persons responsible for the first judgement in favour of Annesley!

The English parliament at last put an end to the farce by passing an important act known as 'The Sixth of George I' – so called because it was passed during the sixth year of his reign. This act declared that the English Parliament had the right to make laws for Ireland and that the Irish House of Lords had no right to hear appeals, thereby reducing the Irish Parliament to a mere debating forum. (The famous Poyning's Law of 1494 had not given that right to the English Parliament and the right was now claimed for the first time.)

Towards the end of King George I's reign another event occurred which strengthened the opposition of the Irish Parliament to control from England. The event is known as the 'Affair of Wood's Halfpence'.

Since the reign of Edward V1 (1546 – 1553) there had been no money minted in Ireland – all the coins circulating in Ireland were made in England. During the time of King George there was a great shortage of small coins in Ireland and this affected the poor in particular. In July 1722 the English Treasury granted a patent to the king's favourite, the Duchess of Kendal, for minting halfpennies and farthings, and she sold the patent to a Wolverhampton Iron Master named William Wood. The patent allowed him to mint sixty tons of copper into halfpennies and farthings to the face value of £108,000. The duchess and Wood hoped to make a very large profit as only £15,000 in small coins was needed. The Patriot Party attacked the gross favouritism shown by the king, but what really rankled with the Irish parliament was the

———— ◎ ————

When Dean Swift died in 1745 he left a legacy for the founding of St Patrick's Psychiatric Hospital   near Kingsbridge in Dublin. He also wrote of the bequest:

> He left the little wealth he had
> To build a house for fools and mad
> And showed by one satiric touch
> No nation wanted it so much.

———— ◎ ————

Dean Swift is buried under the floor of St Patrick's Cathedral at the west end of the nave. The Latin inscription on the wall nearby was written by Swift himself. It has been translated by Yeats as follows:

> Swift has sailed into his rest
> Savage indignation there
> Cannot lacerate his breast.
> Imitate him if you dare –
> World besotted traveller, he
> Served human liberty.

———— ◎ ————

Both Henry Flood and Henry Grattan were lawyers, Flood being tall and handsome while Grattan was a slight, unprepossessing man with a thin sharp voice and awkward gestures. But Grattan had a warmth and imagination that won over his listeners in a way that few other speakers could match.

———— ◎ ————

A strange fact about 'Grattan's Parliament' is that Grattan was always a member of the Opposition.

———— ◎ ————

fact that it hadn't been consulted. The minting of coins was a State prerogative and the granting of the patent by the English Treasury to an individual was regarded as deeply insulting. The Irish parliament protested to the king but a committee appointed by the English Privy Council to look into the matter dismissed their protests and added that the king was not bound to consult the Irish parliament on anything at all.

Perhaps the greatest opponent of the Court Party was not a Member of Parliament at all but a clergyman named Jonathan Swift, dean of St Patrick's Cathedral in Dublin. He had been angered by the destruction of the Irish weaving industry for the benefit of English traders. In an essay at the time encouraging Irish people to retaliate he coined the famous phrase 'Burn everything English except their coal.' The government did not know who the author was, so they prosecuted the printer for sedition. (Nine times the jury was sent out to reach a guilty verdict but they refused to do so every time. So the prosecution was quietly dropped.)

Then early in 1724 a letter was published, under the name of MB Drapier, which vigorously attacked 'Wood's Halfpence'. The author was supposed to be a Dublin shopkeeper but in reality was Jonathan Swift.

Jonathan Swift's 'Irish People' were the colonists –
he had little regard for the ordinary Irish people.

———— ◎ ————

The strange story of 'Half-Hanged MacNaghten' is well known in Derry folklore. John MacNaghten was born in Benvarden, County Antrim in 1722 and when his father died in 1740 he inherited the family estate. That same year he went to Trinity College in Dublin but only spent one year there, being more interested in gambling and the high life of the capital than in studying.

It was not long before he ended up penniless but a strategic marriage to a sister-in-law of Lord Masserine of Glenarm, County Antrim saw him once more financially secure. It was part of the marriage arrangement that MacNaghten took a solemn oath never to gamble again. He kept it faithfully for two years! He then managed to convince his wife and mother-in-law to release him from his vow. Thereafter he took up his old ways and was soon again deeply in debt.

One night in 1756 he was pursued by a group of army officers to whom he owed money and was attacked by them as he was about to enter his own home. It happened that the assault was witnessed by his heavily pregnant wife and the shock caused her death a few days later.

MacNaghten left Derry for a time but by 1760 he was back in the North and gambling again with a group of friends. One early morning he rose from the table having lost everything and was about to leave when James Nesbitt, one of his old gambling adversaries, proposed a final wager. Nesbitt had already won MacNaghten's home, Benvarden House, the previous night and he now proposed that MacNaghten stake the lands attached to the house on the turn of a single card. Nesbitt would stake the deeds of the house and a further 3,000 guineas. One further issue was put at stake – both men were interested in marrying a rich local heiress by the name of Mary Anne Knox and Nesbitt now proposed that the loser would renounce all interest in the lady and he, Nesbitt, would add another 1,000 guineas to the pot.

MacNaghten agreed. The cards were shuffled and placed in the centre of the table. MacNaghten went first and turned over the first card. To his great delight it was a queen but his joy did not last long for Nesbitt's card was a king – MacNaghten had lost everything.

The First Drapier Letter played on the prejudices of the ignorant multitude: the coins were so valueless that it would take twenty-four to equal one penny, ladies would have to bring a cartload of them when they went shopping, a farmer would need three horse-loads to pay his rent and the poor would have to pay thirty-six of the halfpences for a quart of ale! It also claimed that 'Wood's Halfpence' would soon become the sole currency of the Kingdom.

The Second Drapier Letter was not much different but Swift began to show his real purpose in the Third Drapier Letter. He railed against the insults offered to the Irish parliament and asked were not Irish people as free as those of England. (Swift's 'Irish people' were of course the colonists – he had little or no regard for the ordinary Irish people.)

The Fourth Drapier Letter was the most famous of the lot. It appeared in October 1724 and was addressed to the 'whole people of Ireland' (but once more the Catholic population was not included). Again it attacked 'Wood's Halfpence', criticised the assumed power of the English Parliament to legislate for Ireland and pointed out that force alone would make Ireland accept this.

The authorities were outraged and offered the then huge reward of £300 for information on the author. Although many people knew it was Swift, no one came forward to claim the reward. The authorities then prosecuted the printer of the letters but the Dublin Grand Jury refused to accept the charge. The Grand Jury was dissolved and a new one appointed. The new jury not only threw out the charge again but said that anyone who accepted Wood's coins was an enemy of the king.

The authorities gave in; the patent for the coins was withdrawn, Wood was compensated and the king announced in 1725 that the whole affair was at an end.

In the meantime the struggle between the Patriot Party and the Court Party went on. One of the greatest causes of dissension was the Pension List. Large pensions were given to persons who had done little to deserve them and all pensions had to be paid by the Irish Exchequer. By the second half of the eighteenth century the Pension List had grown to excessively large proportions. The leader of the Patriots, Henry Flood, attacked this scandalous system and he was aided by an extremely able and eloquent young

He was furious at losing but said nothing as he left the room. He was determined, however, to marry Mary Anne in spite of giving his word, as marriage to her would solve all his problems.

He was already friendly with Mary Anne's father who had warmly welcomed him as a guest in his home at Prehen House just outside Derry on the Strabane road. MacNaghten now proceeded to visit the house regularly and soon had charmed the whole family with his amusing stories and roguish ways. He paid special court to the lovely fifteen-year-old Mary Anne and succeeded in winning her affections. She even agreed to marry him but only if her father gave his consent. But when MacNaghten asked her father's permission he flatly refused. Although Andrew Knox would not accept MacNaghten as a son-in-law, he did agree not to tell anyone, including Mary Anne, of his refusal. He also told MacNaghten that he was still welcome to visit Prehen House whenever he wished.

MacNaghten continued his underhand scheming by telling Mary Anne that her father had consented to the marriage but wished to keep it secret until she came of age. Later he persuaded the girl to read through the marriage ceremony with him in the presence of a mutual friend. At the end of the reading they both kissed the bible and he then said they were legally married.

When he later claimed the fact publicly the news reached her father who was furious. He placed notices in the local papers denying that his daughter was married and sent her away to stay with her uncle in Sligo.

Meanwhile Andrew Knox brought the whole question of the supposed marriage to both the civil and religious authorities to determine if it was valid and to get it annulled due to the girl being under age if it was. Eventually Knox got the decision he wanted – the marriage was valid but was then declared void.

After the court case MacNaghten went to Bath in England and soon became notorious there for his gambling. He later returned to Derry and made efforts to contact Mary Anne but was rebuffed every time. To add to his misfortunes an inheritance he had expected from his eighty-two-year-old uncle slipped from his grasp when the uncle married a much younger woman and cut him completely out of his will.

man called Henry Grattan. At that time Grattan was not yet a Member of Parliament but he strongly supported Flood in his criticisms.

Another great bone of contention was the duration of parliament. In England it could only last seven years at most but in Ireland the parliament could last as long as the king wished ; the preceding parliament had lasted for the entire reign of George II, thirty-three years!

In 1767 the authorities reluctantly acceded to the repeated requests from the Patriot Party for a seven-year limit by granting the Octennial Bill which limited the Irish parliament's life to eight years. Before the end of the parliament the government tried to get it to agree to a large increase in the number of regular troops supported by the Irish revenue from 12,000 men to 15,200. This was strongly resisted by the Patriot Party which pointed out that the existing 12,000 troops compared very favourably with the total of 17,000 in all of England.

The American War of Independence, which started in 1775, was the catalyst for the relaxation of the penal code in the 1770's. The war went steadily against the English and ended with the surrender of the British at Saratoga in 1777. The loss of the war spread alarm among the British authorities, and this alarm increased with the French recognition of the independence of the United States of America. (An important part in that war was played by Ulster Presbyterian emigrants who had gone to America in large numbers because of the ruinous trade laws.)

The English parliament immediately passed a bill partially relieving English Catholics of their disabilities. This trend was repeated in Ireland with a bill removing many of the restrictions suffered by Catholics in trade and property rights but they were still excluded from the political process.

The events in America also provided the excuse for Protestant patriots to form the Irish Volunteers. They were formed ostensibly to protect Ireland against invasion but they were seen to be a useful lever in wringing concessions from England. They were almost completely Protestant but Catholics were generally favourable towards them and supported them with generous subscriptions.

At the beginning of the American war 4,000 troops from Ireland were sent to America, leaving only about the same number to

MacNaghten then made the fateful decision to risk all by abducting Mary Anne. He knew that the Knox family went to Dublin every year for the opening of parliament and when he heard they would set out on 10 November he decided to ambush them near Ballymagorry on the Derry-Dublin road.

It seems that MacNaghten knew of the decision of the Knoxes to travel in two separate well-armed coaches and had bribed a servant in their household to sabotage their weapons by pouring water into the powder pans on the guns. When the first coach, carrying Mary Anne's brother and uncle and two servants, approached he allowed it to pass unmolested. Shortly afterwards the coach containing Mary Anne, her father and mother and two armed servants came into view. Two other armed servants rode on horseback behind the carriage.

As they approached MacNaghten's hiding place he jumped out on the road and ordered the coachman to halt. He then went round to the carriage door and pointed his gun at the window. One of the servants on horseback aimed his gun at him but MacNaghten fired first and wounded him. Andrew Knox then attempted to discharge his blunderbuss at MacNaghten but the gun would not fire. The same thing happened when he tried to use his pistols. MacNaghten then fired into the coach and critically wounded Mary Anne. Meanwhile one of the servants managed to wound MacNaghten in the shoulder and he and his accomplices fled from the scene. Mary Anne died from her wounds a short time later.

A widespread search for the assassin resulted in MacNaghten being arrested in a hayloft some days later. An accomplice, Dunlap, was also arrested as he made his way back to the MacNaghten estate in Benvarden.

On Friday 11 December 1760 MacNaghten was tried and found guilty of murder although he protested that he loved Mary Anne and did not mean to harm her. For most of the trial he was respectful to the judges but he attacked the Knox family with bitterness and invective. At the end, however, the jury had no hesitation in declaring him guilty. He and Dunlap were then sentenced to death by hanging.

The date for execution was set for 15 December 1761 on the road between Lifford and Strabane. Because

defend the country. The English parliament proposed to send 4,000 Protestant troops from Germany to replace those drafted away but the Irish parliament refused to accept them. Along with the events in America, and France and Spain growing more and more hostile, American and French ships now ranged all around the coasts of Ireland. The Protestant ascendancy realised that if they wanted protection they must provide it themselves.

Early in 1779 the first Volunteer company was raised in Belfast, after which the movement spread rapidly. The Volunteers dressed in colourful uniforms of bright scarlet, orange, green and blue and anyone of any importance was given a military rank. Money was collected to buy muskets and some troops even managed to get a few cannon. Up to 4,000 men enrolled in Antrim and Down by May and, as the movement spread throughout the whole country, over 42,000 had joined before the end of the year. By the end of the following year (1780) they numbered 80,000.

At first Catholics were not allowed to join but later many regiments had large numbers of Catholics. Various professions and classes began to raise their own corps; noblemen and lawyers were two examples. Each corps selected its own uniform, which the men bought for themselves. Where they were too poor to do so, they were provided from a general fund. They bought their own weapons too, although in some cases the Castle authorities very reluctantly handed out a few thousand rifles.

Gradually the threat from external forces receded and the Volunteers began to focus more on domestic issues but they were still loyal to the British connection and still Protestant in control.

In October 1779 parliament met again and the Volunteers made demands for redress of their grievances. Their usual assembly point in Dublin was around the statue of William of Orange in College Green. By this time Henry Grattan had become their spokesman in parliament. He demanded free trade, and a motion to that effect was passed unanimously by the house. Dublin was in a state of great excitement and the House of Parliament in College Green was besieged by huge crowds demanding the quick implementation of the free trade motion. The British parliament subsequently acceded to the petition and in November 1779 passed three Free Trade Acts: the first permitted free export of wool and woollen goods; the second allowed free export of glass

MacNaghten was regarded as something of a romantic hero by the local population no carpenter could be found to build the gallows, so they were constructed by members of the Knox family themselves. MacNaghten was so weak that he had to be carried to the place of execution and had to be supported as he mounted the scaffold.

He calmly placed the rope around his neck and jumped immediately from the platform with such force that the rope snapped. A large number in the crowd took this to be a sign that he was innocent and urged him to escape. He resisted their urgings however and remounted the gallows with the now famous words that he would rather die than be known as 'Half-Hanged MacNaghten' for the rest of his life. He stood patiently on the gallows until another rope was put round his neck and this time his life was ended. Dunlap was hanged shortly afterwards and both bodies were then decapitated. The bodies lie together today in the graveyard of Strabane Church.

———— ◎ ————

During the American War of Independence the famous privateer, Paul Jones, entered Belfast Lough, captured a Royal Navy ship and sailed away with it to Brest. When the people of Belfast called on the Lord Lieutenant for assistance he told them that all he had available was half a troop of invalids and half a troop of cavalry with no horses!

———— ◎ ————

When the Act of Repeal was passed in 1782 the Irish parliament voted to grant £100,000 to Grattan for his great work but he refused to accept such a large sum and could only be persuaded to accept £50,000.

———— ◎ ————

products and the third allowed free trade with British colonies. The news was greeted with great rejoicing throughout the country and the standing of the Volunteers was greatly enhanced.

Having flexed their muscles and tasted victory in these matters, the Volunteers now demanded more, in particular, the repeal of Poyning's Law (which stated that the Irish parliament could not pass any law without the permission of the authorities in England) and 'The Sixth of George I', (which stated that the English parliament could pass laws governing Ireland).

On 16 April 1780 the Irish parliament again met and Grattan, although quite ill at the time, made an impassioned speech in favour of the repeal of the two acts. The motion was not put to a vote, however, as it was felt that the vote might be lost.

Enrolment in the Volunteers continued apace and the movement had over 100,000 men countrywide. During 1781 enthusiastic meetings were held all over the country and in February 1782 a convention of delegates of all the Ulster Volunteers was held in Dungannon, County Tyrone. Two hundred and forty delegates, representing 143 Volunteer corps, attended. The meeting was managed for the most part by Grattan, Flood and James Caulfield, Earl of Charlemont, leader of the Northern Volunteers.

A number of resolutions were passed, among them the following:
  (i) That only the king and the Lords and Commons of Ireland had the right to legislate for the country.
  (ii) That Poyning's Law be repealed.
  (iii) That Irish ports should be open to all countries not at war with the king.

These resolutions were subsequently endorsed by Volunteer corps all over Ireland.

When the Irish parliament next assembled, on 16 April 1782, substantially the same resolutions as those of the Dungannon Convention were put before the house but a decision on the matter was postponed. Later when the action moved to the English parliament, the Commons and the Lords both agreed to end the right granted by 'The Sixth of George I'. The Act of Repeal, as it was called, was communicated to the Irish parliament in Dublin on 27 May 1782. The news was received with great acclaim all over

———— ◎ ————

John Philpott Curran was born in 1750 in 4 Ely Place, Dublin. When he was young he had such a bad stammer that he was given the nickname 'Stuttering Jack'. By practising the speeches of Shakespeare in front of a mirror he completely overcame his disability and became 'the wittiest and dreamiest, the most classical and ambitious member of the Bar'. The writer, Jonah Barrington, describes Curran thus:

> His person was mean and decrepit, very slight, very shapeless - with nothing of the gentleman about it; on the contrary, displaying spindle limbs, a shambling gait, one hand imperfect, and a face yellow and furrowed, rather fat and thoroughly ordinary. But his rapid movements, his fire, his sparkling eye, the fine and varied intonations of his voice – these conspired to give life and energy to every company he mixed with.

———— ◎ ————

During the eighteenth century, stage coaches ran from Dublin to the principal towns in the country. They carried five passengers, one on top and four inside. Gates were put across the roads at many points and a toll had to be paid for the coach to be allowed through. The usual toll for a stage coach was five and a half pence. In 1841 the mail coach from Sligo to Dublin took 15 hours and 15 minutes to complete the journey. In 1866 the train did the same journey in 7 hours 40 minutes for thirty-seven and a half pence.

———— ◎ ————

Ireland and in gratitude the parliament voted 20,000 men and £100,000 to the British Navy.

The following year, in January 1783, the English parliament passed the Act of Renunciation, declaring that Ireland's right to be bound only by the laws made by the king and the Irish Parliament was established forever. From now on, the only connection between the two parliaments was to be that the king was head of both.

Even though the Irish parliament of the time had supported Grattan and others in their efforts, it was still rotten to the core. Of the 300 Members of Parliament over 100 were government hacks who would vote as directed. Electoral areas known as boroughs (like modern day constituencies) had the right to elect one or two Members. Some of the boroughs contained only about a dozen electors and most of the boroughs were in the hands of lords and other rich men. Any man could get elected by paying money to the owner. The borough owner would then direct the people to elect the donor. (Borough owners could make up to £10,000 a seat in this way.) Less than eighty Members were elected in a free democratic way.

Parliamentary reform was obviously needed and the Volunteers next took up that question. They wanted to end bribery and corruption and demanded that all members should be elected by free votes. A general convention of the Volunteers was held on 10 November 1783 in the Rotunda at the top of present-day O'Connell Street in Dublin and the Earl of Charlemont was elected chairman. After much debate, certain reforms were listed and were introduced by Flood in the Irish Parliament shortly after.

Despite a powerful speech by Flood, supported by Grattan and John Philpott Curran (in his maiden speech), the government side voted down the proposals. The result caused great bitterness and for a time there was danger of a clash between the government and the Volunteers. But eventually on 2 December 1783 the Volunteer Convention adjourned, with no fixed date for reassembling. This in effect was the end of the influence of the old Volunteer movement.

From this time on, the Volunteers became more revolutionary in their ideas, influenced greatly by events in France. They now formed themselves into clubs and groups, which held their meetings in secret. They began to drill and arm both Catholics and

Protestants. The government responded by increasing the army to 15,000 men and also revived the militia – a much-hated force. The country saw a great outbreak of violence everywhere. Mobs roamed the streets, attacking and injuring soldiers, ransacking shops and upbraiding shopkeepers for selling English goods.

Some efforts by the Chancellor of the English Exchequer, William Pitt, to remedy the imbalance of trade between the two countries were defeated by the English parliament. Another bill, much less favourable to Ireland, was passed in London but when it was presented to the Dublin parliament there was uproar. Flood and Grattan made eloquent and fiery speeches against the bill. After an angry all-night debate the government had a slender majority of nineteen. So small was the margin that the government thought it prudent to withdraw the bill. So things were to remain as they were until the Act of Union.

During all the foregoing parliamentary agitation the conditions of the Irish peasantry were terrible. They were at the mercy of their landlords and could be evicted from their holdings or have their rents increased without redress.

During the eighteenth century a trend towards pasture farming greatly increased because landlords found there was far more profit for less effort in raising cattle than in tillage. Thousands of tenants were evicted from their holdings and even the bogs which provided the people with fuel and grazing for their animals were more and more being fenced off by the landlords. Indeed in some parts of the country, such as Tipperary, whole villages were demolished to make way for pastures.

With no other source of subsistence the plight of the common people became desperate throughout the country. As a result various secret oath-bound societies grew up to protect the tenants.

Early in the eighteenth century a secret group in Connacht called the 'Houghers' roamed the countryside, ham-stringing ('houghing') cattle and stampeding sheep over cliffs in protest at the growing practice of converting tillage land into pastures for grazing.

Later on one of the most widespread secret society was the Whiteboys who got their name from the white shirts they wore over their coats when they went out on their raids. The counties of

Limerick, Waterford, Cork and Tipperary were the chief centres of Whiteboy activities. Their numbers consisted of both Catholics and Protestants, for their actions were against individuals and not the government. The Whiteboys roamed the country at night in groups of up to 500 men, pulling down new fences, maiming livestock, damaging the pasture lands and threatening small farmers who cooperated with the big landowners.

Gradually they became more extreme and committed terrible atrocities. Finally a large force of soldiers was sent to suppress them and this all contributed to a state of unrest in the south of the country.

Ulster was also very disturbed at this time. The Protestant peasantry there formed secret societies such as the Hearts Oak Boys and the Hearts of Steel. One of their main grievances was that every man had to do six days' work per year (without pay) in constructing and repairing roads and give six days' work of a horse. The Steelboys were formed to combat unjust rents and payment of tithes to the clergy.

All this time the Catholics kept their heads down and got on with using whatever avenues of advancement were open to them. Then in 1771 the first actual relaxation of one of the Penal Laws took place. Catholics were now allowed to take a long lease on up to fifty acres of bog; the bog had to be at least a metre deep and could not be nearer than one mile to any town. The Catholic also had to undertake to reclaim half the bog within eleven years.

From 1785 onwards, great political agitation spread throughout the country. One of the main causes of this was the system of 'tithes' whereby every household had to pay a tax for the support of the clergy of the Established Church. This led to the growth of a group of persons called 'tithe proctors' who made a lucrative business out of collecting the tithes on behalf of absentee clergymen or those who did not want to engage personally in their collection. The activities of these extremely ruthless and greedy individuals caused great hardship and resentment throughout the country.

Another greatly resented tax was the 'Church-rate' or 'Church-cess'. This was a tax to keep the Protestant churches in repair.

Secret societies sprang up, such as the Right Boys and the Defenders on the Catholic side and the Peep O'Day Boys on the

Protestant side. Atrocities were committed by both parties – they fought, maimed and killed each other and caused havoc throughout the country.

In 1792 and 1793 terrible battles between the two factions occurred in the counties of Monaghan, Cavan, Louth, Meath, Tyrone and Down. Pitched battles were fought between the two groups, armed with pikes, scythes, pitchforks, sticks, and sometimes firearms.

In one such battle near Loughgall in County Down, at a crossroads known as The Diamond, on 21 September 1795, the Peep O'Day Boys completely defeated a contingent of Defenders, leaving at least thirty dead. After the 'Battle of the Diamond' the victors marched into Loughgall and there in the house of a James Sloan was founded the Orange Order. The order was pledged to defend the king and his heirs so long as he or they support the Protestant Ascendancy'.

Dublin was as much subject to agitation as the rest of the country and in an effort to quell disturbances in the city a special body of constables was set up to aid the existing watchmen. (This force of constables was in time to become the Dublin Metropolitan Police which was eventually incorporated into the Garda Síochána in 1925.)

The French Revolution of 1789 greatly affected political thought in Ireland at the time. The ruling classes in general supported the Royalist side and the Catholic clergy constantly warned their flocks against the new ideas being promoted on the continent. At the same time there were many in the country who eagerly embraced the new thinking. Political clubs were formed to promote the cause of political reform. Whig Clubs were established in Dublin, Belfast and elsewhere and included among their members such people as Theobald Wolfe Tone, Napper Tandy, John Philpott Curran, Henry Grattan and others.

In October 1791 Tone founded the Society of the United Irishmen in Belfast and later another branch was formed in Dublin with Napper Tandy as its secretary. The stated aims of the United Irishmen were to unite Irishmen of all religions and classes, to reform government and to repeal the Penal Laws.

Tone travelled from Dublin to Belfast on 10 October 1791 to meet like-minded northern reformers. On Friday 14 October they formed the Society of United Irishmen of Belfast in Peggy Barclay's tavern in Crown Entry off High Street. A statement issued at the time said 'We have no national government. We are ruled by Englishmen and the servants of Englishmen.' They wanted 'a cordial union among all the people of Ireland'. They insisted on reform of the Irish Parliament and that it should be open to men of all religions. Most of its members were middle-class businessmen and there were few of the upper or working classes. One member called Hamilton did represent the landlord class, however, and Jemmy Hope was a working-class apprentice weaver.

The United Irishmen were not social reformers, and in 1792 they strongly opposed Antrim weavers who wanted better wages. Neither were they, for the most part, revolutionaries. They expected to attain their objectives by determined persuasion

On 2 December 1791 the more progressive members of the Catholic Committee, which had been founded in 1757 with similar aims to the United Irishmen, now called a meeting in Dublin of Catholic delegates from all over Ireland. They met in the Tailors' Hall in Back Lane, joining Nicholas Street and High Street. (The assembly was often subsequently called the 'Back Lane Parliament'.) A petition to the king was drafted and five delegates were appointed to bring the petition directly to London.

They were introduced to King George III by Edmund Burke and as a result the king sent a request to the Irish parliament to remove some of the inequalities suffered by Catholics. The parliament, however, rejected the request with contempt, but was later forced, in 1793, to grant Catholics substantial concessions in the Catholic Relief Act. The 'Forty-Shilling Freeholders', men who owned property worth at least forty shillings more than the rent they had to pay, were given the vote and were allowed to attend Trinity College and get degrees; they could serve on juries and be justices of the peace. But one thing was still denied them – they could not be elected to parliament. (Of course there was no secret ballot and when landlords directed their tenants to vote for a candidate they were able to know if the tenants had done so.)

The same parliament which reluctantly passed these relief laws also passed two coercion acts: the Convention Act which prohibited any gathering of delegates like the 'Back Lane

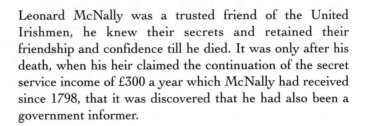

Archibald Hamilton Rowan lived to the age of eighty-three and died in 1834. He was described as a 'majestic figure, a model for the sculptor, with a native oaken sapling in his hand, and two gigantic Danish wolfhounds at his heels.' He was 'an early riser, temperate in his habits, and when not provoked to choler, bland, courteous, amiable, and capable of winning and retaining the most devoted friendship.' A companion who went on a walking tour of England with him describes 'his practice at starting from our inn, of a wet morning, of rolling himself into the first pool he met in order that he might be beforehand with the rain.'

Leonard McNally was a trusted friend of the United Irishmen, he knew their secrets and retained their friendship and confidence till he died. It was only after his death, when his heir claimed the continuation of the secret service income of £300 a year which McNally had received since 1798, that it was discovered that he had also been a government informer.

When a Catholic Convention was organised in Dublin in 1792 to demand more rights for Catholics the Corporation of Dublin sent a petition to the Parliament in protest at the granting of any further concessions. The petition said they wanted 'a Protestant King, a Protestant Parliament, a Protestant Hierarchy, Protestant electors and Government, the benches of justice, the army and the revenue through all their branches and details Protestant'.

In 1792 the United Irishmen organised the Belfast Harp Festival to revive Irish traditional music. It was this festival which inspired Edward Bunting to undertake his great work of collecting Irish songs and airs throughout the whole country.

When Wolfe Tone attended one such harp recital he was not too impressed. 'Strum and be hanged,' he is said to have remarked.

Parliament', and the Gunpowder Act forbidding the importation or sale of gunpowder or arms.

In spite of the Convention Act, the United Irishmen continued to meet and at a gathering held in Dublin in February 1793, Archibald Hamilton Rowan, who had been a member of the Volunteers and was now a United Irishmen, distributed a pamphlet calling on the Volunteers to take up arms in the defence of Ireland and calling for complete Catholic emancipation. Secret government agents were at the meeting and brought the proceedings to the notice of the authorities. Sometime later Rowan was arrested.

When his trial began on 29 January 1794 large crowds gathered in the snow outside the Dublin Four Courts and his defence counsel, Philpott Curran, was chaired home by torchlight procession each evening. Soldiers were on guard inside the building and detachments of cavalry patrolled the surrounding streets. Although eloquently defended by Curran, Rowan was found guilty by the jury after only ten minutes deliberation. He was sentenced to two years' imprisonment and a fine of £500. While Rowan was in prison a Protestant clergyman named William Jackson arrived in Ireland from France to sound out the leading United Irishmen about an invasion by the French. Accompanying Jackson was a London attorney called Cockayne to whom he had confided his plans. Cockayne was in reality an English government spy but he acted his part well. The two men had meetings with Tone, Rowan and others, including Leonard McNally, a Dublin lawyer. During the meetings a statement was issued by Tone at Rowan's insistence to say that the people of Ireland were near to open rebellion, that Ireland was 'a conquered, oppressed and insulted country' and that the Catholics and Defenders 'would throw off the yoke, if they saw any force in the country sufficiently strong to resort to for defence'. Tone later withdrew his statement but allowed Rowan to make a copy of it. Rowan did so and added some embellishments of his own. Jackson later mailed copies of the statement to France. The letters were intercepted and Jackson was arrested. When Rowan heard of Jackson's arrest he decided to escape from prison. He bribed a jailer to allow him to visit his home where he escaped through a back window and eventually made his way to France. The following year Jackson was brought to

————— ◎ —————

When Black Jack Fitzgibbon became Lord Chancellor he had a magnificent golden coach built in 1790 at the then enormous cost of £7,000. On occasions when he used it in the city the coach and its highly unpopular occupant was pelted with stones and once a dead rat was thrown into it. On the death of Queen Victoria the beautiful golden coach was painted black as a sign of mourning. It has now been restored to its former glory and is on view in Newbridge House Open Farm in Donabate in County Dublin.

————— ◎ —————

During the 'reign' of Black Jack an Englishman, Dr Richard Twiss, visited Dublin and later wrote a scathing criticism of Black Jack and his cronies. In retaliation a manufacturer friend of Fitzgibbon printed a portrait of Twiss on the bottom of his earthenware chamber-pots. Black Jack's wife, Lady Clare, then composed the following:

> Here you may behold a liar
> Well deserving of hell-fire
> Everyone who likes may p–
> Upon the learned Doctor T–

————— ◎ —————

trial and convicted of treason. He cheated the hangman, however, as he managed to take a dose of arsenic and dropped dead in the courtroom.

The striking success of republican French forces on the Continent at this time now had an effect in Ireland. Prime Minister Pitt decided on a policy of conciliation, to drop coercion and remove all remaining disabilities suffered by the Catholics in Ireland. In December 1794 he sent over a new Lord Lieutenant, the Earl of Fitzwilliam, to carry out his orders.

Fitzwilliam was a just and liberal man and was received with great enthusiasm by the Catholics of Dublin who knew what his mission was. He immediately set about reforms by removing from office various officials who opposed any improvements. A month later Grattan introduced a bill to give permission to Catholics to sit in Parliament. Just when it seemed that the bill was on the point of being passed a small clique led by 'Black Jack' Fitzgibbon, Lord Chancellor of Ireland, managed to convince Prime Minister Pitt and King George that the Protestant religion would be endangered in Ireland if it was passed. The bill was defeated, Fitzwilliam was recalled, the deposed officials reinstated and the old policy towards Catholics resumed. Fitzwilliam left Ireland on 25 March 1795 amid scenes of great mourning throughout Dublin. To rub salt into the wounds Fitzgibbon was promoted to the title 'Earl of Clare'.

12

◎

'WHO FEARS TO SPEAK OF NINETY-EIGHT?'

The United Irishmen was an open organisation and exclusively Protestant at the beginning but when it was banned by the government in 1794 it changed to being a secret society. Catholics were admitted as members and by 1795 the policy of the United Irishmen was to become more and more republican, influenced greatly by the events in France.

On 9 April 1795 over 4,000 people attended a meeting in Dublin at which they were told by the leaders that they could not hope for any concessions from England by peaceful means. Rumours that a union of the two countries was planned by Pitt as the price to pay for Catholic emancipation invoked passionate speeches. The speakers declared that they would never trade the independence of their country for their own religious liberty and that they would never abandon their Protestant brethren.

When the very popular Fitzwilliam was recalled from Dublin, and hopes of reform began to fade, the leaders began to think more and more of rebellion. The arrival of Fitzwilliam's successor, Lord Camden, in 1795 was greeted by a furious riot in the streets. The military were called to quell the disturbance and two citizens were killed.

All of this added to the unrest which was spreading throughout the country. The United Irishmen's leaders began negotiations with the French government in 1796. Tone, who had told the ill-fated William Jackson that an invasion by France would be welcome, thought it prudent to leave Ireland in 1795. He first went to America but in the following year he made his way to France. In Paris he joined several prominent members of the United Irishmen in negotiations with the French authorities for military aid for an Irish insurrection. Among them was Lord Edward

Lord Edward Fitzgerald was elected to the Irish Parliament and later became one of the leaders of the United Irishmen rebellion in 1798.

Fitzgerald.

Lord Edward Fitzgerald, the son of the first Duke of Leinster, was born at the family home at Carton in County Kildare. His family became Protestants at the time of the Reformation and had supported William of Orange against King James. Edward was a delicate child at first but later developed into an active healthy boy.

At the age of sixteen he joined the British army and by 1781 found himself fighting against American forces in the War of Independence in South Carolina. Subsequently Lord Edward followed a varied career of travel and politics, including election to the Irish Parliament where he caused uproar for supporting the Volunteers when the house condemned them for celebrating French military victories. Gradually he grew more and more republican in outlook and became so involved with the United Irishmen that by 1798 he was one of the leaders of the movement.

Meanwhile the government embarked on a policy of repression, first in Ulster and later in the rest of Ireland. Anarchy, atrocities, burnings and pillaging by soldiers were widespread throughout the country. In May 1797 Grattan made another attempt in parliament to get some concessions on Catholic emancipation but was voted down by the government side by four to one. Grattan and his supporters then withdrew from parliament in disgust.

———— ◎ ————

Lord Edward was described as 'of a cheerful, intelligent countenance, an artless gaiety of manner, without reserve but without intrusion, and a careless yet uneffusive intrepidity both in conversation and in action.'

———— ◎ ————

An escaped slave called Tony Small found Lord Edward Fitzgerald wounded and unconscious on the battlefield at Eutaw Springs in South Carolina, carried him to safety, bound his wounds and undoubtedly saved his life. When Edward sailed for home some time later he took Tony with him and the former Black slave became his devoted servant for the rest of his life.

———— ◎ ————

After Lord Edward Fitzgerald was arrested in the house in Thomas Street, Dublin, the house owner, Nicholas Murphy, was also arrested and spent a year in jail, during which time his house was used as a barracks by the soldiers. He later complained that some fine examples of silverware were stolen by them and that they had destroyed 'six dozen as fine wine as could be found – claret, port and sherry – I purchased it in the wood' and that when the soldiers got tired of drinking his wine 'they were selling it in the morning for sixpence a bottle and buying whiskey with the money'.

———— ◎ ————

The leaders of the United Irishmen now decided that only force would gain the concessions they needed from the government. They fixed 23 May 1798 as the day the rebellion would start with the seizure of Dublin Castle but what they did not know was that every move they made was betrayed to the authorities by informers.

One of these was a man called Thomas Reynolds whom Lord Edward had recruited to the United Irishmen in Kildare. On Lord Edward's insistence he became a colonel in the United Irish army – a fatal move because Reynolds was more interested in his own advancement than anything else. When Fitzgerald revealed to him the plans for the coming rebellion Reynolds negotiated with the Castle authorities a sum of £5,000 and £1,000 a year for life in return for betraying his friend.

Reynolds also told the Castle that a meeting of leaders was to take place in Dublin in the house of Oliver Bond on the morning of 12 March. Shortly after ten o'clock a magistrate called Major Swan arrived at the house with a detachment of constables in uniform. When Swan gave the password 'Where's McCann? Is Ivers of Carlow come?' he was admitted to the house. Swan flung open the door of the meeting room and found the leaders present, but the most incriminating documents were burned before he could prevent it. Thirteen members of the committee were arrested and only Lord Edward of the five-man executive remained at liberty.

Various other houses were raided by the military the same day and more of the leaders taken into custody. They failed to arrest Lord Edward Fitzgerald, however, and a reward of £1,000 was offered for his capture. The Castle sent out two search parties with warrants to arrest him but though they searched his home, Leinster House, they failed in their task. In fact Lord Edward was at home when the search party arrived but his faithful servant Tony smuggled him out the back to safety. In the days and weeks that followed Lord Edward assumed almost mythical proportions in the eyes of his followers, appearing among them in various disguises in spite of intense efforts by the authorities to find him.

In March 1798 the government declared the whole country to be in a state of rebellion and gave the newly appointed army commander, General Lake, a free hand to impose martial law. His

————— ◎ —————

Francis Higgins, the 'Sham Squire' was born in a cellar in
Lord Edward Street. He became in turn a messenger boy, a
shoe-black, a waiter in a pub, a clerk in a law office and
finally a lawyer himself. He became exceedingly rich and
the owner of the *Freeman's Journal*. An unmitigated rogue,
he gained all his wealth and position by underhand means.
He got the nickname 'Sham Squire' because he pretended to
be a landed gentleman in order to get a lady to marry him.
(She is said to have died of grief as a result!) Later it was
proved beyond doubt that he had betrayed Lord Edward
Fitzgerald for £1,000. He was 'to be seen daily with Buck
Whaley on Beaux Walk in Stephen's Green, wearing a
three-cocked hat fringed with swan's down, a canary-
coloured waistcoat with breeches to match, a bright green
body coat and violet gloves.' He died in 1806 aged fifty-six
years of age.

————— ◎ —————

Major Henry Sirr served in the army for three years but
then retired to become a wine merchant in Dublin. In 1796
he was made town major and it was in that capacity that he
was involved in the arrest of Lord Edward Fitzgerald and,
later, Robert Emmet. After he retired he became keenly
interested in the Irish language and history.

————— ◎ —————

soldiery spread terror and savagery throughout the country. Burnings, floggings, mutilations and rapes were the order of the day. 'Croppies', that is men who favoured the United Irishmen and adopted the fashion of cutting their hair short, were especially targeted. Pitch-capping, where the head of the victim was covered with a paper or cloth cap filled with tar and set alight, became commonplace. Another form of torture used was where men were stripped to the waist and tied to a large wooden triangle and flogged until they gave up the name of a secret United Irishman. The named person would then be caught and put through the same procedure.

The United Irishmen's plans for the rising were completed by early May and it was agreed that it would start in Dublin on 23 May by stopping the mail coaches from departing for the provinces. The non-arrival of the coaches in the surrounding towns was to be the signal for the waiting rebels to rise up and in this way the rebellion would spread throughout the country.

Lord Edward had his magnificent uniform of green jacket and matching trousers trimmed with scarlet braid brought to his hiding place in Dublin in preparation for leading the troops into battle. The weather at the time was unusually fine and warm and everything seemed set for successful action.

But then the army of spies and informers at last came up with hard information for the Castle authorities. The informer, Francis 'Sham Squire' Higgins, discovered where Fitzgerald was hiding and told the authorities. On 19 May 1798, at seven o'clock in the evening, Major Swan and a man named Ryan, who was a captain in the yeomanry, entered the house and went up the stairs to the room where Lord Edward Fitzgerald, who had a slight fever, was lying in bed. Swan was confronted by the owner, Nicholas Murphy, who asked him what his business was but when Swan saw Lord Edward in the bed he rushed past Murphy, yelling 'You are my prisoner'. Lord Edward sprang up and attacked Swan with a dagger he had concealed. Captain Ryan then rushed into the room and grappled with Lord Edward who repeatedly stabbed at him with his dagger. The fatally wounded Ryan still grimly held on and Major Swan then joined in the struggle. At that moment Major Sirr, the local town major who had accompanied the party, rushed into the room and shot Fitzgerald twice in the shoulder, causing

———— ◎ ————

The French at this time were at war with England and they thought that a successful Irish uprising would cripple the British war effort. Tone had persuaded the French that the arrival of their troops in Ireland would cause 100,000 Irish to immediately flock to their aid.

A French fleet of forty-eight ships set sail from Brest on 16 December 1796 under the command of Vice-Admiral de Galles. On board were 13,000 battle-hardened troops led by General Hoche. The plan was to land on the south coast of Ireland, join the local insurgents, capture Cork and then march on Dublin.

Many disagreements among the French leaders led to frequent alterations of the plan until in the end the French Directory cancelled the whole thing. A letter to this effect was sent to the port of Brest but before it arrived the fleet set sail.

From the beginning things began to go wrong. Even before they left harbour four boats collided, causing some damage. Vice-Admiral de Galles originally directed the fleet to sail in a southerly direction to avoid a British fleet patrolling off the coast but he changed his mind at the last moment and decided to sail in a westerly direction. By then, however, most of the fleet were sailing southwards and he ordered that cannons be fired to alert them of the change in plans. Unfortunately it happened that one of his ships had hit some rocks and was sinking and the fleet sailing in the wrong direction thought the cannon fire was a distress signal from it. The result was that seventeen ships sailed the wrong way. Most of the fleet came together off Mizen Head in Cork, but the ship carrying Hoche and de Galles did not – it was blown completely off course. In their absence their second-in-commands, Grouchy and Bouvet, assumed command and opened the sealed orders they had been given by the two missing leaders. It was only then that they discovered that they were to land in Bantry Bay.

The fleet by this time was reduced to only thirty-five ships and the extremely strong headwinds battered the remaining ships so much that only fifteen, carrying 6,400 men, made their way into the bay. Grouchy and Bouvet were among them on the *Immortality*.

Even then their troubles were not over. When Grouchy asked the naval commander Bouvet to prepare to land the troops the latter attempted to do so but a strong gale arose and they could not. The storm lasted two days. Then the *Immortality* dragged its anchor and was drifting on shore so Bouvet thought it wiser to leave him to drop the dagger, after which he was overpowered.

After his arrest Lord Edward was taken to Newgate Prison and an armed guard was placed inside his cell in case an effort was made to rescue him.

On 21 May 1798, two lawyer brothers, Henry and John Sheares, who were members of the United Irishmen, were arrested. They were convicted of treason on 12 July and publicly beheaded outside Newgate Prison two days later. Henry was actually reprieved but the order arrived five minutes too late to stop the execution.

On the evening of 23 May Samuel Neilson, one of the United Irishmen leaders, called a meeting of fifteen officers to plan the rising in Dublin city. But the Castle authorities, through one of their many spies, were soon aware of the plans for the rising and troops were immediately dispatched to occupy strategic positions.

Wholesale arrests reduced the United Irishmen organisation within the city to a helpless condition and on-the-spot hanging of prisoners at various points in the city, including Carlisle (O'Connell) Bridge, acted as a powerful deterrent to others. Within a week the threat to the capital was over and the focus of attention shifted to other parts of the country.

On 26 May 1798 about 4,000 rebels occupied the summit of Tara Hill in Meath. It was a good strategic position, offering a clear view of the surrounding countryside and the low stone walls on the hill provided good cover from musket fire. Their instructions were to occupy the hill, erect the revolutionary standard and to place in position 'two pieces of cannon'. They raised their standard all right but they certainly had no cannon. With the arrival of reinforcements from Kildare, bringing some guns stolen from an ironworks in Lucan, their numbers now approached eight thousand. They had also thirty-three sets of arms and about nine thousand ball cartridges which they had captured from a Scottish regiment. They had taken ten Highlanders captive as well and they now made them teach the men how to use the guns.

It was all in vain, however, because when the rebels were attacked by a government force of three hundred Scottish soldiers and the local yeomanry they were decisively defeated. The rebels lost three hundred and fifty dead as against a mere thirteen of the government troops. The battle ended any threat from the United

Bantry Bay altogether but the fierce winds blew the *Immortality* carrying the two luckless leaders nearly 500 kilometres out into the Atlantic. So the second set of leaders were now out of action.

The remaining senior officer, named Bedont, decided that they should leave Bantry and make for the mouth of the Shannon in the hope of meeting the rest of the fleet there. Nine ships did manage to get to the Shannon by 28 December but no other ships made contact, so they decided to head back to France and arrived in Brest on New Years Day 1797.

Meanwhile, some of the ships that had tried to enter Bantry Bay with Bouvet began to straggle in. They anchored just north of Whiddy Island. The senior officer of this group was a man called Durand-Linois. He had eight ships and about 4,000 soldiers at his command but he had no artillery and very little food. He was also convinced that a force of about 5,000 enemy would be waiting for him if he landed. So he decided to bring his little fleet out to sea and wait for reinforcements to turn up. Ironically enough, he was unable to leave for two days because conditions were too calm! When he did reach the open sea he failed to make contact with any other ships and so he returned to France on January 13.

Elsewhere Hoche and de Galles had finally managed to beat their way back towards Ireland but as they got within forty-eight kilometres of the southern coast they met one of the ships which had been with Bouvet. It was in a very poor condition with its complement of 2,000 soldiers almost starving. The two leaders then decided that there was no hope of a successful invasion and set sail for France. (Had they gone into Bantry Bay they would have found Durand-Linois there with his ships and 4,000 men. Whether that would have encouraged Hoche to order a landing we will never know.)

A fleet of forty-eight ships had set sail from France on 16 December 1796 but only thirty-five of them returned. More than 1,500 sailors and soldiers had been drowned and another 2,000 had been captured by the enemy.

The whole expedition was a disaster from the start. Bad planning, poor seamanship, terrible weather and downright bad luck had dogged it from the start. Added to this was an inordinate fear of the British navy. The irony was that the French had the seas around the south of Ireland to themselves – no English ship was in the area from 22 December 1796 to January 1797.

Irishmen of Meath and the North Midlands.

In Kildare the rising met with little opposition at first and the rebels set up four different camps in the county: one on the border between Kildare and Wicklow at Blackmore Hill, one at Knockallen Hill commanding a bridge over the Liffey, one at Gibbet Rath in the Curragh and one at Timahoe in the Bog of Allen. When the rebels at Knockallen Hill found that there was no prospect of success they surrendered to General Dundas, the Midlands Commander. The general generously allowed them to return to their homes on surrendering their arms.

The next day he entered talks with the rebels at Gibbet Rath in the Curragh but before the talks could be completed the 6,000 rebels were attacked from the rear by a newly arrived force under General Sir James Duff. A dreadful massacre followed, with over three hundred rebels slain and no loss to the soldiers. The dead lay in piles on the hillside until the women from Kildare came out that night to claim their loved ones.

Various other calamities occurred in the midlands, particularly in Ballitore and Rathdangan in Kildare and Blessington in Wicklow where the defeat of the rebels again ended in cruelty and butchery.

When the rising broke out in Wexford it was not the result of careful planning – in fact the United Irishmen organisation was relatively weak in the county. The rebellion was a result of the outrageous behaviour of military such as the North Cork Militia over the previous months. This regiment roamed the county, searching for arms and torturing and killing suspects without mercy – twenty-eight suspected United Irishmen were shot dead in Ball Alley in Carnew and a further thirty-four in Dunlavin.

As late as Easter 1798 Father John Murphy, parish priest of Boolavogue near Enniscorthy, refused the sacraments to members of the United Irishmen who would not repudiate their secret oath and he also collected the signatures of 750 of his parishioners to an address of loyalty to the Lord Lieutenant in an effort to stave off martial law.

By May however the activities of the Ferns Yeomanry and the North Cork Militia in the area were becoming intolerable; rumours of massacres and French landings were rife and the massacres in Carnew and Dunlavin created panic. From this time on Father Murphy openly threw in his lot with the United Irishmen, saying,

A large number of Catholic priests were involved in the Wexford Rising.

A Carmelite, Father John Byrne, played an active part in the camps in the south of the county. He had a rather strange death in 1799. He was visiting Clougheast Castle and when the owner thought Byrne was going to attack him he chased him out of the castle. As the friar was fleeing through the main door the portcullis fell on him and killed him.

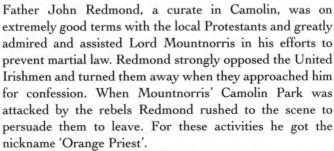

When the nephew of Father Thomas Clinch was killed by yeomen the priest joined the rebels. He cut a remarkable figure, being of huge stature and riding a large white horse. He wore his vestments under his clothes and carried a scimitar on his broad crossed belt. During single combat on Vinegar Hill he was shot and wounded. Although he managed to ride away he died soon after.

Father John Redmond, a curate in Camolin, was on extremely good terms with the local Protestants and greatly admired and assisted Lord Mountnorris in his efforts to prevent martial law. Redmond strongly opposed the United Irishmen and turned them away when they approached him for confession. When Mountnorris' Camolin Park was attacked by the rebels Redmond rushed to the scene to persuade them to leave. For these activities he got the nickname 'Orange Priest'.

After the rebellion Mountnorris sent for him to come to Gorey and Redmond obeyed in all innocence. When he arrived in the town, however, he was knocked to the ground by the yeomen and dragged in front of Mountnorris. A hasty court martial followed and he was sentenced to death. He was rushed to Gorey Hill and hanged, Mountnorris personally firing two bullets into his suspended body.

'Look to the inhuman slaughter in Carnew, and if the reported butchery in Dunlavin is true, it is worse. Our jails are full of the best of our people and it may be our lot to be in company with them before tomorrow night.'

The incident that finally lit the fuse was the burning by the yeomen of the little Catholic chapel at Boolavogue in May 1798. As a result, Father Murphy urged his flock to resist and offered himself as leader. He was joined by another priest, Father Michael Murphy, whose church was also burned.

Unlike most other parts of the country, the rebellion in Wexford soon assumed an unpleasant sectarian character; nearly all the rebels were Catholics, although there were some Protestant leaders.

The poorly armed peasants had an early success over a small company of yeomen and this victory encouraged great numbers of others to join the rebels. Father Murphy established his camp at Oulart Hill and soon had about 5,000 men at his command. When the hated North Cork Militia attacked his position they were defeated with terrible slaughter. Next he marched on Enniscorthy and, by driving a herd of bullocks against the ranks of the defenders, his army broke through and took the town. The garrison and many inhabitants then fled to the town of Wexford about twenty-four kilometres away.

The rebels then marched to Vinegar Hill beside Enniscorthy and established the camp there. During the following four weeks hundreds of Protestant prisoners from the surrounding areas were put to death after perfunctory trials. On May 30 the insurgents attacked and destroyed a body of soldiers at Three Rocks about six kilometres from Wexford.

Later they marched on the town itself but the garrison had already withdrawn, pillaging, burning and killing as they left. When the rebels took over the town they took to drinking and went wild. One local ship's captain named Dixon gathered a mob and broke open the jail in which local Protestant gentry were being held. They then dragged them to the bridge where they killed them one by one and threw their bodies into the river Slaney below. Up to ninety prisoners had been murdered before a local priest, Father Currin, rushed forward and ordered the killings to stop and commanded the rabble to kneel. They obeyed instinctively and he

———— ◎ ————

Father Murphy of Boolavogue is described as being a 'well-built man of medium height, well fleshed, light complexioned, with a high forehead and receding hair over regular features'. He was very popular with his flock but was 'terrible when opposed'.

———— ◎ ————

The exact date of the execution of John Kelly ('The Boy from Killann') is not known but his treatment was particularly gruesome. Badly wounded in the battle of New Ross when a bullet shattered his thigh, he was brought to the gallows on Wexford Bridge. After he was hanged his head was cut off and kicked by the soldiers through the streets of the town. Kelly's own sister was an unfortunate witness to the behaviour of the soldiers.

———— ◎ ————

On 25 June 1798 Matthew Keogh, Father Roche and seven other men were taken to Wexford Bridge for execution. The makeshift gallows was a metal arch that spanned the bridge and the soldiers hanged the men by putting a rope around their neck and hauling them from the ground. The rope round Father Roche snapped the first time and he fell unconscious to the ground. When he recovered he was hauled up again and hanged. The bodies of the men were grossly mutilated after hanging and then thrown in the river. Because Keogh was a Protestant he was treated with great vindictiveness – his head was cut off, stuck on a pike and paraded around the town. Later it was left for months on a pike outside the courthouse.

The same treatment was given to the bodies of Bagenal Harvey and another leader called Cornelius Grogan after they were executed on the bridge on 28 June. Their heads were then placed alongside Keogh's outside the courthouse.

———— ◎ ————

made them repeat a prayer that God might show them more mercy than they had shown the prisoners. One of the released prisoners was a Protestant gentleman called Bagenal Harvey, who was a large landowner and in fact a prominent United Irishman. He was now elected by the rebels to be their leader.

By this time the rebels had three camps – the main camp on Vinegar Hill and two others on Carrickbyrne Hill between Wexford and New Ross and on Carrigroe Hill near Ferns. On 1 June a large group from Carrigroe marched on Gorey but were driven back. Next a force of 1500 soldiers under General Loftus marched from the town to attack the Carrigroe camp but the rebels surprised them on the way on 4 June and utterly routed them. The rebels then occupied the town.

Meanwhile the rebels from Vinegar Hill marched on Newtownbarry on 2 June and took the town. They then began to plunder and drink so that they offered little resistance when the garrison they had driven out returned to attack them. The rebels were routed with the loss of 400 men.

On 5 June Harvey led a force of about 5,000 men in an attack on New Ross and after a fierce battle managed to drive out the garrison. Once more however discipline broke down and they started celebrating and drinking. Even though they repelled two earlier attempts by the soldiers to retake the town, a third attempt late in the evening succeeded. The troops lost 300 men but the rebels suffered much more casualties, losing up to 3,000 men.

That same evening some fleeing rebels broke into Scullabogue House, about thirteen kilometres from New Ross, where a number of loyalist prisoners, nearly all Protestants, were confined. Pretending that they were acting under orders from Harvey, they took out thirty-seven prisoners and murdered them. They then set fire to the barn which contained a further 200 Protestants prisoners, including women and children, and all were burned to death.

The rebels then decided to march on Dublin with an army of up to 20,000 strong but when they attacked Arklow on 7 June it was so ably defended by the garrison commanded by General Needham that they failed to take the town. Father Michael Murphy was killed by a cannon ball in the battle and the men were so disheartened that they retreated and gave up the attempt to reach

———— ◎ ————

When the United Irishmen attacked the barracks in Antrim they had only one cannon, a brass six-pounder which had lain hidden under the floor of the Templepatrick Meeting House. The cannon was now mounted on the wheels of an old coach and was managed by some ex-soldiers who only had pieces of burning peat in an iron pot with which to light the gunpowder. As the rebels approached Antrim town they were fired upon by the defenders and, firing their cannon in reply, the rebels only got two shots off before the gun fell off its mountings.

———— ◎ ————

When Lieutenant-General Lake took command in Belfast in 1797 he declared 'Nothing but terror will keep them in order.' The yeomen were let loose throughout the whole of Ulster, burning, pillaging and flogging. One clergyman reported, 'I saw Samuel Bones of Brouhshane receive 500 lashes – 250 on the back and 250 on the buttocks. I saw Samuel Crawford of Ballymena receive 500 lashes. The only words he spoke during the time were "Gentlemen, be pleased to shoot me." I saw Hood Haslett of Ballymena receive 500 lashes. I believe he was only about nineteen years of age. Before he had received the 500 lashes I heard him exclaiming 'I am cutting through.'

———— ◎ ————

Membership of the United Irishmen was punishable by death. When the army authorities suspected that seventy members of the Monaghan Militia were members Lake ordered that four privates who refused to inform on their comrades should be executed beside their coffins. The rest of the troops were then ordered to file past to view the bodies.

———— ◎ ————

Dublin. They left up to a thousand dead in the fields around the town.

The depleted rebel forces were by now concentrated on Vinegar Hill and General Lake decided to attack the camp, with each of his divisions attacking from a different direction. His troops, numbering about 20,000 and well armed, were in their appointed positions to attack on 21 June with the exception of the division under General Needham, who for some reason did not arrive until the battle was all over.

The attack began with a general bombardment of the rebels' position to which they could make little or no reply but still they resisted bravely for an hour and a half before they broke and fled. Had the hill been completely surrounded as Lake had intended it is likely that few, if any, of the rebels would have escaped alive. The failure of Needham to arrive had left an opening, however, and the main body of the insurgents escaped through what has since been known as Needham's Gap.

The rebels made their way to Wexford where Matthew Keogh was in command. He was aware that General Lake's army was approaching and that his position was hopeless so he released one of his most prominent prisoners, Lord Kingsborough, to ask Lake to spare the town from the brutality of the soldiers. Kingsborough did his best but Lake said he would enter into 'no negotiations and consider no terms'. Shortly afterwards the rebels dispersed and on 22 June a detachment of Lake's regular soldiers marched in and quietly took possession of the town.

The remaining rebel camp at Three Rocks was now abandoned but their leader Father Roche was captured and hanged. Many of the other leaders were also arrested and after a brief court martial they too were taken out and hanged. Among the many who suffered this fate were Bagenal Harvey, Matthew Keogh and Father John Murphy, while on Wexford Bridge alone more than sixty-five prisoners were hanged.

Meanwhile the first opening shots of the rebellion in the North of Ireland were fired when a group of armed United Irishmen attacked a barracks near Larne in County Antrim on 7 June 1798. The plans of the northern revolutionaries had been severely disrupted during the previous years. When General Lake had arrived in Belfast in 1796 he had declared 'Nothing but terror will

─────── ◎ ───────

After the failed attempt by McCracken to take the town of Antrim the troops finished off any captured or wounded rebels. Three days later the bodies of all the dead rebels were thrown into sandpits on the shores of Lough Neagh. Later an onlooker recalled: 'As a cart-load of dead and dying arrived at the sandpit a yeoman officer asked the driver "Where the devil did these rascals come from?" A poor wretch raised his gory head from the cart and feebly answered "I come frae Ballyboley." He was buried with the rest.'

─────── ◎ ───────

Controversy continues to surround Tone's death to this day, some believing that it was the authorities who tried to kill him. Others say that the wound was caused not by a penknife but by a razor given to him by his brother.

His body was taken to High Street in Dublin where his parents were living. He was laid out on the second floor and a plaster cast was taken of his face. His hair was cut off and divided among the family. For two days large numbers of mourners filed past the coffin. He was later buried quietly in Bodenstown, County Kildare.

─────── ◎ ───────

keep them [United Irishmen] in order'. In March 1797 he proclaimed martial law and ordered that all arms should be handed in. Searches and arrests were made all over the province and most of the leaders were arrested and sent as prisoners to Dublin. The yeomen roamed all over the countryside, burning, arresting and flogging everywhere they went. Houses were set on fire, one soldier boasting that he set fire to fourteen houses in the space of one morning.

By the end of 1797 the Ulster United Irishmen were almost completely wiped out by Lake's ruthless campaign. (During all this time no attempt was made to disarm the Orangemen who proved a valuable resource for recruits for the yeomanry.)

It was only when Henry Joy McCracken, a member of a leading Belfast business family, arrived back from Dublin that a semblance of order was restored among the United Irishmen and the insurrection began in Larne on 7 June 1798. Due to the activities of Lake during the previous year the insurgents were extremely poorly armed – most had no firearms and were armed with 'pitchforks, peat spades, scythes, bayonets, sharpened harrow pins fixed on poles, old rusty swords and reaping hooks'. Still they managed to capture Ballymena and Randalstown.

They next turned their attention to Antrim town and as they marched along wearing green cockades and singing 'La Marseillaise' they were joined by other contingents from all over south Antrim. The attackers made little headway and when reinforcements arrived for the garrison the rebels were scattered.

Henry Joy McCracken, Jemmy Hope and others tried to rally the fleeing rebels but failed – the rebellion in Antrim was over. McCracken was later arrested in Carrickfergus and was hanged in Belfast on 17 July 1798. He was among the last of the leaders to be executed.

In County Down the uprising began on 9 June 1798. It started in Saintfield with the burning of a farmstead belonging to a family thought to be informers. The entire family was wiped out – a horrendous deed for which eleven people were later hanged. A detachment of cavalry riding to the scene was ambushed by pikemen and about fifty-five of their number were killed.

Various other actions the same day were not so successful from an insurgent point of view but the news of the success at Saintfield spread quickly and United Irishmen rushed to join the rebels. They had no recognised leader until eventually a Scottish merchant from Lisburn, named Henry Monro, took command. He immediately ordered the rebel army to move to Ballynahinch where he set up his headquarters and established a dug-in position on Windmill Hill just west of the town.

The commander of the government, Major-General Nugent, forces issued a proclamation on 11 June that unless the rebels immediately laid down their arms he would proceed 'to set fire to and totally destroy the towns of Killinchy, Killyleagh, Ballynahinch, Saintfield and every cottage and farmhouse in the vicinity of those places, carry off the stock and put everyone to the sword who may be found in arms'. He carried out his threat the very next day by burning Saintfield to the ground, as well as numerous farmhouses and barns. He waited then for reinforcements from Downpatrick and when these arrived he began pounding the rebel positions with his cannon. The men on Windmill Hill were soon overwhelmed and after a heavy bombardment Ballynahinch was overrun by the Monaghan Militia who engaged in a drunken orgy of killing and destruction.

The next morning the rebels attacked the town but their ammunition was soon exhausted and Nugent's army rapidly overwhelmed them. The cavalry relentlessly pursued the fleeing rebels and hacked them down. Monro was captured two days later and hanged in the market place in Lisburn and with his death came the end of the rebellion in Ulster.

Then, on 22 August 1798, three French warships flying the English flag sailed into Killala Bay in County Mayo. A British army officer who happened to be fishing in the bay at the time went to the ships to give them some of his catch and ended up being made prisoner. He found that the French ships had about one thousand troops aboard and these soon disembarked and took possession of the town. The next morning the leader, General Humbert, raised a green flag bearing the words Érin go Brách (Ireland For Ever) and called on every Irishman to join him. Many did so and were given handsome blue uniforms and muskets but unfortunately some of the men then disappeared with both uniforms and guns, exchanged them for whiskey, and went back for more!

Next Humbert marched south and met with the British forces

near Castlebar. The 'battle' hardly lasted five minutes before the English forces broke and ran, many discarding their muskets, most of which had not even been discharged. The event has since become derisively known as 'The Races of Castlebar'. Not all English troops were as poor as those at Castlebar however and when Humbert was confronted with 20,000 seasoned troops under Lord Cornwallis at Ballinamuck in County Longford he surrendered. Humbert and his troops, cheerfully singing 'La Marseillaise', were taken to Dublin. There the officers were given a banquet in their honour and then allowed to return to France. Some Irish leaders who had accompanied them from France however, were taken and hanged. Among them was Matthew Tone, a brother of Theobald.

A second small French expedition arrived in Rutland harbour in Donegal on 16 September 1798. It consisted of just one ship carrying 200 men and a cargo of arms and was commanded by Napper Tandy. When they landed they made their way to the local post office where the postmaster happened to be an old friend of Tandy's. There Tandy got the bad news that the rebellion was over and that Humbert's expedition had failed. That night Tandy drank himself into a stupor with his old friend and had to be carried back on board his ship. The next morning he sailed back to France.

The third and last French expedition, comprising one large warship and thirty frigates, arrived at Lough Swilly the following month, 12 October 1798. The force was led by Admiral Bompart on board the *Hoche* and was accompanied by Theobald Wolfe Tone. The force was attacked by a squadron of nine warships at the entrance to the lough and a fierce battle ensued. Bompart surrendered when the *Hoche* was on the point of sinking but some of the other frigates were able to escape to France. (Six of them were later captured.)

Tone had been urged to escape before the battle but had refused and in fact commanded a cannon in the battle. Afterwards he made no attempt to hide his identity and was sent in chains to Dublin. He was charged with treason and offered no defence, simply saying that he had done his duty. All he asked was that he be shot like a soldier and not to be hanged like a criminal. Nevertheless he was told on Sunday, 11 November, that he was to be hanged the next day at Newgate Prison but that the part of his sentence requiring

Wolfe Tone, founder of the Society of the United Irishmen.

that 'his head be struck off, fixed on a pike and placed in the most conspicuous part of the city' had been cancelled by the Lord Lieutenant. That night Tone tried to commit suicide by cutting his throat with his penknife. He was found at 4 a.m. in a pool of blood with his windpipe severed. Four surgeons were called in and his wound was sewn up and he lingered on for a week.

He was later told by a surgeon that it would be fatal to him if he moved or spoke and he is said to have replied, 'I can find no word to thank you, sir. It is the most welcome news you could give me', and died immediately. It was the morning of Monday, 19 November 1798, that Wolfe Tone died, aged thirty-five years.

13

◎

'THE UNITED KINGDOM'

As early as 1703 and 1707 the Irish Houses of Parliament had actually petitioned the English government for a union of the two countries but the request was refused outright. With the passing of time the desire for union waned greatly and by 1784 the Lord Lieutenant, Lord Rutland, declared that anyone who suggested union should be tarred and feathered. However, by the end of the century, the English Prime Minister, William Pitt, was convinced that a union of the two countries would indeed be of benefit to both countries. Britain was in grave danger from her old enemy France and Ireland was perceived as being ready to welcome French invaders, so that Britain would be vulnerable to attack from two directions.

Pitt thought that the Catholics might see in the union a means of achieving emancipation but he knew that opposition from the Protestant side would be extremely strong and the opposition from the Dublin ruling classes was certain. The corporation, the bankers, the merchants and members of the Bar would be implacably opposed to the loss of their Houses of Parliament.

Knowing the difficulties he faced, Pitt set about overcoming them. He began a campaign in the press to woo people to the idea. Merchants were told that trade would increase and English capital would flow into the country. The Catholics were told that Catholic emancipation could be granted to them since they could never hope to attain a majority in the new Union Parliament and so would present less of a threat to the Protestant ascendancy.

In February 1799 Pitt brought the matter before the English parliament and got it approved. He then set about preparing for a successful vote in the Irish parliament during the next session. Office holders who were known to be against the measure were dismissed or threatened with dismissal. Those borough owners

———— ◎ ————

'Pocket (or Rotten) boroughs' were controlled by local magnates who appointed their own candidates. Of the 300 members of the Irish House of Commons 178 of them were controlled by thirty rich men

———— ◎ ————

During the buying and selling of votes to achieve the Union one member of the Irish parliament sold his vote in favour of the Union to Lord Castlereagh and then accepted a bribe of £4,000 from the opposition side to vote against it!

———— ◎ ————

Dublin Bay was described by a traveller in 1800 as follows: 'The numerous wrecks which take place every winter, apparent from the masts, which are seen here and there peeping above the surface of the water, as it were, to warn others of their fate, are convincing proof of the assertion that the locality is a most dangerous one to shipping.'

———— ◎ ————

who had the disposal of seats in the Irish parliament were bought off by direct payments – about £15,000 was paid for each seat. The entire cost of buying out the 'rotten' or 'pocket' boroughs was £1,260,000.

To buy individual votes, twenty-eight new peers were created, thirty-two existing peers were promoted, and bribes in the form of pensions, judgeships, government positions and direct cash were offered to others. Pitt's chief agents in this were the Lord Lieutenant (Lord Cornwallis), Lord Castlereagh and Lord Clare (John Fitzgibbon). To give him his due, Lord Cornwallis was disgusted with the methods he was forced to use – 'How I long to kick those whom my public duty oblige me to court', he wrote at the time. He was also convinced that half of those who voted for the union would have been delighted if the bill were defeated.

However, even though the majority vote in favour was obtained by bribery, corruption and coercion, there were some who thought it was the correct thing to do. The country was in a very agitated state over the whole matter and the authorities were fearful that opponents of the Union might resort to arms. Consequently thousands of English troops were poured into the country to resist any such attempt.

When the Irish parliament met in Dublin in January 1799 the king's speech, which was read to the assembly, asked for a discussion on the question of Union. At the end there was a majority of only two in favour of the idea. This was tantamount to a defeat, as the motion was only for a discussion. Pitt, however, would not accept that the cause was lost and said that he would keep bringing the matter before the House until it was passed. In the same month the two Houses of Parliament in England discussed the proposal and very few opposed.

Seven months passed before the matter was brought before parliament again. Bribery and corruption continued unabated and achieved some success in changing the minds of several more opponents of the measure.

On 15 January 1800 the Irish Parliament opened for the last session. This time the king's speech made no reference to the Union but the subject was raised by those opposing the idea. During the debate that followed, Henry Grattan, who had been absent from the House for a long time due to illness, made a

After the ailing Grattan made his famous speech against the Union, Isaac Corry, the member for Newry, stood up and attacked him, accusing him in so many words of encouraging the United Irishmen in their rebellion. Corry had at one time been an enthusiastic supporter of Grattan but when he saw an opportunity for advancement on the government side had switched allegiances. Accepting the challenge, Grattan replied with a devastating speech in which he called Corry 'a political pedlar, an unprincipled trimmer, who prostituted both his principles and his talents, such as they were, first for bread, and then for station.' Corry in turn replied with more charges against Grattan: that he had aided and abetted traitors, had encouraged the rebellion and then run away until it was over. Grattan then accused Corry of being a greater traitor than a rebel. 'I agree that the rebel who rises against the Government should be punished but I missed on the scaffold the right honourable gentleman', and much more in the same vein. A duel followed, as was intended. It took place in a field in Ballsbridge in Dublin. Corry had first sent a message asking for a reconciliation but Grattan refused. When the order to fire was given, Grattan hit Corry in the arm with his shot, while Corry missed. On being told to fire a second time, Grattan deliberately fired above his opponent's head but it is not known if Corry fired. Afterwards Grattan visited Corry while he was recovering from his wound and while he was there Corry's brother Edward came; Corry said 'Here is my brother Edward; Edward, here is Mr Grattan, and he will shoot you whenever you deserve it!' Later when Grattan was living in Brighton in England Corry visited him and was warmly received by him.

When Pitt hinted that Catholic emancipation might follow the Union of the two countries King George III declared 'I would rather give up my throne and beg my bread from door to door throughout Europe than consent to such a measure.'

When the Act of Union ended the Irish Parliament which he had declared independent, Henry Grattan said, 'I sat by its cradle and I followed its hearse.'

dramatic appearance.

Dressed in the blue Volunteer uniform, with red cuffs and collar, he wore his cocked hat, square to the front, and kept it on until halfway up the floor of the house. He then stopped, took off his hat and 'looked round the house with a steady and fearless eye, as if he wished to let them know that, though exhausted, he was yet prepared to give battle.'

Getting permission to make his speech while remaining seated, Grattan spoke eloquently for two hours against the proposed Union. Other speakers joined in on both sides so that the debate lasted for eighteen hours altogether. When the vote was taken, the side opposing the Union lost by forty-two votes, 138 to 96. This caused the Lord Lieutenant, Lord Cornwallis, some uneasiness as forty-two votes were not regarded as a safe enough majority, especially as Grattan's speech was bound to have an effect by the time the final crucial vote was taken.

In March the proposal was again put in front of the two Houses of Parliament in England. It was approved by both. The bill was then drawn up in its final form and put before the Irish Houses of Parliament. The first reading on 21 May 1800 showed a government majority of sixty. At the second reading on 26 May the majority fell to forty. The final step took place on 7 June, when the

One of the most famous Irish highwaymen to practise the 'trade' was Michael Collier, born near Bellewstown in County Meath in 1780. On the wrong side of the law from an early age, he became acquainted with several highwaymen in Drogheda. Later he was to claim that his life of crime started when his girlfriend's father and brothers were arrested for stealing a horse. Collier befriended the policemen escorting the prisoners to gaol in Trim and managed to get them drunk. He then produced files to free the prisoners from their handcuffs. Collier himself then had to go on the run and so began his career as a highwayman.

He and his gang became famous for their activities in the Meath, Louth, Dublin and Kildare area and soon huge rewards were offered for his capture. He was eventually arrested and sentenced to death. The night before his execution, however, he managed to escape by filing through the bars of his cell by means of a file smuggled in to him by a young woman.

Free once more, Collier continued to rob carriages, mail coaches, houses of the gentry and individual travellers such as cattle dealers who had large wallets. In all his actions he appears to have treated employees of his victims with courtesy and when one of his gang mistreated a servant girl during a house robbery he was expelled from the gang. The man then threatened to inform on Collier and a fight broke out during which Collier shot the other man dead.

After a spell in England to escape the authorities he returned to Ireland where he resumed his 'trade'. The authorities reacted with fury at his brazenness and offered a huge award for his capture. Finally after many audacious robberies and hair-raising adventures he was cornered in the Cock Tavern in Gormanstown, County Meath by armed soldiers. He dashed out the back door and was escaping on his horse when a shot rang out and he was wounded and captured. He was brought before the courts and to the surprise of many was sentenced to seven years transportation to Australia instead of the more usual death penalty. On appeal he was allowed to join a British regiment in Africa. Released from the army he emigrated to America but eventually returned to Ireland where he became an extremely successful publican in Ashbourne, County Meath. He died suddenly in Drogheda on 13 August 1849 and was buried the next day in the local Chord Cemetery with no headstone or any memorial to mark his resting place.

Parliament of Ireland voted for its own extinction, most of those opposing the bill having withdrawn in a body. So at the final session there were many empty seats in the chamber although the galleries were crowded. When the final moment came, the Speaker of the House, John Foster, who had vehemently opposed the Bill,

> . . . rose slowly from the chair . . . he looked steadily around him on the last agony of the expiring Parliament. He at length repeated in an emphatic tone, 'As many as are of the opinion that this Bill do pass, say aye.' The affirmative was languid but indisputable; another momentary pause ensued; again his lips seemed to decline their office; at length, with an eye averted from the object he hated, he proclaimed with a subdued voice, 'The Ayes have it.' The fatal sentence was now pronounced; for an instant he stood statue-like; then indignantly, and with disgust, flung the Bill upon the table, and sunk into his chair with an exhausted spirit.
>
> An independent country was thus degraded into a province – Ireland, as a nation, was extinguished.
>
> *Sir Jonah Barrington*

On 1 August 1800 the Act of Union became law and on 1 January 1801 it came into operation. The occasion was celebrated with a gunfire salute and a new standard, the Union Jack, showing the cross of St Patrick, red on a white ground, together with the crosses of St George of England, and St Andrew of Scotland floated for the first time over the Castles of Dublin, London and Edinburgh.

The main provisions of the Act of Union were as follows: the two kingdoms to be henceforth one, The United Kingdom of Great Britain and Ireland; Ireland was to have one hundred members in the British House of Commons and thirty-two peers and four bishops in the House of Lords; the Irish Established Church to be continued forever and united with that of England; Ireland to contribute two-seventeenths of the expenditure of the United Kingdom for twenty years.

The passing of the act seems to have caused little disturbance among the Irish populace. Since the Catholic majority had no say in the Irish Parliament they were relatively unconcerned at its passing and felt that they could not be any worse off in its absence.

Pitt had genuinely intended to make Catholic emancipation part of the terms of Union but the fierce opposition from Protestants forced him to abandon the idea. After the Union came into being he proposed to George III that some measure of emancipation should be introduced but found that the king was implacably opposed to the idea. Pitt resigned from office in February 1801 and the following month wrote to the king that he would never again raise the question during the king's reign.

Pitt became prime minister again in 1804, but when an extensively signed petition for Catholic emancipation was presented to both Houses of Parliament the following year, he did not even support it. Both houses rejected the petition with big majorities. The Catholics constantly presented similar petitions in later years – always with the same result. One MP sneeringly referred to their efforts as 'this annual farce'.

14

◎

FROM THE 'DARLING OF IRELAND' TO THE 'LIBERATOR'

Robert Emmet, who was born in Dublin in 1778, was the younger brother of Thomas Addis Emmet, one of the United Irishmen. In 1798 Robert was a student at Trinity College and he was so outspoken in favour of French revolutionary ideas that he was expelled from the college and came to the notice of Dublin Castle authorities as a dangerous person.

A statue of Robert Emmet now stands in Dublin's St Stephen's Green opposite the house where he was born.

In 1800 he went to France as an agent of the United Irishmen and managed to get an interview with Napoleon. He was given some assurances of assistance for an Irish rising but it seems no firm promises were made. While in Paris Emmet met an armaments expert from America who showed him a new kind of weapon – a

———— ◎ ————

Anne Devlin was one of those arrested after Emmet's abortive rising. She was interrogated and tortured and finally suspended at the end of a rope from the shafts of an upturned cart but she steadfastly refused to give any information about her master. Later she was brought to the gibbet prepared for Emmet in Thomas Street but to no avail. She was then charged with high treason and was imprisoned for three years in Kilmainham jail. After her release she became a servant with another family and finally died in poverty and obscurity in 1851.

———— ◎ ————

When sentenced to death by Lord Norbury, Emmet addressed the judge with these words: 'My Lord, were it possible to collect all the blood that you have shed in a common reservoir your lordship might swim therein.'

———— ◎ ————

primitive land mine. It was a wooden box packed with explosives and shrapnel and Emmet determined to use such a device in the rising he was planning for 1803

When he returned to Ireland he immediately set about organising the insurrection by gathering around him like-minded individuals but no prominent names took up his cause – at least, none became known to the authorities.

His father died in 1802 and Emmet used a legacy of £2,000 to rent two houses to be used for storing arms and in purchasing materials for their manufacture. He soon had gathered a stockpile of hand grenades, pikes and gunpowder which he also stored in various city locations including his house in Rathfarnham in south Dublin where he lived with Anne Devlin as his housekeeper. (Anne was a cousin of the famous Wicklow rebels Michael Dwyer and Hugh O'Byrne and was intensely loyal to her master.)

It seems that Emmet learned the lesson from the '98 rebellion that the fewer who knew the plans the better. His tactics appear to have been so successful that even after an accidental explosion in one of his depots in Patrick Street the authorities did not seem to have been much the wiser.

After the explosion Emmet felt that he had to act quickly, even though he was not completely ready. On the evening of Saturday, 23 July 1803, at nine o'clock, with some of his lieutenants, Emmet sallied out into Thomas Street near Dublin Castle. He had expected over a thousand men to rally to his cause but in the event only about eighty turned up. His followers had no firearms but a good amount of pikes. Waving his sword and calling on passers-by to join him Emmet set off towards the castle. Most of the people in the street merely watched but hangers-on and vagabonds joined the group in the prospect of plunder and loot. Emmet soon realised that to attack the castle was hopeless, so he proposed to his followers that he would lead them out to the Wicklow Mountains where they would wait until reinforcements arrived. The local toughs were in no mood to take this course of action. They murdered an unfortunate soldier who was riding by, they dragged Lord Kilwarden, the Chief Justice and a quite popular man, from his carriage and murdered him and his nephew who was with him.

Emmet was filled with despair and sorrow by these savage acts and made his way to his house in Rathfarnham. He probably could

With the growth of knowledge in human anatomy in the eighteenth and nineteenth centuries was a parallel growth in the need for human bodies to study. This led to the activities of 'the body snatchers'. These were individuals who stole the bodies of recently buried people to sell to hospitals for the medical students to practise on.

In 1825 one such body snatcher by the name of Thomas Tuite was captured in Bully's Acre at Kilmainham in Dublin in possession of five bodies. His pockets were also found to be full of teeth! He confessed that the bodies were worth ten shillings each and a full set of teeth were priced at £1. Tuite was sentenced to six months in jail, but no doubt he considered it worth the risk, as he was a regular supplier to four surgeons in the Dublin hospitals.

Because the activities of the body-snatchers became so commonplace it was found necessary to place a guard on the cemeteries to prevent the robberies. Five watchtowers were built in Dublin's Glasnevin Cemetery and bloodhounds patrolled the grounds. In fact a gun battle took place in January 1830 in the graveyard between the sentries and the body snatchers.

The *News Letter* tells the unusual tale of what happened in February of the same year.

> A few nights ago a corpulent midwife named Maginnis, rather aged, died on the north side of the city and on the night of her burial it was discovered that the leader of those who attempted to disinter the poor woman and deliver her body up for dissection was one of her own sons. On the fellow being accused of the crime he said, 'Sure even if I did so, a tenderer hand couldn't go over her.

In many old graveyards today one can see extremely heavy stone slabs over graves from the period when the body snatchers were active. No doubt they were placed there to protect the bodies of loved ones from the depredations of the robbers. The passing of the Anatomy Act in the British Parliament in 1832 put an end to the work of the body snatchers, for it allowed dissection of legally acquired bodies in the medical schools.

have escaped from the country except that his love for Sarah, the daughter of Philpott Curran, caused him to delay until he could say goodbye to her. He was eventually arrested by Major Sirr in a house in Harold's Cross on 25 August Many other arrests were made and large numbers of prisoners were held in prison ships in Dublin Bay.

A special commission was set up to try him in Green Street Court and unfortunately he chose as his counsel none other than Leonard McNally (McNally was the informer who was in the pay of the Castle authorities and who had 'defended' the United Irishmen). Not that Emmet had much of a defence, as his guilt was all too obvious. In his eloquent speech from the dock he set out his motives and the principles which guided his actions. He then spoke the immortal words which have been quoted so frequently ever since: 'When my country takes her place among the nations of the earth, then, and not till then, let my epitaph be written.'

He was inevitably sentenced to death and at noon on 20 September 1803 he was hanged on a scaffold in front of St Catherine's Church in Thomas Street. His body was then beheaded and his head was given to George Petrie for a death mask to be made. His head was never recovered but the rest of his body was buried near Kilmainham Jail but later removed and reburied in a place unknown to this day. Of the nineteen others tried for taking part in his rebellion, seventeen were hanged.

Shortly after the Union was passed some Catholics, including a few bishops, secretly proposed that the king should have a veto on the appointment of bishops in return for Catholic emancipation. Most Catholics were unaware of this proposal until Grattan made it public in 1808 and immediately there was uproar – most bishops and the generality of Catholics totally opposed the idea. In any case the government refused to even discuss the idea. Among those who were against the move was Daniel O'Connell.

Daniel O'Connell was born near Cahirciveen, County Kerry in 1775. His family were relatively well off, his uncle Maurice (known as 'Hunting Cap') being a skilled smuggler and quite rich. The young Daniel was given a good education both in Ireland and the Continent. While a student in France he saw some of the excesses of the French Revolution and he was twenty-three years of age when the Irish rebellion of 1798 occurred. Both events are said to

———— ◎ ————

There are numerous stories told of O'Connell's extraordinary knowledge of the law and expertise in court. On one occasion he got a client acquitted of stealing a dead cow because he argued that he should have been charged with stealing meat.

———— ◎ ————

In a case about a contested will the witness kept saying the testator was alive when he signed the will. O'Connell noticed that he repeatedly used the Irish phrase '*Bhí beatha ann*' ('There was life in him'). Suddenly Dan had a brainwave. 'When you say "There was life in him" do you deny that there was a live fly in the dead man's mouth when his hand was put to the will.' The shocked witness admitted the deception.

———— ◎ ————

In a murder case the strongest evidence against the defendant was his hat which was found at the scene of the crime and positively identified by the prosecution witness. O'Connell lifted the hat and started to examine the inside, spelling out the accused's name: 'J-A-M-E-S . . . Were these words inside the hat when you found it?' he asked. 'They were,' replied the witness. 'Did you see them in the hat?' he was asked. 'I did.' 'This is the same hat?' 'It is.' 'Now, my Lord,' said O'Connell to the judge, 'that's the end to the case – there is no name whatsoever inscribed in the hat.'

———— ◎ ————

When O'Connell approached King George III at a function immediately after the granting of emancipation, he saw the king's lips move in what he took to be some words of congratulation. Greatly pleased he took the pudgy hand held out to him and kissed it with reverence. Later when he asked the Duke of Norfolk (who had been standing close to the king) what the king had said, he was told the words were, 'There's O'Connell, God damn the scoundrel!'

———— ◎ ————

Daniel O'Connell was one of the greatest democratic leaders
of the nineteenth century. His 'monster' meetings attracted
crowds of many hundreds of thousands.

have had a lasting impression on him, so that all his life he
abhorred the use of violence to attain political ends. He became a
highly successful barrister and for most of his life he pursued the
twin careers of lawyer and politician.

In May 1798 he was called to the Bar – the day after they
arrested Lord Edward Fitzgerald. He was living in Dublin when
the Act of Union ended the Irish Parliament. He heard the bells of
St Patrick's Cathedral ring out in celebration and saw the first flying
of the new flag over Dublin Castle, with the Irish harp relegated to
a little corner. He is reported to have said about that day, 'My blood
boiled and I vowed that morning that the foul dishonour should not
last if I could put an end to it.'

O'Connell soon came to realise that opposition to repeal of the
Act of Union was immense both in England and Ireland. He
decided that he had a much better chance of gaining Catholic
emancipation, which after all, had been promised prior to the act.
Along with his friend Richard Lalor Sheil, he started the Catholic
Association which was to be financed by voluntary contributions.
Each Catholic was asked to contribute one penny per month, the
clergy in each parish to oversee its collection and safe keeping.

The plan was a great success. Even though at best only one
Catholic in twelve contributed regularly, the first eight months saw

In 1815 O'Connell referred to the 'beggarly' corporation of Dublin in one of his speeches. By his standards it was a very mild 'insult' indeed, so he was greatly surprised to be asked by John D'Esterre, a Protestant and member of the corporation, if he had indeed used the expression 'beggarly'. O'Connell replied that he had but that 'no terms attributed to me, however reproachful, can exceed the contemptuous feelings I entertain for that body'. The expected response to this would be a challenge to a duel. D'Esterre was an ex-navy officer and a noted duellist but his next move was calculated to be really insulting. He appeared in the Four Courts with a whip, supposedly to chastise O'Connell. When O'Connell made his way there, D'Esterre had moved to the Liffey quay to parade up and down. One of O'Connell's friends then approached him and told him that if he wanted a duel O'Connell was only too willing. D'Esterre then went to College Green but again when O'Connell went there D'Esterre had disappeared.

The next day the challenge did arrive. Arrangements were made to meet at 3.30 p.m. the following day at Bishop's Court, just outside Dublin in County Kildare. Hundreds of spectators and horse-and-carriages gathered on the snow-covered ground at the duelling place, while a priest hid in a nearby cottage in case O'Connell was shot. His second, a Major MacNamara, changed O'Connell's white tie for a black one to make a less conspicuous target. He also removed various large medallions from O'Connell's watch-chain for he knew they would make a terrible wound if driven into his body.

The two duellists took positions ten metres apart. At the drop of a white handkerchief D'Esterre took a step to the left and a step forward and then fired. His shot was extremely bad for such a skilled marksman and hit the ground in front of O'Connell, who had fired at the same time, aiming low to wound and not kill. D'Esterre was hit in the thigh and fell to the ground.

O'Connell drove back to Dublin, to a rapturous reception. That night bonfires blazed all over the city, while bailiffs rushed to D'Esterre's house in Bachelor's Walk where he lay seriously ill. Two days later he died and was buried at night by the light of lanterns. O'Connell conveyed his 'deep and lasting sorrow' to D'Esterre's widow and vowed that he would never fight another duel – a promise he kept for the rest of his life. For many years after the duel O'Connell would raise his hat as he passed D'Esterre's house on his way to the Four Courts.

£7,573 collected, the next three months, £9,263, and £5,680 in the second half of 1826. The money was used to provide free legal aid to Catholics in trouble with the law and to finance the various political campaigns fought by the association. In the general election campaign of 1826, pro-emancipation candidates (all Protestants of course) were elected in nine counties. In Derry, Westmeath, Roscommon, Louth, Monaghan and County Dublin the tenants voted according to the directions of their clergy and not the landlords. In Waterford a member of one of Ireland's most powerful families, Lord George Beresford was up for re-election. He had been a member for twenty years and his re-election seemed a foregone conclusion. But O'Connell put the full resources of the Catholic Association behind his man, Villiers Stuart, a Protestant with liberal views. The Forty-Shilling Freeholders (those who had a lease for life on land worth at least forty shillings per annum after payment of rent and other charges) were instructed by their landlords to vote for Beresford. However O'Connell organised huge parades and rallies of association members, who wore green scarves, hats, sashes and cockades to represent Irish nationhood, to support Stuart. Strict discipline was maintained and any drunkenness or disorder resulted in the culprits being thrown into the river. When Beresford saw that he had no hope of winning he withdrew from the contest. The Catholic Association had scored an important victory.

Then in June 1828 William Vesey Fitzgerald, the MP for County Clare, accepted an appointment in the Duke of Wellington's government and this meant, by the rules of the day, that he had to stand for re-election. After much persuasion, O'Connell agreed that he himself should stand against him.

O'Connell decided to put himself forward as a 'man of the people' and the election was held amid great excitement. The Catholic Association organised great demonstrations of support and even provided food and housing to supporters who had travelled long distances.

O'Connell had a tremendous victory of 2,057 votes to 982 for Fitzgerald. The British government was greatly alarmed but they saw that public opinion, both in England and Ireland, favoured emancipation for Catholics and so, after stormy debates in the English Houses of Parliament, a bill to that effect received the

———— ◎ ————

When King George IV visited Dublin in 1821 he was warmly welcomed by its citizens. He landed at Howth so drunk that he could hardly stand. Later as he was driven through the streets of Dublin he sported a huge bunch of shamrock in his hat, which he carried in his hand. To make sure everyone was aware of the shamrock he continually pointed to it as he was driven along.

Later in the Viceregal Lodge in the Phoenix Park the king drank the health of the Irish gentry. O'Connell, who wore a blue sash and rosettes for the occasion was so overcome with enthusiasm that he proposed the building of a palace to commemorate the visit. Later, as the king boarded the boat in Dun Laoghaire Harbour, O'Connell presented him with a laurel wreath. (After the king's visit Dun Laoghaire was renamed Kingstown. The name became Dun Laoghaire again in 1922.

———— ◎ ————

The turmoil and unrest in Europe during the early part of the nineteenth century found an echo in Ireland. On Monday 26 July 1813 the 'famous' Battle of Garvagh, County Derry, took place.

The Lammas Fair, the biggest market of the year, had attracted huge numbers of visitors to the town. The streets were packed as about four hundred Catholic Ribbonmen, armed with cudgels, assembled in front of the King's Arms tavern in which they had been defeated in a skirmish with Orangemen at the previous year's fair. At the blast of a whistle the Ribbonmen tied long white sashes round their waists and began throwing stones at the tavern. Unfortunately for them, however, a large number of well-armed Protestants were waiting inside and when they were called upon to 'show their yellow faces' they replied with musket fire. The volley killed one of the attackers, wounded several others, and the rest fled in confusion.

It was only one of a long string of sectarian clashes in the 1790s but it owes its fame to the Orange ballad 'The Battle of Garvagh' which is still sung to this day.

———— ◎ ————

royal assent on 13 April 1829. The act entitled Catholics to become judges, generals and admirals and, most important of all, to be elected to Westminster. Then the government in a spiteful act made sure that the Forty-Shilling Freeholders could never again wield such power by changing the qualification to vote to £10, thus immediately reducing the Catholic vote from 1,160,000 to 86,000.

When O'Connell went to Westminster to take his seat, he was told that the Act of Emancipation only applied to those elected after the passing of the act. He was offered the old oath repudiating the Catholic faith and refused to take it.

This meant that he had to be re-elected before he could take his seat. He stood for election again in Clare and was returned with an even bigger majority. At the opening of the new session of parliament he duly appeared and took his seat.

After his election O'Connell decided to devote nearly all his energies to political work. He actively engaged in the efforts to get reform legislation through Westminster but when the Irish Reform Bill was passed in 1832 it only gave five extra seats to Ireland where O'Connell considered that her large population warranted seventy-five.

He had left agitation for the repeal of the Act of Union 'on the back burner' while working for emancipation. Although the campaign for the repeal of the act had started in 1810, it was not until 1840 that O'Connell started a vigorous campaign, when he founded the Repeal Association. He told those who doubted his capacity to carry out a vigorous campaign at sixty-five years of age, 'My struggle has begun, I will terminate it only in death or Repeal.' He started with A Society for the Friends of Ireland. When this was suppressed he formed The Anti-Union Association; this was in turn suppressed, so he formed The Association of Irish Volunteers for the Repeal of the Union.

In November 1841 he was elected unopposed as Lord Mayor of Dublin. He was the first Catholic mayor for one hundred and fifty years. On his election he promised to abstain from partisan politics and on the whole, he kept his promise but by the end of 1842 he was becoming bored with his life as Lord Mayor and in February 1843 he took up his repeal work again. He began holding huge public meetings throughout the country, the so-called 'monster' meetings attended by hundreds of thousands of people who came

———— ◎ ————

One of the most notorious judges in O'Connell's time was John Toler, Lord Norbury, known as the 'Hanging Judge'. When he died, the gravediggers buried him at twice the normal depth 'so that he should have rope enough'. He was something of a buffoon. He would become more and more agitated as he warmed to a case. He would stand up, throw off his robes, even his wig, pour out the most outlandish gibberish – anecdotes of his youth, snatches of poetry or Shakespeare – rising to a crescendo of roars and bellowing until he would often fall over, only to rise, blowing and laughing.

———— ◎ ————

Lord Norbury once ordered a poor wretch to be flogged from College Green to the quays. When the victim said 'Thank you, my Lord, you have done your worst', Norbury said viciously, '. . . and back again.' Another who had stolen a watch was sentenced to death with the words 'Ha-Ha! You made a grab at time, but you caught eternity.'

———— ◎ ————

Norbury was noted for his savage sentencing and in one day sentenced ninety-seven prisoners to death by hanging. Another time he freed a murderer who was patently guilty and when the Crown prosecutor protested that the evidence clearly showed his guilt Norbury replied, 'I know all that that but I have hanged six men in Tipperary who were innocent so I let this one off to square the matter.'

———— ◎ ————

from miles around in orderly processions. In that first year alone forty such meetings were held, attended by over 100,000 people, where O'Connell made veiled threats of mass revolt if the government did not repeal the Union. Huge crowds assembled in Cork, in Roscrea in Tipperary, at Donnybrook in Dublin, in Ennis, County Clare and in Wexford to listen to O'Connell's powerful voice. In August three quarters of a million people heard him speak at Tara in County Meath. The meetings were well disciplined and organised on army lines and one meeting even saw the appearance of a troop of horsemen in cavalry formation.

Although these meetings were eminently peaceful, the Lord Lieutenant, Lord de Grey, was getting very nervous as he suspected that things were in danger of getting out of hand. Peel's government reacted by sending extra troops and warships to Ireland and passing the Arms Act which allowed the police to raid houses at will.

O'Connell responded with increasingly fiery speeches, hinting that he had physical force behind him and that they would resist if attacked. When he followed this by announcing that he intended holding the greatest monster meeting ever in Clontarf in Dublin and reference was made to 'Repeal cavalry' in a public notice about the meeting, the authorities decided that something had to be done.

Peel was convinced O'Connell was bluffing and decided to call his bluff. On 7 October 1843, a day before the meeting, a proclamation was issued declaring it to be an unlawful assembly, troops were placed in position around the area and heavy guns aimed at the meeting place. O'Connell was in a dilemma; he could call off the meeting and suffer the tremendous loss of face or he could go ahead with it and risk a disaster. But true to his non-violence principles he called it off. Clontarf was a watershed in O'Connell's career – after this his course ran downhill all the way.

In October he and seven others were arrested and charged with conspiring to change government policy by intimidation and demonstrations of great physical force. It was confidently thought that no Irish jury would convict them. But the Castle made its own rules. When the trial started in Dublin on 15 January 1844 the prosecution challenged eleven Catholic jurymen on the grounds that they were 'Repealers'. The end result was that the jury was

————— ◎ —————

In November 1830 an Orange parade through the Catholic village of Maghery, County Armagh was attacked by Ribbonmen and several drums were broken. The Orangemen later burned the village to the ground in retaliation. Two years later the Party Processions Act was passed outlawing Orange demonstrations. This act was eventually to lead to such ridiculous court decisions as those in 1870 when one man was fined forty shillings for cursing the Pope and another the same fine for cursing the Pope and 'the Pope's granny'! A woman was also fined forty shillings for naming her two cats 'Orange Bill' and 'Papist Kate'!

————— ◎ —————

One of the greatest natural disasters ever to hit Ireland occurred on the night of 6 January 1839, when the country was devastated by a storm of such ferocity that the date is forever known as 'The Night of the Big Wind'. The day, a Sunday, began well enough. It was exceedingly calm and snow from previous days still lay on the ground. Gradually, however, the day began to warm up, unnaturally so – one woman describing the air as 'feeling like the air in a hothouse'.

Then around 9 p.m. a light breeze sprang up but by ten o'clock it had turned into a gale. Gradually, inexorably, it grew steadily worse, until by midnight it had become the most destructive storm ever to hit the country. Trees went down like ninepins, whole roofs sailed through the air, walls and houses collapsed, factory chimneys folded and streets became impassable. Nor was the destruction localised, from Kerry to Derry and from Dublin to Galway the story was the same.

The storm reached its peak between two and five in the morning. Torrential rain fell amid crashing thunder and lightning flashes. One curious phenomenon noted in various parts of the country was the fact that many of the rain showers fell as salt water – whipped up, no doubt, by the hurricane as it swept in from the ocean.

The next morning when daylight broke, the sun shone on a shattered, wasted land. Hardly a town had escaped, most resembled sacked cities. Rivers were swollen and choked with debris. Nearly 300 people lost their lives and thousands more were injured.

————— ◎ —————

composed of twelve Protestants, mostly Orangemen. Despite a vigorous defence, all but one of the accused were found guilty and remanded on bail for three months. O'Connell immediately departed for England and held public meetings in Liverpool, Manchester, Birmingham and London!

Eventually O'Connell was sentenced to a year's imprisonment and a fine of £2,000. He was nearly seventy years old. The others were given a sentence of nine months each and a £50 fine and were allowed to choose their place of detention. So they all marched through the streets of Dublin and presented themselves, accompanied by crowds of their supporters, to the Richmond Bridewell. There they were treated with every possible consideration until they were all released three months later on 6 September on direction from the House of Lords. O'Connell was having dinner with the prison governor and assistant governor when a messenger rushed in, shouting 'You're free, Liberator, you're free!' It is reported that the governor fainted on the spot, while the assistant governor wept with relief. O'Connell went home that same evening but returned to the jail the next morning for a public release and a triumphal procession. The Lord Mayor and corporation were there in person to greet him as he left the prison once more.

Things rapidly deteriorated after that. The old spark and drive never returned and anyway the country was soon to be gripped by the deadliest of all foes – famine! In the winter of 1846 O'Connell made a passionate plea in the Westminster parliament for Ireland's starving poor. Shortly afterwards O'Connell began to decline in health, greatly affected by the devastation the famine was causing to the people of Ireland. In 1847 he set out on a journey to Rome, partly on pilgrimage and partly for health reasons but he never reached there. He died in Genoa on 15 May 1847 at the age of seventy-one. In accordance with his wishes, his heart was enshrined in the wall of the Irish College in Rome while the rest of his remains were brought back to Dublin to Glasnevin Cemetery. The 'O'Connell Monument' in the likeness of an ancient Irish round tower was erected over his grave.

15

◎

THE GREAT HUNGER
STALKS THE LAND

Although there had been other famines in Ireland in previous times, particularly in the thirteenth, fourteenth and eighteenth centuries, that which devastated the country in the middle of the nineteenth century was the most terrible. Earlier famines such as those in Donegal in 1830 and 1831 and more widespread ones in the years 1835–37 had caused great local hardship but then in 1845 the potato blight appeared all over Ireland – in Armagh, Antrim, Cork, Kildare, Monaghan, Tyrone, Wexford and Wicklow.

Potatoes played an extremely important part in the diet of the people. Any grain crops they could raise had to be sold to meet rent payments, so families were forced to exist on the potato crop for their entire subsistence. At the same time the diet of potatoes was very nutritious, particularly when combined with buttermilk. The yield from one acre of potatoes was sufficient to feed a family of five or six for most of the year.

Ireland had a low infant mortality rate in the eighteenth and early nineteenth centuries and the population of the country rapidly increased during that period – from about four-and-a-half million in 1800 to eight million in 1841. This meant that land was divided and subdivided in an effort to support more and more people who became increasingly dependent on the potato. It is estimated that over three million of the eight million national population lived in single-roomed cabins and depended on the potato crop as almost their sole source of food. Consequently any potato crop failure produced dreadful results. The early decades of the century saw many such failures and thousands of deaths had already occurred in 1817 when there was partial failure.

Even though July 1845 was particularly wet the *Freeman's Journal* was able to report that 'the potato crop was never before so large and at the same time so abundant'. When the blight hit Wexford some months later all sorts of reasons were advanced as the cause of the trouble: the influence of the moon, lightning and thunder storms, the wind, wrong type of manure, etc. The real cause was a fungus which grew on the underside of the leaves. This fungus produced spores which were rapidly spread by wind, rain and insect. The disease passed down to the tubers, which developed small black spots and then quickly rotted.

In November 1845 the Archbishop of Dublin, Dr Murray, gave orders for prayers to be said in all the churches that God would spare the people in the coming year. The prayers were in vain. The blight was even worse in 1846 – over three quarters of the crop were destroyed countrywide.

The Tory Prime Minister, Sir Robert Peel, decided in 1845 to repeal the Corn Laws which imposed taxes on corn entering the United Kingdom from America. The removal of the protectionist duties on the import of corn was intended to reduce the price of bread but this was of little use to the Irish poor who couldn't afford bread at any price.

Peel also introduced three measures to combat the famine: he ordered £100,000 worth of 'Indian corn' (maize) from America for sale in Ireland, he appointed a Relief Commission in Dublin to oversee the sale of the corn and he introduced work schemes by which the people could earn money to buy the corn. In the first year of operation up to 150,000 people got jobs and it is said that as a result of his efforts no one died of hunger in that first year.

The man appointed to oversee the relief measures was a British civil servant, Charles Trevelyan, a man who firmly believed that no action should be taken which would interfere with market forces. He claimed that the famine was the intervention of divine providence to solve Ireland's chronic overpopulation problem! He also believed that the poor were exaggerating their miseries and that they should do more to help themselves. Constantly complaining about extravagance and waste of money, when a cargo of Indian corn arrived on 8 July 1846 Trevelyan ordered that it be turned back because 'it was not wanted'. By September starvation was widespread, even in the more prosperous eastern part of the

———— ◎ ————

Prior to the Famine the population of Ireland increased from 5 million in 1791 to 8 million in 1841, with about 80% living in the countryside. In the 1830s a survey found that 585,000 labourers, with families of over one million children, had no work for seven to eight months per year.

———— ◎ ————

Some of the habitations of the poor were extremely primitive. In some instances a poor working man would get permission from a farmer to scoop out the centre of an earthen bank between fields. The shell remaining would become the walls and the open top would be covered by branches and rushes.

Mud cabins were also common and were constructed by gathering large quantities of mud which would then be used to build walls up to a metre thick. Armfuls of rushes would be trampled into the mud from time to time to strengthen it. No space would be left for windows or doors. When the four walls were completed in this way they would be slashed smooth and narrower by shovels or spades and allowed to dry out for several days. Openings for doors and windows would then be cut into the walls and a roof of saplings and straw thatch or rushes would be added. The floor inside would always be of dried mud.

———— ◎ ————

A very common system of growing potatoes was by the 'lazy-bed' method. This consisted of laying the potatoes in four or five long rows about 30 cms apart on top of un-dug ground and then covering them with soil dug from a small trench on each side of the 'lazy-bed'. When the tubers had sprouted about 15 cms, more soil would be dug up and used to increase the soil covering the potatoes.

———— ◎ ————

Charles Trevelyan regarded the Famine as
an act of God to reduce Ireland's overpopulation.

country. Desperate starving crowds attacked ships carrying food out of the country and Trevelyan formed a force of 2,000 soldiers to restore order and guard food depots, ships and fields.

Although the Indian corn from America was stored in government depots from January 1846 it was not generally released to the poor until May. Then Trevelyan ordered the closure of the grain depots because too many people were calling on them for food!

Naturally enough, rural Ireland was the first to suffer the effects of the famine. The terrible misery of the starving people was made much worse by the spread of typhus, dysentery, famine dropsy and fever. All this time too, the eviction of the poor peasants from farm and hovel by heartless landlords continued unabated.

Soon so many thousands of destitute people were streaming into Dublin and other cities that guards were placed on the approach roads in an effort to turn back as many as they could. Many of those flocking into the cities were heading for ships to take them to Britain, Canada or America. Here again the poor were exploited when greedy middlemen and ships' captains took their money and filled their ships with up to three or four times the safe number for the hazardous crossing of the Atlantic. More than one fifth of the emigrants died on the voyages in these awful 'coffin ships'.

───────── ◎ ─────────

One famous soup kitchen was set up in Dublin on Croppies Acre in front of the Royal Barracks on the quays near Heuston Bridge (Kingsbridge). A French chef, Alexis Soyer, who worked in the Reform Club in London, was invited to Dublin by the Lord Lieutenant to prove his theory that a bowl of his special soup and a piece of bread were sufficient for a grown man for a day. His 'magic' recipe was oxheads, corn, carrots, turnips, onions, cabbage, peas, leeks and water. His 'New Model Soup Kitchen' in Croppies Acre had a boiler capable of holding three hundred gallons of soup. A wooden hut was constructed on the site with a door at each end. It contained long narrow tables which allowed one hundred clients to be served at a time.

Each client paid about a penny a day and was given a bowl to which a spoon was attached by a short chain. They then entered by one door, ate their soup and bread and exited by the other door. The bowls were taken from them, rinsed, and given to the next batch. The demand was so overwhelming that the crowds fought each other for their share and at the height of the famine, up to 8,750 portions were served in one day.

───────── ◎ ─────────

A magistrate visiting Skibbereen in 1846 reported:

> I have entered some of the hovels . . . and the scenes that presented themselves were such as no tongue or pen can convey the slightest idea of. In the first, six famished and ghastly skeletons, to all appearance dead, were huddled in a corner on some filthy straw, their sole covering what seemed a ragged horse-cloth, and their wretched legs hanging about, naked above the knees. I approached in horror, and found by a low moaning they were alive, they were in fever – four children, a woman and what had once been a man.

───────── ◎ ─────────

But vast numbers had no such plans – all they wanted was food and they thought their chances were better in the towns. The workhouses were filling up rapidly and being stretched to the limit to provide food for them all. The main food staple, potatoes, was obviously not available, so substitute foods had to be found. Two pints of porridge and half a pint of milk was provided for breakfast and rice and milk or bread and soup for dinner.

Soon the workhouses were unable to take in any more, so that whole families were turned away. So many thousands were starving on the streets that the Soup Kitchen Act was passed by which a network of soup kitchens were set up to feed the local communities. Each adult was to get a bowl of soup and a pound of bread per day.

The Soup Kitchen Act gradually began to have an effect. By the middle of 1847 over three million people (nearly half of the total population) were receiving relief. This 'extravagance' raised alarm in the Treasury. Trevelyan's secretary wrote to each Poor Law Union telling them that he suspected that the act was being 'applied solely as a means of adding to the comforts of the lower classes' instead of for 'the utterly destitute'. The remedy was brutal – all government relief under the Soup Kitchen Act was to cease by October 1847.

By the end of September, while a million people were still getting free rations, more than two million others were cut off and had to depend on the workhouses. The workhouses were meant to be just that, the able-bodied would be fed if they worked.

The winter of 1847/8 was as bad as anything that went before. Thousands died from starvation and disease. The hopes of millions rested on the crops of autumn 1848 but these were dashed when the blight was as bad as ever that year.

By 1849 the worst of the Famine was over but then a cholera epidemic hit Dublin, Belfast and other large towns and this combined with the famine had a devastating effect on the population of the country. In 1841 there were just over 8 million people in Ireland and with normal growth it should have been about 9 million by 1851. In fact it was 6.5 million, which means there was a loss of 2.5 million people. Of these, about 1.5 million emigrated, which leaves the horrifying total of roughly one million losses due to famine and disease.

———— ◎ ————

The main food chosen by the government to replace the
failed potatoes during the Famine was Indian meal. This
was a cereal made from crushed maize grain. In its raw state
it was extremely hard and required long soaking and boiling
to make it digestible. Many of the peasants did not know
how to deal with it and anyway few of them had the fuel to
cook it properly.

———— ◎ ————

The loss of a million of the population in Ireland due to the
Famine and disease was seen by Trevelyan as reflecting the
'wishes of an all-wise Providence' as it 'solved' the gigantic
unemployment problem.

———— ◎ ————

An extraordinary story is told of an old man who was dying
all alone – his family had been wiped out by either fever or
hunger. He sent for the priest to come as his one wish was
that he receive the last sacraments before he died. The priest
was unable to attend to him for some time. When he did so
he was astonished to find that the old man had eaten part of
a picture of the Sacred Heart because he thought that he
would die before the priest arrived.

———— ◎ ————

During the Famine *The Times* of London said 'An Irishman
will soon be as rare a sight in Connemara as a Red Indian
on the shores of Manhattan.'

———— ◎ ————

Queen Victoria visited Ireland in 1849 when memories of
the famine were still fresh in people's minds. Nevertheless
she was given a great welcome and was brought to Trinity
College in Dublin to view the *Book of Kells* and see the
autograph of Elizabeth I who founded the college. She then
signed her name on a sheet of parchment which was later
incorporated into one of the volumes. This was later to give
rise to the false report that she had actually signed the *Book
of Kells*

———— ◎ ————

16

◎

'OUT AND MAKE WAY FOR THE BOLD FENIAN MEN'

As O'Connell's career was beginning to wane, a group of young men was gathering around an affluent young Protestant journalist called Thomas Davis, who was born into an upper middle class Dublin family in 1814. The young men were inspired by his ideas and writings. On one occasion he told an all-Protestant audience 'Gentlemen, you have a country . . . You are Irishmen'. This group, who became known as 'Young Ireland', became more and more disenchanted with the non-violent attitudes of O'Connell and grew increasingly outspoken and extreme in their writings and speeches. Among their number were such men as John Mitchel, the son of an Ulster Presbyterian minister, who began to openly advocate rebellion with the aim of

Thomas Davis started the *Nation* newspaper
with John Blake Dillon and Charles Gavan Duffy.

The announcement by members of the County Down Orange Order in 1849 that they intended to march from Rathfriland to Tollymore Park on 12 July greatly alarmed government authorities. The proposed route was to pass through the exclusively Catholic townland of Magheramayo and the obvious intention was to provoke the Catholic Ribbonmen. Because the Party Processions Act had more or less lapsed, the authorities could not ban the march but they felt that the presence of troops and police would prevent trouble. Consequently a military force, a body of police constables and two magistrates were sent to the area.

Early on 12 July 1849 the soldiers took up their positions at Dolly's Brae where there had been trouble the previous year. Shortly after, a force of several hundred Ribbonmen arrived and finding the pass occupied they waited nearby.

The parade of over one thousand Orangemen 'all armed to the teeth' left Rathfriland led by several bands and accompanied by a company of dragoons. Meanwhile the numbers of Ribbonmen at Dolly's Brae had grown to over a thousand, all armed with pitchforks, pikes and muskets. They proceeded to enjoy themselves with shooting practice but no breach of the peace occurred.

At about five that evening the Orange parade approached Dolly's Brae instead of returning to Rathfriland by the same route as they had come. The Ribbonmen had by this stage moved from Dolly's Brae to a hill which overlooked the pass. A man at the head of the Orange parade is reported to have given the order 'Now, my boys, not a shot to be fired', then as they marched along 'there went a bang at the front' which witnesses said later came from the head of the parade. This was followed by a succession of shots from both sides. As shots flew among the police and troops, they charged the Ribbonmen, firing as they went. When the Ribbonmen took to their heels the order to cease fire was given but the Orangemen disregarded it and kept blazing away.

After the battle the police found six dead bodies, eighteen pitchforks, seven pikes and ten muskets. Not one Orangeman was wounded and only one policeman was injured when he was accidentally bayoneted in the arm by one of his companions.

A government inquiry later found that at least thirty Ribbonmen were killed and its report led the government to re-introduce the Party Processions Act, forbidding sectarian parades.

establishing an Irish Republic; twenty-three-year-old Thomas Francis Meagher, the son of a well-off businessman in County Waterford; Charles Gavan Duffy, a Monaghan man who became proprietor and editor of the *Nation* newspaper in 1842; John Blake Dillon, the son of a Catholic businessman in Ballaghadereen in County Mayo who helped Duffy to found the *Nation*; and William Smith O'Brien who joined the Young Irelanders some time later.

As the Young Irelanders, led by Mitchel and Thomas Francis Meagher, grew increasingly militant, openly drilling in the streets and advocating armed resistance to England, the authorities decided to act. Mitchel, Smith O'Brien and Meagher were arrested early in 1848. Smith O'Brien got bail but Mitchel was tried two months later under the Treason Felony Act. He was found guilty, taken in chains to Dublin's North Wall and transported to Tasmania.

While on bail, Smith O'Brien travelled to Paris to meet representatives of the newly declared French Republic and returned with a tri-coloured flag similar to the French one but with green, white and orange sections. Later Smith O'Brien and Meagher were discharged by the court because the jury could not agree and the two were released to cheering crowds in Dublin.

Thomas Meagher was once more arrested in July 1848 along with Charles Gavan Duffy. Their supporters attempted to rescue them but Duffy and Meagher told them to desist as they wanted to let the law take its course. Then on 22 July the government suspended the Habeas Corpus Act and ordered the arrest of all the remaining leaders. Some of those named went into hiding but others resolved to make a stand.

Because the movement was strongest in Munster it was decided to start there. Smith O'Brien and John Blake Dillon travelled throughout the province but everywhere met with discouragement. Leaders and weapons were not available and the clergy warned their flocks about the hopelessness of the enterprise.

When Mitchel was deported, the leadership of the movement had been assumed by William Smith O'Brien – as unlikely a revolutionary as ever there was! He was an upper class Protestant, an MP at Westminster, educated at Harrow and had a pronounced English accent. This was the man who now found himself leading a small troop of about a hundred men, largely unarmed, when the 'rising' took place in August 1848.

———— ◎ ————

The 'Fenian' period of Irish history is remarkable for the large number of men of outstanding talent and dedication to take leading roles. The following is only a small selection of the many to come to the fore: John Devoy (1842-1928) was a Dublin clerk who joined the Fenians in 1861. He was imprisoned for a time and later emigrated to America where he took an active part in organising support for Irish nationalism among the Irish emigrants there. He later took a very active part in Michael Davitt's Land League. In his final years he advocated that the only way to end the partition of Ireland was by the consent of the Unionists in the North. 'Force would accomplish nothing' he said. The old Fenian finally died in 1928 at the age of eighty-six and is buried in Glasnevin Cemetery in Dublin.

———— ◎ ————

Jeremiah O'Donovan Rossa was born in 1831 in Rosscarbery, County Cork. His family had a fairly successful farm and had a happy childhood filled with stories of Irish fairies (which he believed in until old age!) and of the great injustices suffered by the Irish people through the centuries. He was educated in the newly established local national school and grew up speaking both Irish and English. The Famine caused great hardship in the O'Donovan home and they were later evicted from the family farm. The young Jeremiah went to live with relatives in Skibbereen and in the late 1850s he and some other local young men founded the Phoenix National and Literary Society which engaged in political discussions but which also acted as a cover for active drilling and preparation for armed insurrection. When James Stephens got wind of what was going on he made the long trek south to Skibbereen and enrolled all the members in the IRB. Later the government intervened and arrested Rossa and twenty-four of his friends. They were later released however, as it was felt that they posed no threat to the government.

———— ◎ ————

At first large numbers of peasants turned out to follow him but most went home when they found that there were no supplies to feed them. O'Brien refused to allow his 'army' to seize carts loaded with grain and even insisted that they obtain the permission of the owners before cutting down trees for barricades! When the tiny force reached Ballingarry in County Tipperary it attacked a small group of police occupying a house belonging to a widow named McCormack who had a cabbage patch near her home. In a skirmish which later became known derisively as the 'battle of the Widow McCormack's cabbage garden' and during which O'Brien, for humane reasons, refused to set the house on fire, two people were killed. One was simply an onlooker, and the other a man who was standing beside Smith O'Brien.

The long-planned insurrection had lasted just a few hours and O'Brien and his followers made off into the countryside as best they could. Some days later O'Brien was arrested in Thurles and deported to Van Diemen's Land. He eventually escaped to America.

One of O'Brien's lieutenants at the 'battle' was James Stephens, a young Protestant railway engineer from Blackmill Street in Kilkenny. He had charge of forty or fifty men during the skirmish with only a few guns between them. Police reinforcements arrived and Stephens gave the order to fire. When the police returned fire some men dropped dead at Stephen's side. He, himself, was struck by two bullets, one of them in the thigh. As he fled from the scene, he was struck again and rolled into a ditch, half-conscious. Once the police had left, he climbed out of the ditch and eventually made his way to Urlingford, County Kilkenny.

The authorities made a determined effort to arrest all of the leaders of the abortive rebellion but the 'funeral' of Stephens halted the search for him. A sympathetic obituary appeared in the *Kilkenny Moderator* on 19 August 1848 lamenting his death: 'Mr Stephens was a very amiable and, apart from his politics, most inoffensive young man, possessed a great deal of talent and, we believe, he was a most excellent son and brother.' A coffin filled with stones was buried in the graveyard near St Canice's Cathedral in Kilkenny. A headstone over the grave bore the inscription:

> Here Lies James Stephens. Born in Kilkenny AD 1824.
> Died from the effects of a wound at Ballingarry, 1848.
> Aged 24 years. R.I.P.

———— ◎ ————

John O'Leary was appointed by James Stephens as editor of the *Irish People* in 1863. O'Leary was a cranky thirty-three-year-old ex-medical student from a middle-class Tipperary family. He was well educated and earned Stephen's trust even though he refused to join the IRB.

At the age of eighteen he took part in an abortive plan to rescue William Smith O'Brien as he was being brought to trial in 1848. He was arrested but released shortly afterwards. He later came under the influence of James Fintan Lalor, the physically handicapped veteran who had advocated land reform during the Great Famine. In the disastrous attempt at rebellion in 1849 he actively considered kidnapping Queen Victoria during her visit to Ireland at the time.

He was arrested along with Stephens and others in 1865 and after his release went to live in Paris. When he returned to Ireland in 1885 he became an important figure in the Irish literary revival.

———— ◎ ————

Another member of the *Irish People* staff was Charles J Kickham who was born in 1828 and also from Tipperary. At the age of thirteen he had been badly injured when his father's hunting gun exploded, leaving the young Kickham disfigured and almost blind and deaf. He became a voracious reader and eventually wrote the famous novel *Knocknagow* (*The Homes of Tipperary*) about the area around Slievenamon Mountain near Mullinahone in County Tipperary. In his work for the *Irish People* he engaged in strenuous battles with the Catholic archbishop of Dublin who denounced all secret societies and ordered the clergy to deny the sacraments to anyone suspected of membership. Kickham in turn wrote that 'talk of submission to clergymen in politics would astonish the Catholics of any country in the world but Ireland.' When the archbishop called on all Catholics to 'banish' the paper from their homes, Kickham challenged him to produce even 'one ungarbled passage' from his writings to support his arguments and again asserted that the clergy were not to be taken as 'a guide in political matters'.

———— ◎ ————

Shortly afterwards, Stephens, disguised as a lady's manservant, was smuggled on board a ship en route to England. He landed in Bristol and the next day reached France but he was to return again in 1856.

James Stephens took part in the skirmish in Ballingarry, County Tipperary but the police search for him ended when his friends staged a mock funeral for him.

The terrible experience of the famine and the heartless treatment of the tenants by so many landlords left a bitter legacy and a determination by many to never let it happen again. In 1850 various societies for the protection of tenants were established in different parts of the country. In Ulster the tenants generally had more security than elsewhere and they had the right to sell their tenancy to the highest bidder. This was known as the Ulster Custom and after the famine a movement was begun to have the custom more widespread and protected by law.

A national campaign was launched in Dublin in August 1850 including Catholics and Presbyterian representatives from Ulster and the rest of Ireland. The chief instigator was Charles Gavan Duffy. The campaigners established the Irish Tenant League which demanded the 'Three Fs' – Fixity of Tenure, Fair Rent and Freedom of Sale (i.e. tenants should be free to sell their interest in their property).

Meanwhile in 1856 James Stephens returned to Ireland after eight years in France. When he reached Dublin he was depressed

─────── ◎ ───────

One of the most active Fenian recruiters of soldiers in the British army was a rather strange character called 'Pagan' O'Laoghaire. He is credited with getting thousands of soldiers to take the Fenian oath. He was born in Cork but went to America where he studied for the priesthood in his teens. In 1846, when America was engaged in the Mexican war, O'Laoghaire went over the wall of the seminary and joined one of the American regiments. During a battle he was hit in the head by a spent bullet and this occurrence is said to have had a profound effect on him. He dropped his baptismal name 'Patrick' because he said St Patrick had weakened the spirit of the Gael. He renounced Christianity in favour of the religion of the old pagan Irish. He then insisted on being known as 'Pagan' O'Laoghaire.

─────── ◎ ───────

by the lack of enthusiasm in the Young Ireland movement. He lamented that 'the ardour of Young Ireland had evaporated as if it had never existed.' His health wasn't the best at this time, so much so that one old friend thought that he 'was not long for this world'.

Nevertheless he set out the same year to tour the south and west of the country to assess the state of the organisation. He cut an odd figure in his rather dandified Parisian clothes as he walked for over five thousand kilometres, with little more than a walking stick and knapsack, getting the views of everyone he met.

When Stephens returned to Dublin he began a successful career as a French language tutor in Killiney in the south of the county but all the time he was actively engaged in his nationalist work. On St Patrick's Day 1858 in Peter Langan's timber-yard in Lombard Street the Irish Republican Brotherhood was formally established.

Each aspiring member was required to swear an oath saying:

> I, ... , in the presence of Almighty God, do solemnly swear allegiance to the Irish Republic, now virtually established; and that I will do my very utmost, at every risk, while life lasts, to defend its independence and integrity; and, finally, that I will yield implicit obedience in all things, not contrary to the laws of God [or 'the laws of morality'], to the commands of my superior officers. So help me God. Amen.

(The phrase 'now virtually established' was a typical piece of exaggeration by Stephens.)

In October 1858 he went to America to contact leaders of the Irish Republican Brotherhood which had been established there and to organise and assess the strength of the movement in that country. Before he left for Ireland a year later, he appointed John O'Mahony as director of the IRB in America. After Stephens' departure O'Mahony, who greatly admired the mythical Irish hero, Fionn MacCumhail and his Fianna followers, changed the name of the organisation to the 'Fenian Brotherhood' after the ancient warriors. (From then on the term 'Fenian' was applied to all members of the movement and became the name applied to all Irish revolutionaries up to the early 1900s.) The numbers joining

———— ◎ ————

Charles Gavan Duffy later became disillusioned with Irish politics and emigrated to Victoria in Australia in 1855. He eventually became Prime Minister there and was given a knighthood in 1873.

———— ◎ ————

A census carried out in Ireland in 1861 revealed that there were 5.75 million people in the country of which 4.5 million were Catholics and only 700,000 members of the established Protestant Church. Gladstone made effective use of these stark figures in his efforts to redress Catholic grievances.

———— ◎ ————

The chief secretary, William Forster, had gained a good reputation for his Quaker relief efforts during the Great Famine. When he announced in 1880 that the police would be issued with buckshot instead of the far more lethal ball cartridge he was given the derisory nickname 'Buckshot' Forster by the Irish.

———— ◎ ————

When the Gaelic League was formed in 1893 to encourage the use of the Irish language its first president was an Anglo-Irishman named Douglas Hyde. He attacked as absurd the teaching of English to school children when their home language was Irish. He wrote that the children went into school intelligent and bright-eyed, with over 3000 words of Irish vocabulary and came out with perhaps 600 English words which they misused.

———— ◎ ————

were small at first, as the outright condemnation by the Catholic Church of all secret societies had a big effect.

In 1861 Stephens organised a great public funeral for Terence Bellew MacManus, a Young Irelander who had been at Ballingarry in 1848, had been arrested and sent to the penal colony in Australia, had escaped to America and had died in San Francisco. The transport of his body across America was one long demonstration with thousands turning out along the route. His body was first shipped to Cork and was brought from there to Dublin where huge crowds came to pay honour to the dead Young Irelander. Stephens had witnessed the tremendous funeral of Daniel O'Connell and realised the propaganda value of such events. So he set about arranging something similar, with thousands of marchers wearing black badges, carrying torches and accompanied by brass bands and mounted Fenian horsemen taking part in the procession to Glasnevin cemetery.

Next Stephens and an assistant called Thomas Clarke Luby began a recruiting campaign throughout the country and eventually about eighty thousand men had joined the IRB. He was also highly successful in recruiting huge numbers (as many as 26,000) of Irishmen in the British army in Ireland. Thousands also joined in cities throughout Great Britain. In the autumn of 1863 Stephens established the newspaper the *Irish People* not only for propaganda purposes but also to raise much-needed funds. John O'Leary was appointed editor and as a skilful writer he constantly preached Fenian dogma in the paper for many years.

Stephens again went to America early in 1864 to sort out problems in the Fenian organisation there and when he returned to Dublin in August the same year he brought with him $50,000 for the IRB. He again went around the country on foot, on an organising tour. Drilling, making of pikes, gathering of arms and subversion of army personnel proceeded with new intensity. Stephens repeated on every occasion, 'Next year will be the year of action.'

The following year (1865) was indeed the 'year of action' but for the Castle authorities, not the Fenians. On the night of 14 September raids took place all over the country, resulting in the arrests of Thomas Clarke Luby, John O'Leary, O'Donovan Rossa and other Fenian activists. The offices of the *Irish People*, the Fenian newspaper, which were rather daringly situated almost at the gates of Dublin Castle, were raided and many compromising documents were discovered. The Castle had an informer in the *Irish People* offices by the name of Pierce Nagle who had been supplying information to the police all along. A letter urging rebellion 'this year', written on 8 September by Stephens, and stolen by Nagle, alarmed the authorities.

The raids, however, failed to deliver Stephens to the police. He remained free for two months after the raids began. Despite Nagle's best efforts to discover his hiding place, Stephens was living quietly as 'Mr Herbert' in Sandymount in Dublin. And then, as a result of a tip-off, police swooped on the house on Saturday, 11 November between six and seven o'clock in the morning. Because of the large force surrounding the house, Stephens knew there was no sense in resisting arrest. He and three companions were immediately brought to the Lower Castle Yard and there remanded by the Chief Magistrate to Richmond jail until 14 November.

Brought once more before the Chief Magistrate he was committed for trial on 27 November and sent back to Richmond jail. But ten days later he was free! Nine men, led by John Devoy, armed with revolvers and carrying a rope ladder, turned up outside the prison walls on 24 November. The signal was to be a handful of gravel thrown across the wall but it was very slow in coming. At one o'clock a Fenian sympathiser who was a member of the prison staff, unlocked Stephen's cell with a key which had been made from a wax impression taken by the prison's night watchman.

Stephens and his rescuer then went into the prison yard to a high wall between the yard and the governor's garden. They planned to use a ladder in the yard to scale the wall but now found the ladder was too short. They had to bring out tables on which they placed the ladder and thus got over safely. The outer wall was easily scaled by use of the rope ladder and Stephens was quickly brought to a safe house until he left the country.

The police offered a reward of £1,000 for his capture and £300 for information on his whereabouts. A strangely worded description of Stephens was given as follows:

> James Stephens is about 42 years of age, 5 feet 7 inches high, stout make, broad high shoulders, very tight, active appearance, fair hair, bald all round the top of his head; wore

all his beard which is sandy, slightly tinged
with grey, rather long under chin, but
slightly round jaw approaching the ears,
tender eyes which defect seems to be
constitutional, and has a peculiar habit of
closing the left eye when speaking; high
cheek bones and rather good-looking; hands
and feet remarkably small and well-formed,
and he is generally dressed in black clothes.

The escape of Stephens did not prevent the trial of the other
members of the staff of the *Irish People* from going ahead. Rossa
was sentenced to life imprisonment for treason, while Kickham,
O'Leary and Luby got long prison terms in spite of the strenuous
efforts on their behalf by their defence counsel, Isaac Butt.

The following March 1866 Stephens was smuggled aboard a ship
on the Liffey and he eventually reached America. Things didn't go
too well with him there and after many blazing rows with other
Fenian leaders he was eventually deposed as leader of the Fenian
Brotherhood. In January 1867 he went to France.

While Stephens was in France the long-threatened Fenian rising
took place in Ireland. A contingent of Fenians marched out to the
Dublin Mountains on 5 March 1867. They attacked a police
barracks at Tallaght at midnight but suffered two deaths and twelve
wounded when the police opened fire with sixty rifles. The
attackers had few guns and were taken totally by surprise by the
volley. The night was pitch dark and all that the few rebel riflemen
could do was to aim at the flashes. A second volley from the police
caused more casualties and completed the rout

Things went a bit better for the Fenians in other parts of county
Dublin. Police barracks were attacked in Stepaside, Glencullen
and Dundrum. The barracks in the first two locations were
captured by the rebels and large quantities of rifles fell into their
hands. They suffered no fatalities in the operations.

Various other incidents occurred in other parts of the country.
The Fenians in Cork captured a police barracks and a coastguard
station and also derailed the Dublin express train. In Drogheda less
than forty police routed about a thousand Fenians and when
Fenians attacked the police station in Killmallock, County

Limerick they were driven off after a three-hour siege. By the end of March, the 'rising' was over.

On 11 September 1867 an event occurred in England which was to have a profound effect on Irish public opinion. Two Fenian leaders, Colonel Thomas Kelly and Captain Tim Deasy were arrested in Manchester and put in jail. A week later they were brought to court, charged with treason and remanded. As the horse-drawn police van was conveying the prisoners back to prison a group of Fenians jumped in front of the van and ordered the driver to stop. When the Fenians were unable to open the rear door of the van they ordered Sergeant Charles Brett, who was guarding the prisoners, to open the door. When he refused, a shot was fired through the lock and this resulted in the death of the sergeant inside. Another woman prisoner in the van managed to get the keys from the wounded policeman and the prisoners escaped.

A widespread police hunt followed and resulted in the arrest of twenty-six suspects, chief among whom were, in the words of the authorities, five 'principal offenders': William Allen, Michael Larkin, Michael O'Brien, Edward O'Meagher Condon and Thomas Maguire, none of whom had actually fired the fatal shot. The trial, which took place amid virulent anti-Irish hysteria, ended with all five being found guilty and sentenced to death. When each of the condemned men spoke from the dock O'Meagher Condon ended his speech with the words 'God Save Ireland' – a phrase that is familiar still today in a famous song

A tremendous outcry against the verdicts resulted in Maguire (who was patently innocent) and O'Meagher Condon (who was an American citizen) being reprieved. The other three, Allen, Larkin and O'Brien were executed by hanging on 23 November 1867. As so often happens in Irish history the names of the 'Manchester Martyrs', as they became known, became a rallying cry for following generations.

The events in Manchester were followed just weeks later by more tragedy when an attempt was made to free a Fenian prisoner from Clerkinwell Prison in London. The prisoner, Richard O'Sullivan Burke, had suggested in a message to fellow Fenians outside that a gunpowder charge should be used to breach the prison walls during the exercise period.

The first attempt was abandoned on Thursday 12 December

1867 when the fuse failed to ignite. The second attempt on the following day resulted in a tremendous explosion which demolished a row of working-class houses and badly damaged many more. In all twelve people died as a result and about fifty more were injured. This shocking tragedy quickly ended any sympathy the ordinary people of London had for the Fenian cause.

The following April 1868 six people were arrested for the murders. Eventually five of these were acquitted but the sixth accused, Michael Barrett from Fermanagh was found guilty and sentenced to hang. Barrett had been arrested in Glasgow and produced evidence that he was in that city at the time of the explosion but to no avail.

A campaign seeking clemency for the prisoner was organised but powerful people were pressing for revenge, including Queen Victoria, who wrote that she regretted the failure to find the whole six accused guilty and 'it seems dreadful for these people to escape . . . One begins to wish these Fenians should be lynch-lawed and on the spot'.

In spite of the hatreds generated by the killings and hangings the tragic events did have the effect of bringing the problems of Ireland to the forefront and convincing the Liberal leader, William Ewart Gladstone, that something had to be done to solve the 'Irish Question'.

While all these events were happening in Ireland and England, Stephens was in Paris, living in very poor circumstances and watching in silence as the rising fizzled out.

In September 1891 he and his wife came back to Ireland and ten years later on Friday morning 29 March 1901, James Stephens, the Fenian Chief, died in his brother-in-law's house in Blackrock, County Dublin. His coffin was draped in the Fenian flag of green, white and orange. (Just fifteen years later the men of 1916 adopted the same colours.)

The funeral was a massive affair, taking over five hours for the short journey from Blackrock to Glasnevin. Michael Davitt led the mourners and also present were the Lord Mayor of Dublin and John Redmond leader of the Irish Parliamentary Party. His grave has the inscription 'A day, an hour, of virtuous liberty is worth a whole eternity in bondage.'

17

◎

'THE BLACKBIRD OF AVONDALE'

On 27 June 1846 one of Ireland's most famous leaders was born in Avondale, County Wicklow, the seventh child and third son of a rich Protestant Irish landlord and an American mother. His name was Charles Stewart Parnell. (The Stewart part of his name came from his mother, Delia Stewart.)

At the age of six the young Charles was sent away to boarding school in England and later completed his education at Cambridge University. When his father died suddenly in 1859 in the Shelbourne Hotel in Dublin, Charles inherited the family house and estate of Avondale at Rathdrum in County Wicklow.

Charles Stewart Parnell, the 'Blackbird of Avondale'
died at the early age of forty-five.

In May 1870 an important event took place in Dublin. A semi-private conference heard a proposal from a Donegal man, Isaac Butt, to the effect that 'the true remedy for the evils of Ireland' was 'the establishment of an Irish Parliament with full control over all domestic affairs'. The adoption of the resolution marked the establishment of the Home Rule Party, which rapidly became a national organisation. In the elections in 1874 the party won 59 out of the 103 Irish seats for the British House of Commons.

Parnell showed not the slightest interest in Irish politics at the time but when his brother John suggested in 1873 that he should continue the old family tradition and take an active interest in public affairs, to John's surprise Charles replied that he had been thinking about it and that he favoured Home Rule.

In early March 1874 he applied for membership of the Home Rule League at a meeting in Dublin and was gladly accepted. Isaac Butt said at the time, 'We have got a splendid new recruit, an historic name, young Parnell of Wicklow; and unless I'm mistaken the Saxon will find him an ugly customer.'

Parnell was immediately put to the test – a by-election had been called in County Dublin and he was put forward as a Home Rule candidate. Against all expectations he proved to be a nervous, hesitant speaker. It is said that he clenched his hands so tightly behind his back that his nails made his hands bleed. The election ended in defeat. Parnell only got half the votes of the other candidate, a result that was in line with the expectations of his party – the exercise was something of a trial run.

Another chance presented itself in 1875 when a by-election was held in County Meath. The Home Rule Party again put Parnell forward. This time he hit all the right buttons – he spoke in favour of Home Rule, the rights of parents to have their children educated in the religion of their choice and the 'Three Fs' for tenants – Fair Rent, Free Sale and Fixity of Tenure. With the endorsement of so many different groups, it was no great surprise when he had a comfortable victory – gaining nearly twice as many votes as his nearest rival. Parnell was on his way at last.

On Thursday 22 April 1875, he entered the English House of Commons for the first time. He was a tall man, twenty-eight years old, with thinning hair and a bushy beard. In his maiden speech four days later he objected to a colleague referring to Ireland as 'a geographical fragment of Britain'. 'Ireland is not a geographical fragment but a nation,' he said. He spoke thirteen times in the three and a half months of that first parliamentary session.

Prior to his election, the Home Rule Party had already begun to adopt the policy of obstruction in the parliament. They decided that the only effective opposition they could mount against any obnoxious legislation was to obstruct the proceedings at every turn by interminable speeches and the raising of constant 'points of order'. Isaac Butt supported the tactic but it was a Belfast pork butcher, by the name of Joseph Biggar, MP for Cavan, who used it to the limit. The very first day that Parnell attended parliament Biggar gave a typical display. He spoke for nearly four hours against a Coercion Act.

Parnell adopted the tactic with enthusiasm and when Butt responded to a plea for help from desperate government ministers in 1877 by reproving Parnell for his conduct he was pushed aside and Parnell elected leader.

As president of the Home Rule Party Parnell gave many rousing speeches both in Ireland and England. One particular speech in Castlebar, County Mayo included the famous words, 'Let no man lightly define the measure of Irish independence. Let no man assign a *ne plus ultra* to the march of a nation.' And later he added the words 'Let no man say "Thus far shalt thou go and no further."'

Meanwhile in America a new group called Clann na nGael (The Irish Family) had replaced the Fenian Brotherhood as the main Irish revolutionary organisation. One of its leading members was a dark-haired, blue-eyed Kildare man, called John Devoy. He had been arrested for his activities for the IRB and on his release after the amnesty for Fenians had emigrated to America in 1871. Another member of Clann na nGael was O'Donovan Rossa who continued to make inflammatory speeches about the necessity of continuing the war with England.

In April 1879 a meeting was held in Irishtown, County Mayo, to protest against the excesses of a landlord who refused to reduce his rents and the Mayo Land League was formed as a result. The driving force behind the league was a thirty-two-year-old Mayo man called Michael Davitt. His family had been evicted from their home in Straide, County Mayo during the famine of 1850 and had emigrated to Lancashire in England. At the age of nine Davitt went to work in the local cotton mill, working twelve hours a day, six days a week. Two years later, in spite of his protests that he was too small, he was ordered to work on a piece of machinery. Within thirty minutes his right arm was caught in the machine and was so badly mangled that it had to be amputated.

Because of his injury he could no longer work, so he went to school and soon became an avid reader of Irish history. He then took the Irish Republican Brotherhood oath and in 1870 was sentenced to fifteen years hard labour for taking part in an attempted raid on Chester Castle. Because of his lost arm he was unable to use a pick or shovel in the prison stone quarries and was harnessed to a cart like a horse for his day's work. In December 1877 he was released on parole, mainly as a result of the representations made by Parnell on his behalf.

A few days later he met Parnell in London to thank him and each man came away with a very favourable impression of the other. When Parnell asked Davitt what he intended doing next his reply was 'I shall rejoin the revolutionary movement, of course.'

He was as good as his word – he rejoined the IRB and was appointed to the Supreme Council of the organisation. In 1878 he went to America where he conferred with John Devoy and both agreed that the land question was the most important issue to be resolved in Ireland.

Meanwhile back in Davitt's native County Mayo there were ever-increasing signs that famine was again threatening. The harvests were very bad and the number of evictions increased from 183 in early 1878 to 261 in the same period in 1879. The numbers of agrarian crimes more than doubled in the same period. Davitt set about organising the tenant farmers and when he asked Parnell to speak at a rally in Irishtown in Mayo the latter readily agreed. On 8 June 1879 Parnell told the farmers 'You must show the landlords that you intend to keep a firm grip on your homesteads and lands.' Other protests were organised throughout the summer and in 1879 Davitt founded the Land League of Mayo. The nationwide nature of the problems facing tenant farmers led to a meeting in Dublin on 21 October 1879 at which the Irish National Land League was formed with Parnell as president.

The league became the greatest mass movement since the time of O'Connell. Its aims were to lower rents, reduce evictions and

———— ◎ ————

Captain Boycott was intensely disliked by his workers. He would punish them for the slightest fault and even fined them one penny for every hen that trespassed on his fields.

———— ◎ ————

In 1854 Lord Leitrim, William Clements, inherited an estate of over fifty-four thousand acres in Donegal and he immediately set about evicting both Protestant and Catholic tenants in a ruthless manner. He removed so many tenants simply to improve the shape of his estate that it became known as 'The Straight Lined Estate'. The local farmers were forbidden to keep goats without his permission and he ordered one farmer to kill every one of his flock before his eyes for breaking the rule. More reprehensible still, he considered his tenants' daughters as fair game and forced himself on any who took his fancy.

His behaviour was so outrageous that he made enemies of all classes of local society and several attempts were made to kill both him and his henchmen. One bailiff was shot and only escaped death because the bullet hit a gold sovereign in his pocket. Another attempt on Lord Leitrim himself only failed when the attacker fainted before he was able to fire his blunderbuss.

On 2 April 1878 another more carefully planned attempt was made. Early that morning three men waylaid Leitrim on his way from Manorvaughan to Manorhamilton. A fusillade of shots were fired, during which the lord's driver was killed, his clerk mortally wounded and Leitrim himself so badly hit that he was unable to defend himself. His attackers then grappled with him and finished him off with blows of their musket butts. During the struggle Lord Leitrim grasped the beard of one of the men who had to cut it off to free himself from the victim's death grip.

A huge reward was later offered for information leading to the arrest of the murderers but it was never claimed. The police knew the perpetrators' names but could find no one to give evidence against them in court. It has been suggested that the police themselves did not try very hard.

———— ◎ ————

increase peasant ownership of the land. The early days of the Land League were filled with optimism but the mood was soon to change as the extremely wet summer that same year led to great hunger and shortages during the winter.

The landlords continued their policy of getting rid of tenants who could not pay the rent. Evictions continued to rise – more than 1,893 families were evicted in 1880 compared with less than half that number in 1879, while agrarian crime soared from 297 to 2,590 in the same two years.

In September 1880 Parnell gave a speech in Ennis, County Clare during which he referred to the problem of a man taking over the farm from which another had been evicted. There were shouts from the crowd of 'Shoot him' but Parnell quietly pointed out that there was a better way. 'When a man takes a farm from which another has been evicted, you must show him on the roadside when you meet him, you must show him in the streets of the town, you must show him in the fair and the market place, and even in the place of worship, by leaving him severely alone – putting him into a kind of moral Coventry – you must show him your detestation of the crime he has committed.'

His listeners were electrified by Parnell's words and just three days later wholeheartedly put them into practice. Captain Charles Boycott, an estate agent for Lord Erne at Lough Mask in County Mayo issued an eviction notice to one of the lord's tenants for non-payment of rent. On 22 September 1880 a process-server, accompanied by twenty-two policemen, attempted to carry out the eviction but were repulsed by a determined group of tenants. The local Land League led by the parish priest proclaimed Boycott under ban. All his workers deserted him; shopkeepers would not sell provisions to him; no tradesmen would serve him and his letters and telegrams had to be delivered by the police. Other landlords who opposed the Land League now decided to come to the aid of Boycott and a number of Ulster Orangemen organised an expedition to harvest his crops. The chief secretary, William Forster, feared that there would be grave disorder and set a limit of fifty men on the expedition and at the same time promised to protect them.

With great excitement and fanfare the expedition set out by train from the North under police escort and arrived in Claremorris on

Among the most notorious evictions carried out in Ulster during the 1860s were those in the north Donegal estates of Gartan, Derryveagh and Glenveagh. A County Laois landowner by the name of John Adair gradually bought these estates from 1857 onwards.

From the very start Adair antagonised the local people; he ruthlessly impounded stray animals and made the owners pay stiff fines to redeem them; he brought in shepherds from Scotland to tend the Scottish sheep he bought to the anger of the local workers. The new shepherds were disreputable and violent men who caused a great deal of trouble. When the police investigated a claim by them that locals had killed some of their sheep they found sixty-five of them dead from exposure and neglect and another sixteen fleeces drying in the house of James Murray, the steward of the estate. Sometime later, on 15 November 1860, Murray's body was found with its skull crushed by a heavy stone. The bloodstained rock lay near the body.

The killer of James Murray was never revealed but grave suspicion fell on one of the Scottish shepherds who moved into the widow's bed within three days of her husband's funeral.

Shortly after Adair had bought the Derryveagh estate he served notice to quit on his tenants and now that he was convinced that they had some part in his steward's murder he was determined to evict them all. On Monday, 8 April 1861, accompanied by a large body of police, Adair's men systematically moved from house to house and after putting out the families, knocked down the walls of every house. At the end of three days had they evicted 244 people and levelled twenty-eight houses. The police were not called upon to take any action as the tenants offered no resistance.

These terrible evictions got international attention and a fund was set up to assist many of the evicted tenants to a new life in Australia.

Adair subsequently built Glenveagh Castle and died a natural death fifteen years later in America. By a curious turn of fate an American, Henry McIlhenny, a direct descendant of one of the evicted tenants bought the estate in 1937 and later made a gift of Glenveagh to the Irish people. Today it is a national park.

11 November. The new labourers, guarded by 160 soldiers and fifty police, successfully harvested the crops at a cost of £3,500 to save crops worth £35.

In the general election of 1880 Parnell stood in three constituencies, in Cork, Mayo and Meath. He won all three seats but chose to sit for Cork City. On 24 January 1881 the government introduced a bill in parliament called the Protection for Person and Property Bill. It would allow the authorities to arrest and imprison 'any reasonably suspected person'. The next day the Irish members kept the parliament in session for twenty-four hours by speech after speech. At one point they forced the house to sit through a forty-hour debate. They kept up the obstruction for a week, much to the disgust and fury of many English MPs, and Queen Victoria wrote to one lord 'The Queen trusts that measures will be found to prevent the dreadful Irish people from succeeding in the attempt to delay the passing of the important measures of coercion.'

The parliamentary protests and the agitation by the Land League did, however, bear fruit when Gladstone introduced the Land Act of 1881 which granted the league's demands for the Three Fs. For very good reasons it has been called the Magna Carta of the Irish tenant and it began the process of breaking the landlords' stranglehold on Irish land.

In the same general election of 1880 in which Parnell was so successful a minor Clare landlord, by the name of Captain William O'Shea, was also elected as a member for Clare for the Home Rule Party. The event was to have a profound effect on the subsequent career of Parnell.

Catherine, the captain's wife, was then thirty-five years old. She was described as being 'a beautiful woman, tall and dark with a mouth expressive of tenderness and sweetness and wistful eyes and a head crowned with a wealth of soft, glossy black hair.' She had married Willie O'Shea when she was twenty-one and by this time had three children; a boy aged ten and two daughters aged seven and five years.

Some time later when she visited the London Parliament she met Parnell for the first time. When he came out she saw 'a tall gaunt figure, thin and deadly pale. He looked straight at me smiling and his curiously burning eyes looked into mine with a wondering intentness that threw into my brain the sudden thought, this man

Willie O'Shea challenged Parnell to a duel
over his friendship with his wife, Catherine O'Shea.

is wonderful – and different.'

That summer Parnell went to the Ladies' Gallery in the House to meet Catherine O'Shea several times. He also took her on drives out in the country and seems to have met her on many occasions before the summer recess of parliament. Later he wrote:

> My own love, you cannot imagine how much
> you have occupied my thoughts all day and
> how very greatly the prospect of seeing you
> again very soon comforts me. Yours always,
> C.

The activities of the Land League, as branches and numbers increased, seemed to be leading to a clash with the English authorities. Land League meetings became increasingly militant. They were accompanied on many occasions by groups of horsemen dressed in green and carrying long staves tipped with metal so that they resembled lances. The British government under Gladstone was increasingly determined to act.

On Wednesday 3 November 1880 while Parnell was at lunch in Dublin he was approached by a plain-clothes police officer and handed an indictment for conspiracy on nineteen counts. Among other things he was charged with conspiracy to stop tenants paying their rent, to stop legal evictions, to prevent others taking over farms from which tenants had been evicted, and with advocating boycotts. Thirteen other men were also served with indictments. The charges came to nothing however, when the jury declared that 'they were unanimous about disagreeing'.

All this time he was deeply involved with Katie O'Shea. It seems that Captain O'Shea was unaware of the affair at the time, at least he gave no sign in his dealings with Parnell that he was aware of anything. However, Katie told a friend that her husband knew well what was going on and that he knew Parnell stayed with her during her husband's absences. Be that as it may, on 12 July 1881, Captain O'Shea wrote to Parnell challenging him to a duel because he said he had just discovered that Parnell had been staying with Katie in the O'Shea home unknown to him. When he had gone home to Katie that day he had found Parnell's suitcase in the house. After a furious row with his wife he had gone back to London and written the letter. Some time later O'Shea seems to have accepted Parnell's 'assurances' that there was nothing going on and no more was mentioned of a duel.

The concession of the Three Fs failed to end agitation and unrest over the land issue. The response of the government was to introduce a policy of coercion but Parnell continued his opposition.

Catherine O'Shea eventually married Charles Stewart Parnell and had several children by him.

———— ◎ ————

When Michael Davitt was in goal he noticed the name of John Devoy carved into the jamb of the same cell as he was in himself.

———— ◎ ————

After Parnell and Davitt were released from prison they met in England and Parnell said he would resign from public life if the Ladies Land League continued its militant activities. Later as they discussed Home Rule and the possibility of an Irish government, Parnell, in a rare light-hearted mood suggested that he would appoint Davitt as director of prisons since he had so much experience in that field!

———— ◎ ————

Archbishop John McHale of Tuam very much disapproved of the activities of the Ladies Land League saying that they were 'forgetting the modesty of their sex and the high dignity of their womanhood'.

———— ◎ ————

When the scandal broke about Parnell's relationship with Katie O'Shea, Cecil Rhodes of South Africa fame sent him the following laconic telegram: 'Resign – marry – return.'

———— ◎ ————

James Carey, who informed on the perpetrators of the Phoenix Park murders, was given a free pardon and sent out of the country to South Africa for his own safety. However, he was tracked there by a man called O'Donnell and shot dead.

———— ◎ ————

In a speech in Wexford he said, 'We won't get anywhere until we remove English misrule.' When one of his fellow-Irish members of Parliament asked him if he had any instructions for them if he were to be arrested, he is said to have replied, 'If I am arrested, Captain Moonlight will take my place.'

A few days later, 13 October 1881, Parnell was arrested and brought to Kilmainham jail. A succession of arrests of other leaders followed and this led to the Land League proposing a rent strike. Parnell reluctantly came round to the view that there was no other option.

On 18 October 1881 a manifesto was issued by the leaders in Kilmainham jail calling on all tenants to pay no rents until the government restored the constitutional rights of the Irish people. The manifesto was signed by Parnell, John Dillon, Thomas Sexton, AJ Kettle and Thomas Brennan. The names of Michael Davitt and Patrick Egan were also included. The manifesto was condemned by the Catholic hierarchy and the government finally suppressed the Land League two days later.

Parnell spent six months in Kilmainham jail and while he was still there Katie gave birth to their first child, a baby girl, on 15 February 1882. Although the child was quite healthy at first, her condition deteriorated later and when Parnell, on parole due to the death of a nephew, visited Katie in Eltham in England, he found the baby seriously ill. He and Katie were alone at the time when baby Sophie died. Captain O'Shea was unaware that he was not the father of the baby; he wrote on 25 April 'My child is to be buried at Christchurch this afternoon.'

On the day of his daughter's funeral, Parnell was back in Kilmainham jail but was released on 2 May 1882 along with Davitt, Dillon and some others. Their release was due to an understanding reached between Parnell and Gladstone which became known as the Kilmainham Treaty. They had agreed that, in return for the release of Land League prisoners, the relaxation of the coercion laws, the amendment of the Land Act and the protection of tenants in arrears of rent, Parnell would use his influence to calm the country and get his followers to accept the new Land Act. The prisoners were released and thus set in motion the chain of events which culminated in some dreadful murders.

The chief secretary, William Forster, who had ordered the

leaders' arrests, resigned in protest at their release and Gladstone appointed Lord Frederick Cavendish in his place. TH Burke, a Catholic but regarded by ultra-nationalists as a 'Castle rat' or traitor, was appointed undersecretary.

On the morning of Saturday 6 May 1882 Cavendish and the new viceroy, Lord Spencer, went to Dublin Castle to meet their staff. Afterwards Spencer rode off under escort to the Viceregal Lodge in the Phoenix Park, while Cavendish decided he would walk there. On his way Cavendish was overtaken by Burke in a horse-drawn cab, who then decided that he would walk the rest of the way with Cavendish. It was seven o'clock in the evening and there were a lot of people about, many of whom were watching a polo match.

Meantime Lord Spencer had arrived at the Viceregal Lodge and sat down at an open window towards the front to work on some papers. The next moment he heard a cry that he said later he would never forget. He looked out and saw a man rushing towards the Lodge shouting, 'Mr Burke and Lord Cavendish are killed.'

The two men had been killed by men using twelve-inch-long surgical knives which had been bought in London and smuggled into the country hidden in women's skirts. The assassins then escaped on a sidecar and it was not until the following year that they were arrested and charged with the murder. All the murderers were members of a secret society called the Invincibles and one of them, James Carey, was a Dublin town councillor who was regarded by his neighbours as a very respectable and religious man. When the trials began in 1883, Carey turned state witness. The four other defendants were convicted and hanged in Kilmainham Jail. It emerged from the trial that Burke was the primary target of the assassins and Cavendish was killed simply because he happened to be in Burke's company.

Parnell was in Eltham with Katie when he read the news of the atrocity in the *Observer* on Sunday 7 May. Katie saw him go suddenly rigid with shock and when he showed the headline to her he said, 'I shall resign.' He made an offer of resignation to Gladstone but his resignation was not accepted.

After the assassinations the government immediately rushed through another Coercion Act but Gladstone and Parnell went ahead with the terms of the Kilmainham Treaty. Parnell's outspoken condemnation of the atrocity was a big factor in the continued co-operation The increasing rapport between Parnell and the English liberals greatly annoyed the Conservatives, whose organ was *The Times* newspaper. It had always been virulently anti-Irish and in 1887 it published a series of articles entitled 'Parnellism and Crime'. One of these articles contained what it claimed was a facsimile of a letter written by Parnell to a friend, in which he said that his opposition to the Phoenix Park murders was a necessary piece of policy and that Burke had got 'no more than he deserved'. Parnell immediately denounced the letter as a forgery but *The Times* insisted it was genuine and that they had other similar letters.

The source of the letters was a man called Richard Pigott, who was born in 1828 in County Meath. He was a political journalist who owned several newspapers with patriotic titles like *Flag of Ireland*, *The Irishman* and *The Shamrock*. In 1881 Parnell bought Pigott's newspapers for £3,000 and replaced them with his own newspaper *United Ireland*. It was during this transaction that Pigott acquired samples of Parnell's hand-writing.

In 1885 when he was short of money Pigott proposed writing a pamphlet to be called 'Parnellism Unmasked' which would supposedly prove the connection between Parnell and political crime in Ireland. Pigott was finding the task of providing any tangible evidence against Parnell extremely difficult and soon came to the conclusion that his only hope lay in forging some evidence. When that 'evidence' reached *The Times* it was so eager to discredit Parnell that on 18 April 1887 it published the 'facsimile'.

Parnell didn't pay much heed to the newspaper article and later in the House of Commons he merely dismissed the letter as a forgery. The affair seemed to be about to peter out naturally when one of the Irish MPs decided to sue *The Times* for libel because he too was mentioned in the articles. This seemed to spur the newspaper to increase its campaign and it published another Parnell letter. This was dated 9 January 1882 and was supposedly written by Parnell before the murders, when he was still in Kilmainham.

> Dear E,
> What are these fellows waiting for? This
> inaction is inexcuseable; our best men are in
> prison and nothing is being done. Let there

be an end to this hesitency. Prompt action is
called for. You undertook to make it hot for
old Forster and co. Let us have some
evidence of your power to do so. My health
is good, thanks.
Yours very truly,
Chas. S. Parnell

The House appointed a special commission to investigate. The
commission had a majority of Conservative members and there was
little doubt what conclusion they would come to.

Richard Pigott had a photographic business
where he dabbled in pornography and blackmail.

Meanwhile Parnell and Katie embarked on a complete study of his
handwriting and those of 'possible imitators . . . [and] we made
some interesting discoveries'.

On 21 and 22 February 1889 Pigott was called before the
commission. He gave a fairly convincing performance until the
second day when he was asked to write down certain words. He
misspelled 'inexcusable' and 'hesitancy' in the same way as in the
letter. With these gaffes Pigott's guilt was blindingly obvious.
Parnell's counsel, Sir Charles Russell 'with short sharp questions
drove Pigott deeper and deeper into the mire of confusion and self-
contradiction.'

When the cross-examination finished Parnell correctly forecast that Pigott would leave the country before the commission met again. Pigott did indeed flee to Spain and registered in a Madrid hotel under the name of Ronald Ponsonby. As luck would have it, he was spotted walking down the street by none other than Willie O'Shea! The police were alerted and were waiting in his room when he returned but before they could arrest him he took a gun from a bag, put it to his mouth and killed himself. (Parnell was later paid £5,000 in damages by *The Times* which also suffered £200,000 in costs.)

After the 'Pigott affair' Parnell seemed to be in an unassailable position but then on Christmas Eve 1889 Willie O'Shea cited him as co-respondent in his divorce case against Catherine. The divorce hearing began on 15 November 1890 in the same room where Pigott had been unmasked. Katie's counsel told the court that he intended to produce no witnesses and that he would not cross-examine. The result was, therefore, a foregone conclusion: the jury found for Willie on all counts. The judge then granted him custody of the two youngest girls, who were in fact Parnell's children. Katie wrote later that when the *decree nisi* was brought to her house by a solicitor, 'We were very happy that evening and Parnell declared he would have the decree framed.'

The Irish leaders continued to support Parnell and in Dublin shortly after the close of the divorce proceedings, on 25 November, Parnell was almost unanimously re-elected as leader of the Home Rule Party. But shortly afterwards Gladstone sent a message that it would be impossible to get the British Parliament to pass a Home Rule Bill for Ireland as long as Parnell was leader. This caused consternation in the party, as they knew that Gladstone was their only hope for Home Rule and at the same time they had overwhelmingly chosen Parnell as their leader. Parnell told his party that he would only quit if Gladstone would introduce the Home Rule Bill immediately. This Gladstone refused to do and things remained as they were until 6 December 1890 when the 'anti-Parnellites' withdrew their support and elected Mr Justin McCarthy as their chairman. The split had happened at last and the anti-Parnellites were in the majority.

Early in 1891 a by-election in North Kilkenny was fought with unusual bitterness but at the end of the day Parnell's candidate was beaten by nearly two to one, 2,527 votes to 1,362. The following March the Parnellite candidate was defeated in the Sligo election but a more happy event occurred on June 25 when Katie and Parnell were married in a registry office in England. The honeymoon was short-lived, however, for Parnell had to return to Ireland to fight another by-election in Carlow in which his candidate again lost. Although Dublin was still solidly behind him he was losing support throughout the rest of the country.

Still he threw himself whole-heartedly into campaigning in the forthcoming general election. He travelled around the country making speech after speech in an effort to regain lost ground.

When he returned to Brighton to Katie he looked worn out and ill. She was thoroughly alarmed, so much so, that Parnell told her he would give up the struggle if she asked him to but she admitted that when she looked into his eyes, 'I knew I could not say it.'

One week later he was back campaigning in Ireland and got thoroughly wet when he spoke bareheaded at a meeting in Galway. Some days later, in spite of his doctor's advice not to travel, he went back to England promising, 'I shall come back on Saturday week.'

Under Katie's care Parnell's health improved somewhat but he had a restless night that Thursday 1 October 1891. On Saturday he was a bit better but by Sunday he was again unwell and Katie called the local doctor. On Monday he was too weak to leave his bed and had another bad night that night. By Tuesday he was feverish and late that evening he was dozing but suddenly opened his eyes and said, 'Kiss me, sweet wifie, and I will try to sleep a little.'

Katie wrote later:

> I lay down by his side, and kissed the burning lips he pressed to mine for the last time. The fire of them, fierce beyond any I had ever felt, even in his loving moods, startled me, and as I slipped my hand from under his head he gave a little sigh and became unconscious. The doctor came at once but no remedies prevailed against this sudden failure of the heart's action, and my husband died without regaining consciousness, before his last kiss was cold on my lips.

Charles Stewart Parnell died on 6 October 1891. Katie wanted him buried in Brighton but was prevailed upon to allow him a public funeral in Dublin. His coffin was brought to Ireland via Holyhead on the lower deck of the ship the *Ireland*. A large green flag was draped over it.

Many thousands of mourners followed the coffin to Glasnevin Cemetery to a plot not far from the grave of Daniel O'Connell. When the coffin was lowered into the grave the wreath from Katie was placed on top of it first. Then many mourners dropped flowers on the coffin in tribute.

18

◎

THE DAWN OF THE
TWENTIETH CENTURY

In 1896 there arrived in Dublin a man who was destined to play a large part in the politics of the next century. James Connolly accepted an invitation to become the paid organiser of the Dublin Socialist Club. He was twenty-eight years old at the time and had already become deeply involved in the socialist movement in his native Scotland.

From a very poor family his father was a carter, employed to remove manure from the streets of Edinburgh at night. At the age of fourteen, James enlisted in the Royal Scots Regiment of the British army where he spent almost seven years. (During his service on Spike Island in Cork harbour he guarded an Irishman who was to be executed. The experience is said to have turned him completely against the British establishment.) Strangely enough, all his army service took place in Ireland and he met his wife (Lillie Reynolds from County Wicklow) while he was in Dublin with the army.

When he arrived in Dublin in 1896 to take up his new position with the Socialist Club, he set up home with his wife and three daughters in a one-roomed tenement flat in Charlemont Street. Shortly afterwards along with seven like-minded socialists he formed the Irish Socialist Republican Party. The aim of the new party was 'The establishment of an Irish Socialist Republic based upon the public ownership by the Irish people of the land and instruments of production, distribution and exchange.'

Connolly vigorously engaged in the great cultural revival, which was taking place at the time in Ireland but declared:

> If you could remove the English army
> tomorrow and hoist the green flag over
> Dublin Castle, unless you set about the

organisation of the Socialist Republic, your
efforts would be in vain.

While Ireland was growing more and more nationalist Britain was
becoming increasingly imperialist. The Golden Jubilee of Queen
Victoria in 1897 was celebrated with great enthusiasm in Britain
but in Ireland things did not go so smoothly. A 'jubilee' procession
was organised by James Connolly in which the centrepiece was a
big black coffin bearing the words 'British Empire'. The police
attacked the procession, and a full-scale riot developed. When the
procession reached the Liffey the coffin was thrown into the river
to the shouts of 'Here goes the coffin of the British Empire. To hell
with the British Empire.' Connolly was among those arrested and
lodged in prison for a short while.

The following year, 1898, Connolly brought out the first edition
of his newspaper the *Workers' Republic*. It carried the now famous
slogan, 'The great appear great to us because we are on our knees.'

In October that year the Boer War broke out. Many Irish people
supported the Boers against the British on the principle 'the
enemies of Britain are our friends'. At a meeting in Dublin that
month a large number of people pledged support for the Boers and
condemned the idea of Irishmen joining the British army to fight
against them.

James Connolly was born in Edinburgh 1868. He came to Dublin in 1896
and later commanded the forces that occupied the GPO in 1916.

Queen Victoria visited Dublin for the last time in 1900 and the Royal Dublin Society decided to erect a statue in her honour in front of their headquarters in Leinster House in Kildare Street. When Leinster House later became the seat of the Irish Parliament the presence of the statue, depicting the ample proportions of the ageing monarch, proved objectionable to many of the deputies and it was decided to remove it. The discoloured black figure lay for some years in the grounds of the Royal Hospital, Kilmainham, until it was transported to Australia to be erected in Sydney.

In 1906 a Dublin coalman by the name of O'Carroll had a fine of ten shillings imposed on him because he did not have his name displayed on his cart in a 'legible' manner. He refused to pay the fine and had a ton of coal confiscated as a result. The fact that his name was clearly displayed in the Irish language carried no weight with the court.

In 1907 Ireland was probably the tenth richest country in Europe. The average Irish income was on a par with the European average. Top salaries were about £2,000, while a labourer earned around £50 a year. Huge numbers were unemployed, however, and up to a quarter of Dublin's population lived in 22,000 single rooms. As many as 13,000 of these were occupied by three or more people.

Prostitution was widespread. In an area between O'Connell Street and Amiens Street, known as Monto, there were an estimated 4,000 prostitutes plying their trade.

The registration of motor cars was first introduced in Ireland in 1904 at a fee of one pound. Cars also had to display number-plates, while the speed limit was set at 20 miles an hour. By 1913 the price of petrol rose to about 3 cent a litre in present day prices.

Later an Irish Transvaal Committee was set up to stop army enlistment and was proving so successful that Queen Victoria was enlisted in the government's counter-efforts. She first decreed that Irishmen in the army must wear the shamrock on St Patrick's Day. (A far cry from the days when they 'were hanging men and women for the wearing of the green'!) A state visit to Dublin was then arranged and she arrived on 4 April 1900 to be greeted by impromptu protest demonstrations.

The pro-Boer campaign so annoyed the British authorities that over forty prominent nationalists, including eleven MPs were sent to prison for their political activities in 1901 and 1902.

In 1900 the Irish Parliamentary Party, up to now divided into the Parnellite and anti-Parnellite factions, was re-united at last under a new leader, John Redmond. He was a Parnellite, an upper-class Catholic and a graduate of Trinity College. Elected MP in 1881, he opposed Irish independence and instead sought Home Rule within the Empire.

John Redmond reunited Parnell's party and concentrated
his efforts to achieve Home Rule by purely parliamentary methods.

That same year an organisation called *Cumann na nGaedheal* (Association of the Irish) was also established. The founders of the new body included Arthur Griffith, Maud Gonne and Major John MacBride, who had fought for the Boers in South Africa, Tom Clarke, who had been imprisoned for his Fenian activity in

———— ◎ ————

In December 1907 the *Freeman's Journal* carried a report on the death in Dublin of one 'Banker' Patterson, who left £80,000 to charity when he died. 'Banker' made his money by giving loans of single shillings at one penny a week interest. He was illiterate and so miserly that he sat in the dark to save money, wore no trousers in summer, and his only possessions when he died were a cup, a plate and a knife.

———— ◎ ————

The theft of the so-called 'crown jewels' from Dublin Castle in July 1907 (at the time of the visit of King Edward VII) is one of the great unsolved mysteries of the last century. The regalia of the Order of St Patrick were placed in the office of the Master of Arms on 15 March, was verified by the official in charge, the Ulster Knight of Arms, as being still there on 11 June but had disappeared when the safe was opened in July. The regalia, including the Grand Master's jewelled star and badge, to the then total value of £30,000 (about €2.5 million in today's money), had mysteriously vanished and the culprits were never caught.

In 1927 Taoiseach W T Cosgrave was approached by certain persons with an offer to sell back the jewels for £2,000–£3,000 and it is believed he did buy them back to keep them in the state's possession. Although the culprits have never been identified the suspicion is that they were nationalists, particularly as the Fianna Fáil party at the time purchased a fleet of cars for £3,000 when, according to Sean Lemass, they hadn't a penny in funds.

———— ◎ ————

Tom Clarke was born in England of Irish parents and went to live in South Africa when he was ten years old. Later he returned to Dungannon in County Tyrone and then in 1879 went to America where he joined the local Fenian organisation. Four years later he returned to England and was arrested for taking an active part in the Fenian dynamiting campaign. He was sentenced to fifteen years penal servitude. He was released in 1898, broken in health, and retired to Dublin. He married Kathleen Daly, the daughter of John Daly, the Limerick Fenian leader, in 1901. The historian FS Lyons described him thus: 'With his large, cheap spectacles, drooping moustache and frail figure he looked the small tradesman's part to perfection.'

———— ◎ ————

Arthur Griffith, founder of the Sinn Féin movement in 1905, advocated political and economic separation from England.

England, and John Daly, who was mayor of Limerick. Their aims were to promote Irish economic resources and Irish culture.

In 1905 Griffith started a new organisation, which later became known as Sinn Féin. As the name, 'Ourselves Alone', implies, its aim was self-reliance in all things. Part of its policy was the withdrawal of Irish MPs from Westminster, the setting up of Irish courts, civil service, stock exchange and central bank. It would also appoint Irishmen to represent Irish interests abroad.

After Tom Clarke was released from prison in 1898 he came back to Dublin and opened a small newsagent's shop in Parnell Street. The old revolutionary soon attracted young political activists. Together they founded the *Irish Freedom*, a militant newspaper that preached the doctrines of the Irish Republican Brotherhood. The vibrant 'new' IRB recruited members from Sinn Féin, the Gaelic League and the Fianna, (a sort of revolutionary Irish Boy Scout organisation).

The arrival of 'Big Jim' Larkin in Dublin in 1908 greatly boosted the trade union movement. Born in Liverpool of very poor parents, he developed into a man of great physique. From an early age he was passionately concerned for the poor, having a deep hatred for unscrupulous employers who exploited them, and he was outspoken in trade union matters from an early age. In 1909 he

———— ◎ ————

The leader of the Unionists at the time of the Home Rule agitation was Edward Carson, who was born in Dublin in 1854. He attended Portarlington School and Trinity College. He did not distinguish himself as a student and was completely overshadowed by another fellow student at Trinity whom he hated – Oscar Wilde. By a quirk of fate he was later to oppose Wilde in a libel case taken by the latter. Before the case began, Wilde remarked 'No doubt he will perform his task with all the added bitterness of an old friend.'

Later Carson was elected leader of the Ulster Unionists and was the founder of the Ulster Volunteers. Carson was also responsible for the gunrunning in 1914 by which the UVF smuggled in 30,000 rifles and three million rounds of ammunition.

———— ◎ ————

Andrew Bonar Law (1858-1923) was born in America but brought up in Glasgow. He became leader of the British Conservative Party in 1911. At all times he wholeheartedly threw his weight behind the Unionist opposition to Home Rule.

———— ◎ ————

Even though there was a rush to sign the Solemn League and Covenant the organisers left nothing to chance. Employers told their employees that failure to sign might have consequences for those who did not do so. Tenants were given the covenant to sign by their landlords, shop-owners requested their customers to add their names. Anyone in the Belfast shipyards who did not sign were run off the job as a 'papist'.

———— ◎ ————

formed the Irish Transport and General Workers Union and over a thousand workers joined the first day. The ITGWU soon spread from Dublin to Cork, Limerick, Galway and other ports and was to play an important role in subsequent events. The membership increased rapidly from 4,000 in 1911, to 8,000 in 1912 and 10,000 in 1913.

The constitutional efforts to achieve Home Rule continued all this time. The 1886 bill had been defeated in the English House of Commons; the 1893 bill was passed by the Commons, but defeated in the Lords. The third attempt at getting the measure passed saw an enormous increase in tension in Ireland as the loyalists of the North, with the active backing of the British Tory party, vowed to resist Home Rule by force of arms if necessary.

In March 1912 a huge demonstration was held by nationalists in Dublin. O'Connell Street was packed from one end to the other by thousands who listened to speeches by John Redmond and others. One of the speakers was a young Dublin schoolteacher called Pádraig Pearse, who gave the prophetic warning to Britain:

> . . . if we are tricked this time there is a party
> in Ireland . . . that will answer with the
> strong hand and the sword's edge. Let the
> *Gall* [English] understand that if we are
> cheated once more there will be 'red' war in
> Ireland.

On 11 April 1912 Prime Minister Henry Asquith introduced the third Home Rule bill to a full House of Commons. The first and second readings were carried by approximately 100 votes each time in spite of the bitter opposition of the Tories. The bill then went to the committee stage when amendments could be considered.

While agitation for Home Rule was occupying John Redmond's constitutional nationalists, Edward Carson, James Craig and Andrew Bonar Law were stirring up resistance to any such concession in Northern Ireland. Bonar Law urged Orangemen and Unionists in Derry to evoke the spirit of the siege of Derry in 1689 and told them 'You are a besieged city. The government has erected a boom against you, a boom to cut you off from the help of the British people. You will burst that boom.'

Carson held a massive rally in Belfast which was attended by thousands of Unionists eager to sign a 'Solemn League and Covenant' that would 'use all necessary means to defeat the present conspiracy to set up a Home Rule parliament in Ireland and solemnly and mutually pledge ourselves to refuse to recognise its authority.' On another occasion he declared 'We must be prepared . . . the morning Home Rule passes, to become responsible for the government of the Protestant province of Ulster.' (This ignored the fact that the province had about 690,000 Catholics to almost match the 885,000 Protestant population.)

After many such meetings all over Ulster another massive rally was held in Belfast on 28 September 1912. A huge procession made its way through the city's streets to the City Hall where Carson led the way by signing the covenant. His example was followed by thousands of others. So great was the crowd that tables for the signing stretched for over 500 metres. Many of the signatories signed in their own blood and at the end of the day 218,206 men had signed and even more women, 228,206. The date, 28 September, was known thereafter as 'Ulster Day'.

The following January 1913 the Ulster Unionists went a step further by raising a Volunteer Force which would defend the independence of Ulster against any threat, no matter from which quarter it came. The force soon numbered about 100,000 men between the ages of seventeen and sixty-five. Its officers were mostly men who held commissions in the British armed forces and the rank and file were well armed with either rifles or revolvers.

Later that year Carson advocated in the House of Commons that the whole nine counties of Ulster should be excluded from any Irish Home Rule. Asquith made a counter proposal that individual Ulster counties would be allowed to opt out, first for three years and then for six. Redmond reluctantly accepted this but Carson rejected it out of hand.

Meanwhile the ITGWU went on energetically organising the unskilled workers of Dublin. Eventually most companies, with varying degrees of cooperation, were organised but two remained unrecruited. Guinness's brewery workers were so well treated and had such good wages and conditions that there was no hope of recruiting them. Another company outside the 'fold' was the Dublin United Tramway Company owned by William Martin Murphy.

Murphy had made his money constructing tramways and railways in England and further afield. In Ireland he owned not only the Tramway Company, but also the *Irish Independent* newspaper, the Imperial Hotel (now Clery's) and the largest department store in Dublin. Although he was not a bad employer he bitterly resented any attempt to organise his workforce. As a counter to the ITGWU he organised in 1911 the employers of Dublin into the Dublin Employers Federation.

He warned his employees not to join Larkin's union and in August 1913 he sacked 100 employees from the Tramway Service and Jacobs biscuit factory who had disobeyed him in joining the ITGWU. Then on 26 August, the day the Dublin Horse Show was to open, Larkin called more than 700 employees of the Tramway Company out on strike. The police reacted violently to the strikers and one man was killed in a melee. Larkin roundly condemned both the employers and the police. He was arrested for his 'seditious' speeches, brought to court and released on bail.

A meeting to be held in front of the GPO in O'Connell Street the following Sunday, 30 August 1913, was banned by the authorities. Larkin refused to accept the ban and promised he would speak at the meeting. The police on the other hand were on the alert to arrest him if he showed up. Larkin spent the Saturday

Big Jim Larkin organised the workers' strike in 1913.

———— ◎ ————

In the first days of the 1914–18 war Prime Minister Asquith declared to the House of Commons that 'Ireland is the one bright spot in the landscape.'

———— ◎ ————

Larkin departed to America in 1914 and did not return to Ireland until 1923. He died in January 1947 and an immense crowd attended his funeral to Glasnevin Cemetery in Dublin. In 1980 a dramatic statue of him with arms upraised was erected in O'Connell Street opposite Clery's. One of the quotations inscribed around the base is 'The great appear great because we are on our knees; let us rise.'

———— ◎ ————

night in the house of Countess Markievicz and on Sunday morning the countess and some of her theatrical friends disguised him as an elderly clergyman. Because Larkin's strong Liverpool accent would be easily recognised he was to pretend to be stone deaf; his 'niece' (a part played by one of the women) would answer any questions for her deaf 'uncle'. They booked rooms for the 'clergyman' and his 'niece' in the Imperial Hotel in O'Connell Street. Shortly after the meeting began, Larkin stepped out onto the balcony in the front of the hotel and began to address the meeting to the cheers of the crowd. The police, however, were in the hotel and arrested him before he had a chance to say more than a few words and after ferocious baton charges the crowd in the street was dispersed, leaving over four hundred people injured.

A few days later tension in the city increased when the employers, led by William Martin Murphy, organised a lockout of all employees who had joined the ITGWU. All over the city workers found themselves locked out, so that by the end of the week over 25,000 employees were out of work. Women working in Jacobs biscuit factory were sacked for refusing to remove their Women Workers' Union badges.

The lockout caused incredible hardship both to the workers and their families. The union headquarters at Liberty Hall was turned into a relief station, providing food and clothing for thousands of families.

When Larkin was again brought before the courts he was sentenced to seven months in prison and brought to Mountjoy jail under a heavily armed guard. The following Sunday a huge protest meeting was held in London and among the speakers was George Bernard Shaw and James Connolly. In his speech Connolly asked that everyone work and vote against the Liberal Government until Larkin was released. He pointed to the absurdity of jailing Larkin for his 'seditious libel' when Carson and the Unionists were openly preaching treason and drilling a private army. Two by-elections were held shortly afterwards with disastrous results for the Liberals. Two days later Larkin was released from prison, having served only seventeen days of his sentence.

Next Larkin and Connolly appealed to the British TUC to refuse to handle Dublin goods but for tactical reasons the TUC refused their request. This effectively ended the dispute – the workers in

The staging of John Millington Synge's *The Playboy of the Western World* in the Abbey Theatre in 1907 led to incredible scenes in the theatre. The fact that the play dealt with Irish peasant life, lauded by the Gaelic League as being 'morally' on a higher level, made it a sensitive subject. Douglas Hyde maintained that Irish speakers were cleaner, more virtuous and better mannered than others. They were also regarded as being more religious and with stronger faith.

The play opened on 24 January and the following day the *Freeman's Journal* in its review said, 'a strong protest must be entered against this unmitigated, protracted libel upon Irish peasant men and worse still on Irish peasant girlhood' and 'No adequate idea can be given of the barbarous jargon, the elaborate and incessant cursings of these repulsive creatures. Everything is b****y this or b****y that.'

The paper also published a letter from 'A Western Girl' which deplored the use in the play of the word 'shift'. The writer declared that the word, 'indicating an essential item of female attire' was one 'which the lady, (Miss Sarah Allgood, who played the part of the Widow Quin), would probably never utter in ordinary circumstances, even to herself'.

The following Monday-night's audience was even more demonstrative. During the part of the play where Pegeen Mike is left alone with Christy Mahon a storm of protest broke out. Booing, shouting, the singing of 'God Save Ireland', shouts of 'Sinn Féin Forever' and banging on the seats with sticks, filled the theatre. One voice was heard to shout 'Such a thing could not occur in Ireland'. The police were called and things quietened down but at the end of the play the audience started singing patriotic songs such as 'A Nation Once Again' and 'The West's Awake'.

Trinity students attended the next night's performance with the intention of preventing any interruptions. When the play started there was such uproar that the police were again called and hardly anyone could hear the actors' words. WB Yeats, who had earlier appealed for calm, ran up and down the aisles, pointing out trouble-makers to the police to get them ejected. One of these was Padraic Colum's father who was later fined forty shillings by a magistrate. Yeats was one of those who gave evidence against him.

The Wednesday performance saw further disturbance but by Thursday night, the more 'objectionable' passages were removed from the play and things quietened down after that. A police presence was maintained in the theatre, however.

Dublin saw no further hope of success and were forced back to work. The strike, however, had given the workers a new awareness of their power and the alliance which grew between workers, nationalists and intellectuals was to have a significant impact on future events.

Political activity did not cease, of course, during the years of labour troubles. In the middle of the lockout the ITGWU established the Irish Citizen Army to defend workers. Another more 'nationally' minded force, the Irish Volunteers, was also founded in 1913. The formation of the Citizen Army was announced by Connolly to celebrate Larkin's early release from jail. In his speech he said,

> I am going to talk sedition. The next time we are out on a march, I want to be accompanied by four battalions of armed men. I want them to come with their corporals, sergeants and people to form fours. Why should we not drill and train our men in Dublin as they are doing in Ulster? But I don't think you need any training.

Eoin MacNeill became Chief of Staff of the Irish Volunteers.
He was not involved in the plans for the 1916 Rising
and did his best to stop it.

Thousands of recruits enrolled, among them, Countess Markievicz. The new army trained regularly in Croydon Park and soon became quite proficient in their defence of the workers against the police and employers. The example of Carson and the Northern Unionists in setting up their own army was a powerful incentive to the nationalists to do the same. The Irish Republican Brotherhood also started drilling in secret in Dublin and began buying a few rifles when funds permitted.

When the nationalists decided to imitate the Unionists they looked for a respectable figure to head-up their organisation. They chose Eoin MacNeill, a history professor at University College Dublin, who readily agreed to their request. On 11 November 1913 a meeting to establish the Volunteer force was held and among the committee members elected were Roger Casement, Pádraig Pearse, Thomas MacDonagh, Eamonn Ceannt, Con Colbert and Joseph Plunkett – all of whom would be later executed for their part in the 1916 Rising. An enrolment meeting was called for 25 November and the organisers were overwhelmed by the response. Over 10,000 men attended and signed up. More than 5,000 others had to wait for another day.

In April 1914, the women's organisation, which became known as *Cumann na mBan*, was also inaugurated. Their first objective was to aid the Volunteers by collecting money for the purchase of arms.

Meanwhile the Unionists in the North were stepping up their campaign for the exclusion of Ulster from any Home Rule arrangement. Under intense pressure, Redmond reluctantly agreed that if one tenth of the voters in any county demanded it, that county would be able to vote itself out of Home Rule for a given number of years.

Redmond's concession dismayed nationalists throughout the country but it only stimulated people like Connolly, Pearse, Clarke and others to more radical solutions. The Irish Citizen Army, which had languished somewhat when the lockout ended, became invigorated. Larkin was elected chairman, Seán O'Casey, the playwright, was secretary and Countess Markievicz, treasurer.

In 1914 with the imminent prospect of Home Rule and no agreement on Ulster's right to opt out, the question arose as to what the British army in Ireland would do if they were ordered to

Tom Clarke was born in England and lived for a time in South Africa and America where he joined the Fenian organisation.

proceed against the Ulster Unionists. The officers based in the Curragh Camp in Kildare were asked what their choice would be if they were ordered to move against Ulster or be dismissed. Sixty officers of the Cavalry Brigade led by General Gough said they would choose dismissal. The government backed down in the face of such opposition and the determination of the officers was never put to the test. The 'Curragh Mutiny', as it was called, never actually took place therefore.

The Curragh Mutiny and the open landing of nearly 25,000 rifles and three million rounds of ammunition for the Ulster Volunteer Force in Larne, Bangor and Donaghadee on 24 April 1914, without any interference from the authorities, sparked a surge of recruits to the Irish Volunteers. By the end of May 1914 they numbered nearly 130,000 men. They openly marched and drilled but were still without weapons. Pearse remarked that 'the Orangeman with a rifle is a much less ridiculous figure than the Nationalist without a rifle.'

The growth of the Volunteer army alarmed Redmond, who now sought to exert some control over the organisation. When Eoin MacNeill sought Redmond's approval for the Volunteer movement, the latter insisted on representation on the Volunteers' committee, otherwise he would create an alternative Volunteer movement. Eventually, to avoid a split, the Volunteer committee agreed to accept the Redmondite nominees.

The urgent need for guns and ammunition for the Volunteers resulted in a plan to purchase a consignment of 1,500 second-hand Mauser rifles and 45,000 rounds of ammunition in Hamburg. The conveyance of the arms to Ireland was entrusted to Erskine Childers, the son of an English father and Anglo-Irish mother. Childers was an expert sailor and had fought against the Boers in South Africa and his experiences there had changed him from being a unionist to being a fervent nationalist.

The consignment of arms was brought out of Hamburg harbour on board a tug to a meeting point in the North Sea where Childers' yacht, the *Asgard* and another yacht, the *Kelpie* (owned by the grandson of William Smith O'Brien, the leader of the 1848 rising) were waiting. Part of the cargo, 900 rifles, was transferred on board the *Asgard* and the other 600 were transferred to the *Kelpie*. On board the *Asgard* were Childers, his wife Molly, Mary Spring Rice, who was a Gaelic League supporter, an English army officer called Gordon Shepherd and two Donegal fishermen, Patrick McGinley and Charles Duggan.

The *Asgard* then sailed for Howth harbour near Dublin, while the *Kelpie* sailed to Wales where its cargo was again transferred, this time to the *Chotah*, a steam-yacht which brought its cargo to Kilcoole in County Wicklow.

The *Asgard* took four weeks to complete its journey, running the gauntlet of gales and the British navy on the way. But on Sunday 26 July the ship entered Howth Harbour and a body of Volunteers marched out from Dublin to meet it. Apart from some of the officers, they had no idea of the purpose of the march When the Volunteers realised what was afoot there was great excitement and they rushed to the quayside so that the officers, who included Eamon de Valera, had great difficulty restraining them. It only took twenty minutes to land the cargo. The ammunition was taken away in motorcars to secret locations and a thousand rifles were handed out to the men but no bullets were issued.

The Volunteers had taken the precaution of cutting the telegraph wires but the authorities soon knew about the landing. The police and a detachment of the King's Own Scottish Borderers were sent to intercept the Volunteers. At Clontarf the marching

Volunteers were stopped by the police and soldiers with fixed bayonets. Some of the police refused to obey orders to seize the rifles and were dismissed on the spot. The Volunteer leaders proceeded to parley with the police thus giving time to many of the Volunteers to disappear with their guns over garden walls to safe hiding places. In all the police only confiscated nineteen rifles.

The successful gunrunning caused great excitement in the city when the news spread. There was also great anger at the behaviour of the authorities when contrasted with the open connivance of the forces of the Crown in the Larne Gun Running. The false rumour that some of the Volunteers had been bayoneted added greatly to the tension.

A crowd of men, women and children followed and jeered the Scottish Borderers as they marched back to the Royal (now Collins) Barracks at Arbour Hill. As they passed along Bachelor's Walk on the quays and neared the Halfpenny Bridge, stones and verbal abuse were showered on them. The officer in charge brought the troops to a halt. It was claimed later that he had intended warning the crowd that unless they stopped harassing his men he would order them to shoot. At the subsequent inquiry an Alderman Byrne claimed that there was no stone throwing, while an ITGWU official said he had seen more stone throwing at soccer matches in Belfast without interruption of the game. At any rate, the raised hand-signal of the officer in charge, Major Haig, was taken as an order to shoot. Several volleys rang out, leaving three dead and at least thirty-five wounded, fifteen seriously. One of the dead and several of the wounded were subsequently found to have bayonet wounds. The dead were later given a public funeral. The coffins were followed by Volunteers in military formation and a salute was fired over the grave.

19

◎

'A TERRIBLE BEAUTY IS BORN'

T he assassination of the Austrian Archduke Ferdinand in Sarajevo on 28 June 1914 precipitated World War I. When the British government announced on 3 August that for all practical purposes Great Britain was at war with Germany, John Redmond immediately offered the unqualified support of nationalist Ireland.

Although Redmond's speech was received with warm applause from both sides of the House of Commons it was not universally approved in Ireland. Most did approve, particularly with the belief that at last Home Rule would be granted, but a section of Irish nationalists adhered to the old principle that 'England's difficulty is Ireland's opportunity'.

James Connolly spelled it out at a commemoration of the three workers killed during the 1913 lockout:

> If you are itching for a rifle, itching to fight,
> have a country of your own; better to fight
> for our country than for the robber empire.
> If you ever shoulder a rifle let it be for
> Ireland . . . Make up your mind to strike
> before your opportunity goes.

It must not be forgotten, however, that those opposing the Redmond campaign were in a decided minority. Countrywide, over 180,000 members of the Volunteers sided with Redmond and only about 11,000 men opposed him, while in Dublin city the numbers 'for' were 2,375 and 'against' were 1,103.

The first anniversary of the outbreak of the war led to a clash between the pro- and anti-war factions. The first week of August 1915 was designated 'Dublin War Week' – a week of intense recruiting for the British army. But that same week the funeral of an old Fenian, Jeremiah O'Donovan Rossa, took place. Rossa had suffered greatly in English prisons for his Fenian activities and when he died in America it was decided to bring him home to Ireland for a hero's funeral. The coffin lay in state in Dublin's City Hall and huge crowds gathered to pay homage as the funeral passed through the streets to Glasnevin Cemetery on 1 August 1915. Both Redmond's unarmed National Volunteers and the armed Irish Volunteers, led by Pádraig Pearse in full Volunteer uniform and wearing a sword, agreed to marshal the crowds. At the graveside Pearse gave the famous speech which ended with the words:

> The Defenders of this Realm have worked well in secret and in the open. They think that they have pacified Ireland . . . They think that they have foreseen everything, think that they have provided against everything; but the fools, the fools, the fools! – they have left us our Fenian dead, and while Ireland holds these graves, Ireland unfree shall never be at peace.

Pádraig Pearse was the son of an English stonemason.
He founded St Enda's school in Rathfarnham.
One of the signatories of the 1916 Proclamation, he was later executed.

———— ◎ ————

By the time the First World War ended over 300,000 Irish men and women had served in the British forces and about 35,000 Irish soldiers had been killed. In spite of the generous response from so many Irish men and women from 'Southern Ireland' they were treated with scant respect by the army authorities who were very pro-Unionist. While Northern volunteers were brigaded together and allowed to take the Red Hand of Ulster as their emblem, the Catholic regiments were refused permission to use the emblem of the Irish harp. Ulster volunteer officers were granted immediate commissions while Irish Volunteer officers had to undergo further training and in any event the vast majority of the officers appointed to Irish regiments were British. All this was done in an effort to prevent the growth of any sense of nationalist self-confidence or pride.

———— ◎ ————

On Wednesday 19 April 1916 a curious document was published which, it was alleged, had come from the Castle authorities and which showed that they planned to arrest all the leaders of the Volunteers. The document, which became known as the 'Castle Document', had almost certainly been forged by Seán Mac Diarmada and Joseph Mary Plunkett with the intention of providing an excuse for the rising and strengthening the resolve of any waverers among the leadership.

———— ◎ ————

The GPO in O'Connell Street was first opened to the public in January 1818. At one time it had been suggested that the site should be used for the new Catholic Cathedral but the authorities did not think it appropriate to allow it in such a prime location.

After the 1916 Rising the GPO had to be practically rebuilt as only the front section was relatively undamaged. (Some bullet holes can still be seen there to this day.)

———— ◎ ————

The dilemma for the British government continued into 1916. The Volunteers were openly drilling, holding recruiting meetings, marching in their green uniforms, or the belts and soft hats which became a substitute for a uniform. They even carried out a mock attack on the GPO in O'Connell Street in rehearsal for the real thing which was to come later. At the same time it was important for the government to get as many as possible to join the British army, so the government did not know how to react.

The Volunteer executive issued a warning that any attempt to disarm the men would be met with force and the Irish leaders such as Connolly, Pearse and Clarke were pressing for bold action to awaken the dormant nationalism which they believed still existed in the Irish people. Connolly, in fact, insisted that the Citizen Army would, if necessary, take action on its own. The great fear of the leaders was that if they delayed too long the unrivalled intelligence system of the Royal Irish Constabulary would discover all their plans.

Finally the Supreme Council of the IRB made the fateful decision to start the rising on Easter Sunday, 23 April. Because of the absolute necessity for secrecy, and because of the tendency of Connolly to take precipitate action, the council actually decided to arrest him and keep him under guard. Only the threat of action against them by the Citizen Army and Countess Markievicz persuaded them to release him. His enthusiasm for immediate action was undiminished and from then onwards he was taken into the confidence of the supreme council of the IRB, even though he was never an IRB man.

The decision was kept such a closely guarded secret that among those not informed were Arthur Griffith, Bulmer Hobson (secretary of the Volunteers), The O'Rahilly (treasurer), Commandant JJ O'Connell (head of the military sub-committee) and Eoin MacNeill (Chief of Staff). (They were not told the plans because they maintained that the Volunteers should not take any action except in a defensive capacity.) Next the council appointed Pearse as Commander-in-Chief, and Thomas MacDonagh told his adjutant, Eamon de Valera, about the plans.

Easter Sunday was confirmed as the day of action and on 3 April Pearse issued orders for a three-day march and manoeuvres to be held by all the Volunteers on that Sunday. MacNeill, Hobson and

The person the police referred to as 'the woman known as Countess Markievicz' was born Constance Gore-Booth in London in 1868. She was the daughter of Sir Henry Gore-Booth of Lissadell, County Sligo. She was a noted horsewoman and beauty in her youth. While in England she was presented at the court of Queen Victoria. She later went to Paris to paint and there she married a Polish count called Markievicz. They returned to Dublin shortly afterwards and there she became involved in the Gaelic movement through her readings of the Sinn Féin newspaper. On the weekend of the rising Countess Markievicz decided to make an appropriate flag for the occasion but, since the shops were closed for Good Friday, she had to improvise. She took a green bedspread and cut it down to a manageable size. The small tin of gold paint available had only a tiny amount left and was nearly dry but undeterred, she mixed some mustard with the paint and wrote the words 'Irish Republic' on the flag. Later this flag was to fly over the GPO during the rising.

Countess Markievicz

Joseph Mary Plunkett was one of the signatories of the 1916 Proclamation of the Republic. The night before he was executed for his part in the rising, he married his childhood sweetheart, Grace Gifford, in Kilmainham jail.

others were becoming suspicious by this time and MacNeill demanded that no action should be taken without his permission. To preserve the secret the council gave him that assurance because they knew he had the power to wreck the whole enterprise.

Some alterations to the plans were made. It was decided that Easter Monday 24 April would be the day because the Fairyhouse Races on Easter Monday would be sure to take large numbers of English army officers out of the city.

The plans called for a force of about 3,000 men of the Volunteers and the Citizen Army to take immediate action in Dublin. A simultaneous uprising was to take place in the rest of the country. Precise and detailed plans were made for the occupation of strategic buildings and positions throughout the city to contain the British forces and prevent reinforcements arriving. The plans were daring but impractical in the event, as the numbers required to carry them out successfully were never available.

A week before the planned rising a Provisional Revolutionary Government of seven men was constituted, and a Proclamation of the Irish Republic was printed. Each of the seven members of the 'Revolutionary Government' signed the proclamation: Thomas Clarke, Pádraig Pearse, Seán Mac Diarmada, Thomas MacDonagh, Eamonn Ceannt, James Connolly and Joseph Plunkett.

Thomas MacDonagh signed the 1916 Proclamation.
He was shot at dawn on 3 May 1916 in Kilmainham jail.

By Holy Thursday the suspicions of those leaders not in on the plans led them to confront Pearse with their fears that something more than routine manoeuvres was involved. Pearse told them then that a rising was intended. MacNeill was enraged and told Pearse that he would do everything he could, short of telling the authorities, to stop the rising.

He issued orders giving Bulmer Hobson control of all the Volunteers in the city and cancelling every order not made personally by himself or Hobson. (MacNeill's countermanding order was conveyed to Limerick by The O'Rahilly on Easter Sunday but when he heard that the rising had started he immediately returned to Dublin to take part.) However, Pearse, MacDonagh and Mac Diarmada managed to persuade MacNeill on Friday morning to countermand his orders because a large shipment of arms was arriving from Germany which would greatly increase their chances of success. The Germans had refused to send troops but had agreed to send 20,000 rifles in a German steamship called the *Aud*. Because the IRB military council wanted the arms to arrive after what they hoped would be a successful rising they cabled the Germans to instruct the captain of the *Aud* to delay until 23 April. The message arrived too late – the *Aud* had already set sail and could not be contacted as she had no radio. It so happened that the Americans raided the offices of the German military attaché in Washington and discovered the message. They immediately informed the British authorities, who sent destroyers to intercept the *Aud* off the coast of Kerry. When the warships did so they ordered her into Queenstown (Cobh) harbour but the German captain abandoned ship on Saturday morning, 22 April, and scuttled her and her cargo.

None of the IRB of the leaders was aware of the interception of the *Aud* at the time but by Saturday morning, the Dublin Castle authorities knew of her sinking and later that day the Volunteer leaders also heard the bad news. MacNeill once more changed his mind and sent out messages at midnight on Saturday to Volunteers throughout the country that no manoeuvres were to take place. He also asked the *Sunday Independent* to print this message the following day:

> Owing to the very critical position, all orders given to Irish Volunteers for tomorrow, Easter Sunday, are hereby rescinded, and no parades, marches, or other movements of Irish Volunteers will take place. Each individual Volunteer will obey this order strictly in every particular.

The message was read with consternation and anger by Volunteers throughout the city. Early that morning the military council met in Liberty Hall and in spite of the setbacks and confusion they decided to go ahead with the original plans. The rising would take place in Dublin on Easter Monday at noon. Orders were sent out to country units confirming MacNeill's order but Volunteers in Dublin were all ordered to remain in the city.

The following order was conveyed to the Dublin battalions:

> 24 April
> 1. The four City Battalions will parade for inspection and route march at 10.00 a.m. today. Commandants will arrange centres.
> 2. Full arms and equipment and one day's rations to be carried.

It was signed by Thomas MacDonagh, Brigade Commandant.

————— ◎ —————

When James Connolly saw the Irish flags flying over the GPO in Easter Week 1916 he grasped Tom Clarke by the hand and with tears in his eyes declared, 'Thanks be to God, Tom, that we both have lived to see this day.'

————— ◎ —————

On the afternoon of Easter Monday 1916 a column of elderly part-time soldiers had been out on a route march in the Dublin Mountains. They were derisively known as the 'Gorgeous Wrecks' from the words 'Georgius Rex' on their belts. They all carried rifles but no ammunition and as they marched back into the city, unaware of what had happened since they had left that morning, they were suddenly shot at. Five were killed and eight wounded.

————— ◎ —————

Eamonn Ceannt was one of the signatories of the Proclamation of the Irish Republic. He was among those who occupied the South Dublin Union in Mount Brown during the rising and was executed on 8 May 1916.

————— ◎ —————

The following was added in Pearse's own handwriting: Coy E 3 will parade at Beresford Place at 10 a.m. PH Pearse. Comdt.

On Easter Monday morning about 1,200 Volunteers and 200 members of the Citizen Army answered the order. They marched through the Dublin streets in small companies, the officers and many of the men wearing the green Volunteer uniform. Others simply had a bandolier over one shoulder and a yellow badge on one arm to show that they were indeed soldiers. They carried an assortment of weapons – old Italian rifles, a few German Mausers smuggled in on the *Asgard*, rifles bought or stolen from British soldiers and most plentiful of all, the traditional Irish pike. The sight of marching men was such a common sight that little attention was paid to the companies led by Connolly, Pearse and Plunkett as they marched up O'Connell Street to the GPO. Here they halted and the order was given to take over the building. No opposition was encountered inside the GPO and the few British troops inside surrendered without a fight. The reason became clear when they were called upon to hand over their ammunition – they revealed that they had none!

A green flag bearing the words 'Irish Republic' was hoisted over one corner of the GPO and the Irish tricolour was raised at another. Across the street a flag showing a plough and stars was raised over the Imperial Hotel. (Seán O'Casey's play *The Plough and the Stars*, about the events of Easter Week, was later to be the cause of much controversy.)

Seán Mac Diarmada was a close friend of Tom Clarke and became the paid organiser of Sinn Féin. One of the signatories of the 1916 Proclamation of the Republic, he was executed on 12 May in Kilmainham jail.

Maud Gonne was one of Ireland's best-known woman activists. She was the daughter of English parents (her father was a British army officer of Irish descent) and grew up to be an extremely beautiful, unconventional and inspirational girl. She also became a life-long revolutionary and a private income allowed her to move easily through Irish, French and English society. Her first political activity was campaigning against evictions in Donegal. She became involved in the Irish literary movement in Dublin where William Butler Yeats fell deeply in love with her. She acted in his play *Cathleen Ní Houlihan*, which he wrote specially for her. Even though she and Yeats were life-long friends – and perhaps lovers – they did not agree politically; her deep concern for the poor was not shared by him. In the 1890s she had an affair with a Frenchman, Lucien Millevoye, who was already married, and had two children by him. Millevoye left her for a singer and she later married Major John MacBride who was a hero of the Boer War. That marriage did not last very long under the strains of his drinking and alleged womanising. They were divorced after the birth of their son, Seán. It was only after the execution of her husband for his part in the Easter Rising that she adopted the MacBride name.

Maud Gonne

Next Pearse went outside the GPO and read out the proclamation which declared that Ireland was a republic. It was signed by Tom Clarke, Seán Mac Diarmada, Thomas MacDonagh, Pádraig Pearse, Eamonn Ceannt, James Connolly and Joseph Plunkett. The document reminded the Irish people of their heroic dead and their right to freedom; it guaranteed religious and civil liberty for all and cherished all the nation's children equally. Inside the GPO the Volunteers made improvised sandbags by stuffing mailbags with paper, rubbish, coal, and anything else they could get their hands on. The windows were smashed to allow the Volunteers to see and fire at their attackers. Some windows were barricaded with wax dummies taken from an exhibition in nearby Henry Street; consequently some of the GPO 'defenders' were 'King George V', 'Queen Mary' and 'Lord Kitchener'!

The first casualties of the rising was a party of Lancers riding down O'Connell Street just after the GPO was occupied. They were totally unaware of the occupation of the building until they were suddenly shot at. Four of the Lancers and two of their horses were shot dead. The two dead horses were to lie in the street for the rest of the week.

Other buildings throughout the city were also earmarked for occupation. The Citizen Army quietly took over St Stephen's Green, closed the gates and began digging trenches. Later on Tuesday when they came under heavy fire from high houses around the Green they withdrew to the College of Surgeons on Stephen's Green West and Little's public house on the corner of Cuffe Street.

The South Dublin Union in Mount Brown was taken by the Fourth Battalion under Eamonn Ceannt and Cathal Brugha after a stiff fight and the Mendicity Institute on the quays was taken by Seán Heuston and his men. Boland's Mill was occupied by de Valera's battalion to hold the line at the canal and also because it commanded the area from Westland Row to Beggars Bush barracks. His troops also took over the buildings commanding Mount Street Bridge. Jacobs biscuit factory in Bishop Street was occupied by Volunteers under Thomas MacDonagh and Major John MacBride, mainly for the large supplies of food it contained. The Volunteers occupying the factory were jeered by hostile crowds waving Union Jacks and calling them cowards for not going

———— ◎ ————

The gunboat *Helga*, which shelled Liberty Hall, had been built in Dublin and later became the Irish fishery protection ship the *Murchú*. During World War Two it served in the Irish Marine Service.

———— ◎ ————

During the rising in Easter Week various volunteers came forward to join the ranks of the garrison in the GPO and among them were two sailors, a Finn and a Swede, who knew very little English. Declaring that 'they had small nationalities and didn't like England' they asked that they be allowed to join the fight. They were given rifles and placed on the roof where they actually took part in the shooting.

———— ◎ ————

About 150 women took part in the rising in Dublin, with more than thirty of them serving in the GPO. The most famous of course is Countess Markievicz but Maud Gonne, Kathleen Clarke, Nora and Ina Connolly, Áine Ceannt and Muriel McDonagh all played an important part. The Citizen Army accepted women in its ranks more readily than did the Volunteers but de Valera was the only Volunteer commander who absolutely refused to have any women under his command.

———— ◎ ————

Arthur Griffith, who was born in Dublin in 1871, became a printer by trade and in 1899 he founded the *United Irishman* newspaper which expounded his policy of self-reliance. In furtherance of this philosophy he launched Sinn Féin (Ourselves Alone) in 1904 which openly advocated the establishment of an independent Irish state. Griffith was rugged, tough, single-minded and hard-headed, with practical objectives such as the establishment of Irish merchant shipping, protection for Irish industry and Irish control of the civil service in Ireland. It cannot be said that the Sinn Féin organisation was much of a success at the time, having very few members but subsequent events were to change all that.

———— ◎ ————

to fight in France. The Four Courts was occupied by Commandant Edward Daly. Other places taken over were the railway stations at Harcourt Street and Westland Row.

A group of Volunteers took over the Magazine Fort in the Phoenix Park by the simple ruse of pretending to play a football match beside the fort and when they went to retrieve the football which was 'accidentally' kicked near the sentry, they overpowered him and took over the fort. They failed to get the main store of arms however and an explosion they set off to destroy the fort was only partially successful.

One important position not taken was Dublin Castle. Part of the Citizen Army had been detailed for that task but so few men turned up that it was decided not to occupy it but to try to prevent any soldiers leaving it. Unknown to the insurgents there was only a small group of soldiers under the command of a corporal guarding the Castle and it could have been taken easily. A policeman on duty was shot dead but when the soldiers on guard duty returned fire the attackers were driven off. So instead of taking the Castle the small Citizen Army group occupied the City Hall and some other buildings nearby.

There were about twelve hundred British troops in various barracks in the city at the time and when news of the rising reached England two brigades were sent over to Kingstown (Dun Laoghaire) so that by Tuesday the British army strength in the city was about five thousand.

Trinity College became a British garrison manned by the students of the College Officers' Training Corps. By Wednesday a line of British army posts stretched from Trinity to Dublin Castle and to Kingsbridge Station. This effectively divided the insurgent army in two.

By Wednesday the British had managed to get the gunboat *Helga* into position on the Liffey near the Customs House and they attempted to shell Liberty Hall. They were unsuccessful at first as the shells only fell on the nearby Loopline (railway) Bridge. They then tried further downstream but this time the shells fell in the Phoenix Park. Finally they brought guns to the corner of Tara Street and George's Quay and managed to destroy the building.

Then, together with artillery pieces in the grounds of Trinity College, they started shelling other rebel strongholds. The GPO was badly hit and the upper storey destroyed. Several other buildings in O'Connell Street were also demolished or set on fire with incendiary shells.

Later that same Wednesday evening, battalions of the Sherwood Foresters arrived in Kingstown. One column approached the city by the Stillorgan Road and met little opposition. Another column came in by Ballsbridge and met fierce resistance from de Valera's Third Battalion at Lower Mount Street Bridge By the time they had taken the bridge, eighteen officers and two hundred and sixteen other ranks had been killed or wounded.

James Connolly was wounded on Wednesday when he ventured from the GPO into Prince's Street to dispatch a squad to Abbey Street. Almost at once a shot from a sniper shattered his ankle. He was carried back into the GPO and even though he was seriously wounded he later insisted on being brought around on a stretcher to supervise operations.

On Thursday the British troops started to shell O'Connell Street from a nine-pounder gun positioned at Trinity College. Because they were using incendiary shells the effect was devastating. By evening the Imperial Hotel, the Royal Hibernian Academy, Elvery's Sports Shop, the offices of the *Freeman's Journal*, and many other buildings were engulfed in flames. By Friday the GPO was in flames and no longer capable of being defended. The garrison was called together and told to prepare to evacuate the building. The plan was to dash out a side door into Henry Street, make their way up Moore Street and occupy the Williams and Woods jam factory in Parnell Street.

The first group to try the manoeuvre was led by The O'Rahilly. He led a small group out the door and was to report back about conditions in the streets. He never did, however, for he was shot dead in Moore Lane.

Pearse, Plunkett and Mac Diarmada did manage to reach a house at the end of Moore Street unscathed and Connolly was carried out safely on a stretcher.

On Saturday morning they held a consultation and agreed that the situation was hopeless and at 3.30 p.m. that afternoon Pearse surrendered his sword to Brigadier-General Lowe at the British post in Parnell Street. He also sent Elizabeth O'Farrell with an order of surrender to the other Republican commanders. James

Connolly countersigned the order to units of the Citizen Army, as he knew they would obey no one else. The order was dated Saturday 29 April 1916 at 3.45 p.m.

One by one all the rebel positions were surrendered, although the men in Jacobs biscuit factory held out until 3.00 p.m. on Sunday afternoon. Many of the surrendering Volunteers were taken to the open ground in front of the Rotunda hospital. The prisoners were kept out in the open all night and the next morning were marched to Richmond Barracks (Keogh Square) in Inchicore and the injured Connolly was taken to Dublin Castle.

Wholesale looting occurred in the city during the rising. The poor descended on O'Connell Street, Henry Street, Grafton Street, Camden Street and other shopping areas. and everything that could be carried was taken away.

A well-known and tireless pacifist called Francis Sheehy-Skeffington tried to organise some citizens to prevent the looting. On his way home on Tuesday evening he was arrested by a Captain Bowen-Colthurst and taken to Portobello Barracks. Later that night Bowen-Colthurst brought him out with his patrol as a hostage. He was told that if the patrol was shot at, he would be shot dead.

Then Bowen-Colthurst arrested two editors, Thomas Dickson of the *Eye-Opener* and Patrick McIntyre of the *Searchlight*, and brought them to Portobello Barracks also. The next morning he ordered that Sheehy-Skeffington and the two journalists be shot. Their bodies were buried in sacks in the yard of the barracks that night. (Bowen-Colthurst was later court-martialled in June and found guilty but insane. He was imprisoned in Broadmoor Criminal Mental Asylum but was released in 1922. He emigrated to Canada and died there in 1966.)

The rising had proved costly. Over 200 civilians were killed and 600 wounded. The rebels suffered 64 dead and 200 wounded while the forces of the Crown had 134 killed and 381 wounded. Many parts of the city, especially O'Connell Street, lay in ruins. Nearly 3,500 men and eight women were arrested. Of these 1,836 men and five women were interned in England and Wales.

Decomposing carcasses of horses and unburied, or poorly buried, corpses posed a great threat to public health. Many shallowly buried bodies of soldiers were discovered and handed

⎯⎯⎯ ◎ ⎯⎯⎯

When the leaders of the 1916 Rising were executed in Kilmainham Jail they were blindfolded and a piece of white paper or cloth was put on each chest as a target. The execution party passed their rifles behind them to be loaded and as one of the rifles was loaded with a blank round none of them knew for certain if they had shot anyone.

⎯⎯⎯ ◎ ⎯⎯⎯

Roger Casement was born in Dublin but spent much of his earlier life working in Africa and Brazil for the British Consular Service. He wrote scathingly about the terrible conditions of the workers in the rubber industry there and was knighted in 1911.

When he returned to Ireland in 1913 he espoused the nationalist cause and went to Germany to purchase arms for the rising. He landed by U-boat in Tralee Bay on Good Friday 21 April 1916 but was arrested the next morning. He was executed in Pentonville Prison on 2 August and was later buried in Glasnevin Cemetery.

Roger Casement

⎯⎯⎯ ◎ ⎯⎯⎯

over for reburial to the military authorities. Coffins were so scarce that many bodies were left lying in the city morgue. Over sixty unidentified bodies taken off the streets were taken to pits behind Dublin Castle for burial. Many of these were later claimed by relatives and were given a proper burial.

There were a few other attempts at a rising in other parts of the country. In County Galway a small band of men led by Liam Mellows took over the small towns of Craughwell and Athenry and cut the railway lines to Athlone and Limerick. They then marched along the coast road to attack Galway city but they were dispersed by shelling from British warships in Galway Bay. At Ashbourne, County Meath, Thomas Ashe led a group which ambushed a party of forty policemen and the battle lasted five hours until the police surrendered.

Some rebels in County Wexford captured the town of Enniscorthy and held it for three days against all efforts by the police to dislodge them. Others camped on Vinegar Hill but dispersed to their homes when they learned of the Dublin surrender. In Cork over a thousand Volunteers were prepared to act until they received the countermanding order from MacNeill. By the time the new instructions arrived from Pearse the British army had secured the city.

For the leaders of the Easter Rising retribution was swift and they were shot one by one. Pádraig Pearse, Thomas MacDonagh and Thomas Clarke were tried by court martial and shot at dawn on Wednesday 3 May in the yard of Kilmainham Jail.

Joseph Plunkett was also sentenced to death and married his sweetheart Grace Gifford in Kilmainham Jail the evening before he was shot. On Thursday 4 May he, Edward Daly, William Pearse (Pádraig's brother) and Michael Hanrahan (MacDonagh's second-in-command at Jacobs factory) were executed; Major MacBride on 5 May; and Eamonn Ceannt, Michael Malin, Con Colbert and Seán Heuston on 8 May. The next day Thomas Kent (Ceannt) was shot in Cork for shooting a policeman when he and his brother resisted arrest.

Countess Markievicz was also sentenced to death but the sentence was commuted to penal servitude for life. Eamon de Valera was one of the last leaders to surrender and he too was sentenced to death on 10 May. However his connections with

America and the widespread revulsion and anger at the executions, which spread throughout the country and abroad, led to his sentence being commuted to penal servitude for life. Finally, on Friday 12 May, Seán Mac Diarmada and James Connolly were executed. Connolly, who was being held in Dublin Castle and was dying from his wound which had become infected, was carried on a stretcher to an ambulance and brought to Kilmainham Jail. There he was put sitting on a chair at the opposite end of the stone-breakers yard to where the others had been shot and was executed. Mac Diarmada had also to be carried to the place of execution as he was crippled with arthritis. In all ninety-four leaders were sentenced to death but only fifteen were executed.

As the news of the executions spread throughout the city and country the antipathy towards the rebels changed to admiration and what sympathy there was for the British forces soon evaporated. The newspapers and the general public took to calling the rising the 'Sinn Féin Rebellion' because so little was known about the real leaders that a connection with the Sinn Féin movement seemed the only explanation. In fact the Sinn Féin organisation played little part in the rising and Griffith was unaware of the planned rising beforehand. This did not prevent him from being interned, however, and Eoin MacNeill, who had tried to prevent the rising was sentenced to life imprisonment in Dartmoor.

The Prime Minister, Henry Asquith, visited Dublin on 12 May to assess the situation for himself. He halted the executions and returned to England convinced of the urgent need for a settlement. (There was some evidence that General Maxwell ignored a telegram from Asquith to halt the execution of Connolly.) Roger Casement meanwhile was brought to London and went on trial on June 26 in the Old Bailey. He was found guilty and hanged in Pentonville Prison, on 3 August 1916, having converted to Catholicism before his death.

20

◎

'BLACK AND TANS'
AND 'AUXIES'

After the rising people began to call it the 'Sinn Féin Rising' even though Sinn Fein had little to do with it and was generally a pacifist organisation at the time. Meanwhile the prison camps provided fertile conditions for the development not only of the IRA (the extremist wing of the Volunteers) but also the more secretive Irish Republican Brotherhood (IRB). One of the most active organisers was a young man from Cork named Michael Collins who had taken part in the Easter Rising and had fought in the GPO.

In spite of being at the top of the authorities' wanted list
Michael Collins moved freely around the city.

By Christmas 1916 most of the prisoners were released and they played a significant part in some crucial by-elections which were held in the first half of 1917. The success of candidates standing for the revitalised Sinn Féin astounded the country and shocked the Redmondites. These victories further helped to influence Irish public opinion, so that when the remaining prisoners were released in July 1917 they were welcomed home by huge crowds waving Republican tricolour flags in the streets.

The Castle authorities continued to harass the Volunteers and eighty-four men were arrested in August 1917. Among them was Thomas Ashe, who had led a detachment of Volunteers in a battle against armed police in Ashbourne, County Meath, during the Easter Rising. He had been later sentenced to death but released with the other Volunteers. On this occasion he was sentenced to one year's hard labour in Mountjoy jail. In September the Republicans demanded that they be treated as prisoners of war. The demand was refused. The prisoners then went on hunger strike, Ashe was forcibly fed, and died as a result on 25 September 1917.

The Irish Volunteers greatly increased in numbers during the succeeding months and soon were estimated to number between 50,000 and 60,000 throughout the country. But things did not go their way politically all the time. The Sinn Féin party lost three by-elections in a row in early 1918. But then the British made a massive blunder – they announced that conscription to the British army would be applied to Ireland. Despite wholesale protest and opposition all over Ireland the bill was passed in the House of Commons on 16 April 1918 by 301 votes to 103. The Home Rule party members walked out in protest. (In the event conscription was never introduced in Ireland and Sinn Féin got the credit for that rather than the Home Rule Party.)

The fury of the protests in Ireland led the authorities to believe another rising might take place. In May 1918 they arrested scores of Sinn Féin leaders, including Eamon de Valera, Countess Markievicz, Arthur Griffith and Kathleen Clarke. They were deported to England and interned. To appease American opinion the authorities claimed to have discovered a 'German plot' but no charges were ever brought against the arrested men and no details of the 'plot' were ever given, then or later.

A general election took place on 14 November 1918 for the first time in eight years. The Sinn Féin candidates had an overwhelming victory, helped immeasurably by impersonation and vote-rigging by their supporters, it must be said. The old Home Rule party was practically wiped out. Sinn Féin won nearly three-quarters of the seats: Sinn Féin 73 seats, Unionists 25 seats, and the Home Rule Party 6 seats. The Sinn Féin candidates stood for an abstentionist policy and consequently none of their elected members took their seats in Westminster, including Eamon de Valera, who had a dramatic victory in East Clare and who was in Lincoln jail.

Those successful Sinn Féin candidates not in jail met in Dublin on 7 January 1919. Twenty-six elected candidates were present and they decided to convene *Dáil Éireann* (Assembly of Ireland), 'an Irish Parliament for a sovereign independent Irish Republic'.

The first Dáil met amid great excitement in Dublin's Mansion House on the afternoon of 21 January 1919. When the role call was made the constant refrain in answer was 'In a foreign prison'. In the case of the Unionists the response was simply 'Absent'.

On that very first day of the new Dáil Éireann, nine Volunteers, led by Dan Breen and Seán Treacy, shot dead two policemen, Constables Mac Donnell and O'Connell, who were guarding a cart carrying gelignite to a quarry at Soloheadbeg in County Tipperary. Both constables were Catholics and one was a widower with four children. The terrorist action had not been ordered by the leadership but it proved to be the beginning of a bitter two-and-a-half-year guerrilla war.

In February de Valera escaped from Lincoln jail in England and at the Dáil meeting in April he was elected president.

In March 1919 Volunteers of the Dublin Brigade attacked Collinstown Aerodrome (now the headquarters of Aer Rianta) and seized a large amount of arms and ammunition. More incidents occurred throughout the country, month after month, in which men were killed on both sides. Martial law was declared in various parts of the country, so that Ireland was approaching a state of war.

The guerrilla campaign, led by Michael Collins and Cathal Brugha, became highly organised and was run on military lines. Police barracks all over the country came under attack. In Dublin Collins concentrated on eliminating a key part of the British intelligence system. He organised a group of hit men, known as 'The Squad' to kill members of the Dublin Metropolitan Police 'G' Division, the heart of the authorities' information gathering. The first member to be shot was Patrick Smith on 31 July 1919. (He was unarmed at the time but was shot in the back five times. He died some weeks later, leaving a wife and seven children.)

Following a series of similar incidents the British government declared Dáil Éireann a dangerous association and suppressed it on 10 September 1919. The banning of all Republican newspapers followed on 20 September. The Republicans responded by launching a stencilled information sheet called the *Bulletin*, which carried accounts of atrocities perpetrated by the Crown forces. Secret and incriminating information obtained by the Republicans during raids on British mail, or supplied by well-placed informers inside Dublin Castle or government offices, were also frequently published in the *Bulletin* to the embarrassment of the authorities.

The RIC were being stretched to the limit, so the British forces were augmented by large numbers of men brought over from England. These recruits were so numerous that there were not enough proper uniforms for all of them, and they were therefore dressed in khaki coats with black trousers and caps. They promptly got the name of 'Black and Tans' – after a well-known pack of foxhounds. Yet another armed force, named the Auxiliary Division, made up of British ex-army officers, started recruiting in July 1920 and was sent to aid the RIC the following year. These 'Auxiliaries', who were paid £1 a day, had no pension rights, were not under military discipline and were not subject to trial by the civil courts.

The Black and Tans and the Auxiliaries quickly established a pattern of ruthlessness. When the IRA shot a policeman or soldier the 'Tans' and 'Auxies' took revenge by burning houses or whole villages; prisoners were murdered while 'trying to escape'; property was stolen or destroyed; passers-by were shot dead. In August when two of their number were set upon and tied to a tree in a Limerick public park, a group of Tans attacked Carey's Road in the city and smashed the windows and much of the contents of over a hundred houses. They also set alight a large part of the centre of the city, destroying shops and houses in the process.

When local men cut the hair of an eighteen-year-old girl in Tipperary for 'walking-out' with an English soldier a group of his companions retaliated by burning the creamery in Newport to the ground. Although the British authorities publicly disapproved of the actions of their forces in Ireland, Lloyd George and Winston

Churchill privately assured Major-General Tudor, the chief of police, of their full support.

The IRA, under the direction of Michael Collins, fought fire with fire. He was a man who was utterly ruthless, completely fearless and although sought by the authorities from 1919 onwards he seldom bothered to adopt a disguise, cycling openly through the streets of Dublin, depending on his Squad and intelligence network to protect him.

During 1920 the struggle between the British forces and the IRA continued all over Ireland, apart from the northeastern counties. Black and Tan atrocities were countered with shootings, assassinations and ambushes. When the local elections were held that year Sinn Féin won 422 seats, Labour 324, Nationalists 213, Unionists 297 and Independents 128. Even in the North the nationalists were successful with the election of a nationalist corporation and mayor in Derry city after 230 years of Unionist domination. The new corporation immediately declared its allegiance to Dáil Éireann.

In March 1920 a policeman was shot near Cork and the next morning a group of men with blackened faces burst into the home of Tomás MacCurtain, the local IRA commander newly elected Lord Mayor, and shot him dead. The authorities put it about that he had been shot by Sinn Féin but the coroner returned a verdict of wilful murder against Prime Minister Lloyd George, Lord Lieutenant French, three named policemen and some others unknown.

Terence MacSwiney was immediately installed as the new Sinn Féin Lord Mayor and he made the now famous declaration in his inauguration speech, 'It is not those who can inflict the most but those who can suffer the most who will conquer.'

On Easter Monday 5 April 1920 eighty-eight nationalist prisoners in Mountjoy prison went on hunger strike demanding that they should either be treated as prisoners of war or be released. Huge crowds gathered outside the prison singing and praying.

A week later the Labour Party and the Congress of Trade Unions declared a general strike. It was completely successful and all commercial activity came to a halt. Two days later Lord French gave in, released the prisoners and declared that from then on all persons arrested for political offences would be treated as political prisoners. Meanwhile the 'war' between the IRA and the police and military continued. Many of the smaller police barracks had to be evacuated and over sixty-six policemen were killed. Hundreds of barracks were burned to the ground so that the pro-British *Irish Times* reported that 'The King's Government virtually ceased to exist south of the Boyne and west of the Shannon'

By May of that year things escalated as dockers around the country refused to handle any goods they regarded as war material. Then the railway workers refused to move the trains if there were police or troops on board. In late May of that year the Connaught Rangers Mutiny occurred in India in protest at the behaviour of British troops in Ireland. The men of the Connaught Rangers regiment were mostly recruited in the West of Ireland and the regiment had a proud tradition. After court martial sixty soldiers were sent to prison in England and one, twenty-two-year-old James Daly, was executed for leading the mutineers on an abortive raid on the regiment's arms magazine.

In June loyalist workers attacked Catholic areas in Derry city and in the disturbances which followed over eighteen Catholics were killed.

Even worse was to follow in Belfast in July. Spurred on by rabble-rousing speeches from Carson and others, and angered even further by IRA attacks on police officers, Protestant workers from the shipyards proceeded to attack Catholic workers, homes, churches and convents all over the city. Over twenty people were killed and three hundred wounded in that first weekend of violence and more than 5,000 workers were driven out of their jobs.

The rioting died down for a while but erupted again when the IRA shot dead District Inspector Swanzy as he returned from church services in Lisburn on Sunday 22 August 1920. Swanzy was suspected of being involved in the killing of the Cork Lord Mayor, Tomás MacCurtain, and consequently was high on the IRA's target list. His killing provoked Loyalist mobs in Lisburn to go on the rampage against Catholics. Within days the whole Catholic population of the town was driven out and the refugees streamed into Belfast for shelter. The violence then spread to Belfast with the Catholics of Ballymacarrett being the chief target. A ferocious battle in York Street resulted in five deaths, and all the time the military and police simply looked on and made no attempt to stop the carnage. Finally when a night-time curfew was imposed on 30 August things calmed down somewhat but still a further twenty-three people were killed in September.

Efforts were made by trade unionists to get the 8,000 or more expelled workers re-instated in their jobs with little success. Many of the trade unions were only half-hearted in their efforts, with the honourable exception of the carpenters' union which took a very courageous and principled stand on the matter.

The rest of the country had looked on in horror at the events in the North and nationalists throughout the country now started a boycott of all Belfast goods to put pressure on loyalists to mend their ways. The boycott affected Northern business considerably, although Unionists dismissed it by pointing out that the greater part of Belfast's output was sold to Britain.

In August 1920 the Lord Mayor of Cork, Terence MacSwiney, was arrested for having in his possession documents 'likely to cause disaffection to His Majesty'. He immediately went on hunger strike, was convicted and sent to Brixton prison in London. In spite of worldwide sympathy and the protests of thousands outside the prison the authorities refused to release him.

Meanwhile the mayhem continued throughout the country. Milltown Malbay in County Clare was attacked and ransacked by the Tans early in September. Later that same month, 20 September 1920, over 100 police attacked Balbriggan in north County Dublin to avenge the shooting of two of their comrades (one of whom died). They roamed the town in a wild drunken state, killing two men, firing their rifles, burning houses and the local hosiery factory and threatening to repeat the dose the following night. These horrendous events were repeated in towns and villages all over Ireland during the last months of that year.

During those terrible months Terence MacSwiney died on hunger strike on 25 October. After a lying-in-state attended by thousands in Southwark Cathedral, the body was put on a train to Holyhead for transport to Dublin where a huge funeral was planned. Troops removed the coffin at Chester however and brought it direct to Cork where it lay in state in the City Hall. While huge crowds paid their last respects inside the building, troops in armoured cars patrolled the streets outside.

Kevin Barry was executed at the age of eighteen
for his part in an attack on a British army lorry.

In November an eighteen-year-old Dublin medical student named
Kevin Barry was captured after an IRA attack on a British army
lorry in the city. Three soldiers, one of whom was also aged
eighteen, were killed in the attack and the British soldiers were in
no mood for kid-glove treatment. Barry was repeatedly beaten in
an effort to get him to reveal the names of his companions. He was
sentenced to death even though it was quite clear that his gun had
never been fired and he was hanged in Mountjoy jail on 1
November 1920.

Another traumatic event occurred at the end of the same month.
On Sunday 21 November members of Collins' Squad entered
various hotels throughout Dublin city and shot dead fourteen
people, including eleven British Intelligence officers (some in front
of their wives) and wounded several more. The IRA claimed that
they were all undercover agents for the Crown but at least one was
an innocent veterinary surgeon shot dead in bed in the Gresham
Hotel as he was reading a newspaper.

That same afternoon there was an important Gaelic football
match at Croke Park between Dublin and Tipperary. The military
surrounded the grounds and proceeded to search for IRA men.
The Auxiliaries suddenly opened fire without warning, killing
twelve men and women and wounding sixty more. (One Tipperary

player called Michael Hogan was among the dead and the Hogan Stand in Croke Park was later named after him.)

Later in the evening three prisoners in Dublin Castle (Peader Clancy, Dick McKee and Conor Clune) were shot dead 'while trying to escape'. Contrary to some accounts, they were not tortured beforehand. One observer of the bodies, a Dr MacLysaght, stated categorically that they were not. However, a medical doctor who examined Conor Clune's body found thirteen bullet holes in his chest. (This day, 21 November 1920, became known as 'Bloody Sunday' until the name was later applied to the events in Derry on Sunday 30 January 1972.)

The funerals of Clancy, McKee and Clune were huge events in the tradition of Irish political funerals. In spite of the constant efforts of the authorities to capture Michael Collins, he went to the Pro-Cathedral for the funeral service and helped to carry the coffins. He later appeared openly at the graveside, without disguise, to lay a wreath on the graves. A woman bystander was so surprised to see him that she blurted out, 'Look! There's Mick Collins'. Collins' reaction was to mutter in disgust, 'You bloody bitch!'

The weeks succeeding Bloody Sunday saw a steady increase in violence throughout the country with the IRA adopting guerrilla tactics forming small groups of men into what became known as 'flying columns'. These groups moved constantly around the country, depending on sympathetic householders to shelter and feed them as they were 'on the run'. One of the most famous of these flying columns was the thirty-six-strong group in West Cork, commanded by Tom Barry, a twenty-three-year-old veteran of the Great War. Their most spectacular exploit was the ambush of two lorry-loads of Auxiliaries at Kilmichael on 29 November 1920 in which sixteen Auxiliaries and two IRA men were killed. The Crown forces later took their revenge by burning homes, farm buildings and shops in the area.

The Unionists in the North felt under constant threat during 1920 and were suspicious of the RIC because nearly 80% of the force was Catholic. To counteract this, Loyalists took to organising vigilante groups in various counties such as Armagh, Tyrone and Fermanagh. One of the leading organisers of the groups was Sir Basil Brooke of Fermanagh.

In 1918, just before the First World War ended, a German submarine sank the Dublin-Holyhead mailboat, *Leinster*, just outside Dun Laoghaire harbour. The ship was carrying almost five hundred British soldiers at the time. The total number of lives lost in the disaster was five hundred and one.

Seán Treacy who, along with Dan Breen, had fired the opening shots in the War of Independence was cornered in a security sweep in Talbot Street in Dublin in 1920. In the ensuing gun battle Treacy and a British intelligence officer named Price were shot dead. A newsagent and a young boy were also killed by flying bullets.

During the lying-in-state of Terence MacSwiney in Cork City Hall in 1920 a large placard on the front door repeated the inscription on the coffin: 'Terence MacSwiney, murdered by the Foreign Enemy, in the Fourth Year of the Republic.'

Although the Six Counties was the part of Ireland that had most resisted Home Rule, the Government of Ireland Act of 1920 in effect made them the only part of Ireland to get Home Rule.

Later that same year Craig and Carson reactivated the defunct Ulster Volunteer Force. Next Craig urged the formation of a special full time force of 2,000 armed constables. This later resulted in the establishment in November 1920 of Special Constables, of which there were three types: 'A-specials', who would be full time, paid, and armed; 'B-specials', who would be part time, paid, and generally armed, and 'C-specials', who would be unpaid, and called on only in emergencies. (The UVF surged into the new special forces and by July 1920 there were over 16,000 B-specials and 3,500 A-specials.)

The 'specials' soon showed their true colours – in December 1920 in Enniskillen they shot at the Catholic church and then marched through the town singing sectarian songs. On 23 January 1921 a band of A-specials broke into a pub in Clones, County Monaghan and started to drink freely of its stock. The RUC ordered them to leave and they replied by shooting at the police. One special was killed and several were wounded in the gun battle which followed. The following February another group of specials burned eight houses to the ground in Roslea, County Fermanagh.

On 11 November 1920 the Government of Ireland Act setting up parliaments for what was called 'Northern Ireland' and 'Southern Ireland' was passed in the House of Commons. The territory of Northern Ireland was the area covered by the six counties of Antrim, Armagh, Down, Fermanagh, London/Derry and Tyrone. Southern Ireland encompassed the other twenty-six counties. Members of both parliaments were to be elected by proportional representation to protect the Unionist minority in the South and the nationalist minority in the North and the two areas would have their own taxation and judicial systems. There were various restrictions on the powers of both parliaments, such as being forbidden to have an army or navy and not having control over custom affairs.

The bill finally received the royal assent on 23 December 1920 and came into effect on 1 May 1921. The 'border' between the Six Counties and the rest of Ireland was established for the first time. (This boundary followed no definite line but conformed to boundaries of ancient baronies.)

That same month in which the new Northern state came into being saw the proclamation of martial law in the counties of

Munster. From 10 December 1920 possession of firearms or ammunition was a crime punishable by death; any meeting of more than five adults was forbidden and every householder had to attach a list of all the house's occupants to the inside of the front door.

Just one day after the proclamation of martial law the Black and Tans showed their disregard for all law by burning and looting the centre of Cork city. Three hundred buildings, including the City Hall and the Carnegie Library, were destroyed, with the damage later reckoned at the enormous sum of three million pounds at the prices of the time.

The martial law regulations allowed 'official reprisals' to be carried out by government forces after IRA attacks. The first such reprisal took place on 1 January 1921 when General Strickland ordered the burning of seven homes in Midleton in County Cork. This was followed by similar reprisals all over Munster. In County Clare alone one judge found 139 cases of 'criminal acts by the Crown forces' without any evidence of the guilt of the victims.

The ferocity of the forces of the Crown was matched by the ruthlessness of the IRA. In the first three months of 1921 they executed seventy people suspected of being spies and informers. In one case in County Cork they shot a seventy-year-old woman landowner for passing on information about a planned ambush. Six Volunteers had been arrested for the planned attack and the IRA then threatened that if they were shot that the woman would die also. The authorities ignored the threat and executed all six Volunteers and five days later the IRA executed their prisoner.

Tom Barry's West Cork flying column was also active at this time and in a spectacular ambush at Crossbarry in County Cork thirty-five British soldiers were killed for the loss of three Volunteers.

Around this time the IRA threatened to burn two Loyalist homes for every Republican one destroyed by the Crown forces. When the British commander ignored the threat the IRA proceeded to burn many large country mansions and castles in reply.

It is estimated that over the first two months of 1921 317 Volunteers and civilians were killed and 285 were wounded. The Crown forces suffered 174 killed and 288 wounded. During the following months the turmoil continued.

On 14 March 1921 six prisoners were hanged in Mountjoy jail

for 'high treason'. Two of them were accused of taking part in the Bloody Sunday shootings. The day of the executions was a day of public mourning in the city. Businesses were closed and a crowd of 20,000 gathered outside the jail. When the bells tolled for the executions the crowds fell to their knees in prayer.

A state of war existed in Dublin. Collins' men carried out ambushes and the military replied with raids and shootings. An 8.00 p.m. curfew was imposed and military lorries roared through the streets every night carrying raiding parties all over the city. The colossal reward of £10,000 was offered for the arrest of Collins.

On 25 May 1921 120 men of the Dublin Brigade of the IRA, at the instigation of de Valera, attacked the Customs House on the docks. It housed nine departments of the British administration and its destruction would be a severe blow to the authorities. The men entered the building and forced the staff to leave. They then set fire to the building but before they could escape the place was surrounded by British forces. Five Volunteers were shot dead and seventy were captured. The next day only the walls of the once beautiful building were left standing. Incalculable amounts of historic Irish documents and civic records were destroyed along with the building. The operation had been at the same time a great success and a great disaster for the IRA. Collins was furious with de Valera for his lack of understanding of proper guerrilla tactics.

During that year (1921), however, the first tentative moves were made to come to some agreement between the British government and the Irish executive. Elections for separate parliaments for 'Northern Ireland' and 'Southern Ireland' took place in May 1921. There were 128 seats to be contested in the South and fifty-two in the North. Sinn Féin was the only party to nominate candidates to contest the elections in the South, except for the four Trinity College seats, where the candidates were also unopposed – the Labour Party had generously decided not to put forward any candidates to avoid splitting 'the democratic forces'. Sinn Féin 'won' the 124 seats to the great shock of the British cabinet who had been led to believe that many of the seats would be strongly contested. In actual fact no voting took place in the South for any of the seats and all the nominees were deemed elected. Countess Markievicz had been the only woman in the first Dáil but now she was joined by five other women, including Kathleen Clarke, wife of the 1916 leader, Tom Clarke, and Margaret Pearse, mother of Pádraig and Willie.

In the Six-County elections all the seats were contested. The Sinn Féin and nationalist organisations agreed to cooperate in the contests and since the election was conducted under the proportional representation system each agreed to give their number two vote to the other.

The days of the election campaign and polling day itself were marred by violence and intimidation. The *Manchester Guardian* wrote:

> It would be hard to find, even in the rather corrupt history of Irish politics, an election fought with such ruthlessness, such corruption and such unfairness as the election for the Northern Parliament which ended today.

When the results were counted it was found that the Unionists had secured forty seats, and Sinn Fein and Labour had got six each. The first Prime Minister was James Craig who boasted later, 'I have always said that I am an Orangeman first and a politician and a member of this parliament afterwards.'

On 1 April an RIC constable was shot dead by Republicans and less than an hour later uniformed police raided Catholic homes in Belfast's Arnon and Stanhope streets, beat a man to death with a sledgehammer, shot three other men to death and wounded three children, one of them mortally. The government refused to set up an investigation,

These events were followed by the burning of fifty Catholic homes in Antigua and Stanhope streets in Belfast and this provoked the IRA to reply in kind by burning factories, business premises and mansions throughout the province. A ferocious campaign of tit-for-tat killings ensued which left forty-four Catholics and twenty-two Protestants dead during the month of May alone.

A new police force, the Royal Ulster Constabulary, with the reserve part-time force, the B-specials, were set up on 5 April 1922 and were overwhelmingly filled with Orangemen. By the autumn of that year there were fifty thousand regular and part-time policemen in the Six Counties, that is, a policeman for every six families (or one policeman for every two Catholic families).

On 7 April 1922 the Special Powers Act, which conferred draconian powers on the government and police authorities, was passed by the Northern parliament at Stormont. Citizens could be interned without trial, police could search homes without a warrant and Republican political organisations could be banned. Special courts could impose sentences of penal servitude for life, order males to be privately whipped or pass sentence of death.

The Unionists then turned their attention to drawing up the boundaries to the local electoral divisions to ensure that the Catholic vote was stymied as much as possible. Probably the worst example of this was in the city of Derry, where one electoral ward was drawn to enclose 90% of the Catholic population and the remaining Catholic 10% was scattered over two Protestant wards where their vote would be ineffectual. The result was that the minority Protestant population had control of the city for generations.

Meanwhile on 28 June 1921 the 'Parliament of Southern Ireland' had its first meeting. But it was all over in minutes – the only persons present were the Lord Lieutenant, nominated senators and the four lower-house members for Trinity College. On 13 July it met once more and then adjourned, never to meet again.

The tentative feelers for peace which were put out early in 1921 eventually bore fruit. Hostilities ended on 11 July 1921. The truce was signed in the Mansion House by General Macready and Assistant Secretary Cope acting for the Crown, and Commandant Robert Barton TD and Commandant Edmund Duggan TD acting for the army of the Republic. The next day de Valera and a group of other Republicans, not including Collins, travelled to London to meet Prime Minister Lloyd George.

Real negotiations did not begin until 11 October 1921. The leaders of the Irish delegation this time were Michael Collins and Arthur Griffith. After very difficult and sometimes deadlocked negotiations the Anglo-Irish Treaty was signed in London on 6 December 1921. One of the factors that persuaded them to sign was the promise by Lloyd George that if eventually the Unionists rejected unity with the rest of Ireland he would set up a boundary commission to redefine the border and it would undoubtedly

Kevin O'Higgins was elected to the Dáil in 1918 and became
Minister for Justice in the new government of 1923.

recommend the restoration of large parts of the Six Counties to the
South. He also threatened that the war would be resumed in three
days if his terms were rejected. He waved two letters in the air,
which were addressed to the Northern leader, James Craig, and
asked the Irish delegation which should he send, the one accepting
his terms, or the one rejecting them. The Irish side retired for the
night and the next morning told Lloyd George that they accepted
his terms. The twenty-six counties would now officially constitute
the Irish Free State.

The British Cabinet was satisfied that at last the age-old 'Irish
problem' was solved but Collins took a more realistic point of view.
He is reported as saying after he signed, 'I have signed my death
warrant.'

The Dáil debate on the Treaty began on 14 December and it
soon became apparent that the deputies were split down the
middle in their attitude to it. De Valera, having refused to lead the
delegation in London, now strongly opposed the Treaty. His stance
was supported by deputies Cathal Brugha, Austin Stack, Rory
O'Connor, Erskine Childers and others, including nearly all of the
women delegates. Collins defended the agreement as the best that
could be achieved. He had strong support from Kevin O'Higgins,
Richard Mulcahy, Eoin O'Duffy, William Cosgrave and others. The

Dáil went into recess for the Christmas period and when it reconvened on 3 January 1922 the arguments continued. Finally in a vote taken on 7 January 1922 the result was in favour by 64 votes to 57.

De Valera then resigned as president of Dáil Éireann and stood against Griffith in the hope that he would be re-elected, thus enabling him to sack those members of the cabinet who were pro-Treaty. However, Griffith won by 60 votes to 58.

Negotiations between the Irish authorities, led by Collins, and the British army culminated in the Lord Lieutenant surrendering Dublin Castle to Michael Collins in mid-January and a provisional government being installed. The British forces were then returned to England, the disbanding of the RIC began and a new unarmed police force, the Garda Síochána (Civic Guards), was established

In June there was a general election in which de Valera got only thirty-six seats out of a total of 128. It was plain that most of the Irish people favoured the Treaty.

The anti-Treaty Republican Army Council decided to set up its headquarters in the Four Courts on Dublin's quays. The Dublin Brigade entered the building on the night of 13 April 1922 and barricaded the windows with sandbags.

The British Cabinet then told Collins that unless he acted against the Four Courts they would regard the Treaty as being abrogated and so, early on 28 June, the Free State army attacked the Four Courts. Collins had given the occupants twenty minutes to surrender and when they refused, he gave the order to start shelling the building. The Irish Civil War had started.

21

◎

'BROTHER AGAINST BROTHER' AND 'THE HUNGRY THIRTIES'

Churchill and Lloyd George were reported to be delighted with the commencement of hostilities between the pro-Treaty and anti-Treaty supporters. When the attack on the anti-Treaty forces holding the Four Courts was largely ineffectual due to the lack of proper high-explosive shells (shrapnel shells were all they had), Lloyd George threatened to use British troops if Collins was not able to dislodge them. The provisional government resisted any such moves and by 30 June had forced the Four Courts garrison to march out of the blazing building in surrender. (Many invaluable historical documents and records were destroyed in the fire.)

The 'Irregulars', as the anti-Treaty side became known, had also occupied two hotels in O'Connell Street but these troops were easily removed. On Monday 3 July 1922 Eamon de Valera, Austin Stack and Oscar Traynor left the Hamman Hotel and passed unrecognised down the street and over O'Connell Bridge to safety. On Wednesday Cathal Brugha darted out of the blazing hotel with a gun in his hand. When ordered to surrender he refused and was shot several times. He died two days later.

The fighting in Dublin lasted for eight days and at the end of it O'Connell Street once more lay in ruins. Sixty people had been killed and over 300 wounded.

The Free State troops also had considerable success in the south of the country, capturing in succession, Waterford, Limerick, Cork city, and Fermoy from the Irregulars. In October the Dáil gave the army's military courts the right to sentence prisoners to death for treason against the new state.

Eamon de Valera commanded the Volunteers in Boland's Mills in 1916

On 12 August 1922 Arthur Griffith died, probably from stress and overwork. His death was a great shock to the people of Ireland but an even greater shock was to come ten days later when Michael Collins was shot dead in an ambush by anti-Treaty forces at Béal na mBláth in West Cork. He was actually on his way to meet IRB officers in the county with a view to finding a way to end the war when he was spotted by an anti-Treaty soldier as he and his companions passed through the area. In expectation that he would pass along the same route on his return, an ambush was set in place. After waiting in vain all day, most of the ambush party departed, leaving six men behind to dismantle the barricades and a landmine. While they were doing this Collins' convoy returned and, in a brief exchange of fire, Collins was killed by a bullet which struck him in the back of the head. He was thirty-one years old.

Collins' body was first brought to Cork city where it was received with scenes of great distress and mourning. From Cork it was brought by sea to Dublin on the *Classic*. From Friday to Sunday the body lay in state in Dublin's City Hall flanked by a guard of honour, including members of the Squad. The funeral on Sunday was the greatest since that of Parnell, with thousands marching behind the coffin carried on a gun carriage, which, ironically, had been used in the shelling of the Four Courts. At the graveside in

The first trade dispute faced by the new Free State government was the national postal strike which took place in 1922. It was provoked by the decision of the government to impose a wage cut on all civil servants in March of that year. When poorly paid postal workers pointed out that their wages had hardly increased in thirty years, an independent commission was set up to investigate wages and conditions in the postal service. The commission found that the workers were indeed badly paid, that their wages should be increased and the cuts be halted. Far from agreeing with these findings the government announced further cuts early in September and the postal strike began on the tenth of the month.

The government refused to recognise their right to strike and ordered the police and military to remove any picketers. Armoured cars were then used to clear peaceful pickets from the streets and in one incident a telephonist, Ms Olive Flood, was shot at by a soldier while she was on picket duty. Luckily for her, the bullet was deflected by a suspender buckle and she was only slightly injured. The public was outraged by the event and increasingly supported the strikers but the attacks continued.

Another bizarre incident occurred at Limerick post office when an army officer, dressed as a woman, tried to pass the picket line. When a postal worker challenged him he punched the man in the face and twenty other soldiers immediately attacked the picket line. Fifteen workers were injured in the fracas - five of them women.

Eventually the strike ended after three weeks, with the little gain to the workers beyond a promise of a further investigation of their grievances. In a final bitter twist the strikers lost their pension rights.

When Michael Collins' body was being brought from Cork to Dublin, a moving tribute to the dead leader was paid by the British navy in Cobh Harbour as the *Classic* passed down on its way to the sea. The navy ships were all drawn up in line – astern with their sailors lining the decks in salute as the Last Post was sounded.

Glasnevin Cemetery Richard Mulcahy, Collins' Chief of Staff, made a short speech and old comrades fired a volley over the grave.

After the death of Collins the new leaders of the Free State side were William Cosgrave, who had fought in 1916, Kevin O'Higgins, a young capable lawyer, who had been elected to the Dáil in 1918, Ernest Blythe, a Northern Presbyterian who had been a supporter of Arthur Griffith, and Richard Mulcahy. These men were determined to consolidate the Free State and to crush the Irregulars.

On 9 September 1922 the Dáil reassembled without the presence of the Republicans and William Cosgrave was elected as President of the Executive Council (head of government) of the Irish Free State.

William Cosgrave took part in the Easter Rising and
was later elected head of government of the Irish Free State.

In October 1922 the Republicans decided to form a 'national government' with Eamon de Valera as president and Austin Stack, Seán T O'Kelly, Liam Mellows and others as ministers. Erskine Childers was appointed as Minister for Publicity. Childers had been on the run in Cork and Kerry and was now asked to come back to Dublin. On his way he was arrested on 10 November by Free State troops in Wicklow and was found to be in possession of a revolver – this was a capital offence under new government legislation. (The revolver was an ornamental one which had been given to him sometime before by Michael Collins.) He was tried secretly in a military court on 17 November, found guilty and executed seven days later in Beggars Bush Barracks.

Childers was not the first to be executed under the new powers, however. On the same day as his trial, four other young men who had been found in possession of guns were shot. On 30 November three more prisoners were executed. They had been captured immediately after they had attempted to blow up a building occupied by Free State forces.

The Irish Free State officially came into existence on 6 December 1922, having received the Royal Assent the day before. The man appointed to represent British interests as Governor-General was Timothy Healy, who had done much to blacken Parnell's character at the end of his career. Healy now took up residence in the Viceregal Lodge in the Phoenix Park.

On 27 November Liam Lynch, the Irregulars' Chief of Staff, stated that all TDs who had voted for the emergency powers and the military courts, would be shot on sight.

The next month, 8 December 1922, four more Republican prisoners, Rory O'Connor (former secretary to Kevin O'Higgins and best man at his wedding), Liam Mellows, Joseph McKelvey and Richard Barrett, who had surrendered in the Four Courts, were taken from their cells and executed. There had been no trial and the reason given for the executions was that they were a warning to others but they were principally as a reprisal for the shooting dead, near the Ormond Hotel on the Dublin quays, of a Free State officer and TD, named Seán Hales.

The shooting of Dáil TDs ceased but the Republicans then started a campaign against the property of supporters of the government. Houses, offices, business premises, even a passenger train, were all destroyed. On 13 January 1923 Beechpark, the home of William Cosgrave, was burned to the ground. The government side replied in kind; a supporter of de Valera, called Fintan Lalor, was taken from his lodgings and his body was later found near Milltown Golf Club in South Dublin. Finally on 24 May the Republican leadership gave the order to cease fire and dump arms, but they still did not accept the legitimacy of the Free State.

The civil war had cost the state enormous amounts of money and hundreds of deaths. (A figure of 4,000 to 5,000 military deaths has been estimated for the combined pro- and anti-Treaty forces. The seventy-seven Republicans executed by the Free State forces were later to loom large in the pantheon of heroes for Fianna Fáil supporters.)

A general election was held in August 1923 in spite of the extremely unsettled state of the country. The newly founded Cumann na nGaedheal party led by William Cosgrave, which represented the pro-Treaty side, won 63 seats. The anti-Treaty side led by Eamon de Valera gained 44 seats and Labour won 14 seats.

When the Dáil convened after the general election the successful Republican candidates refused to take their seats because to do so would mean they would have to take the Oath of Allegiance to 'HM King George V, his heirs and successors'. The Labour TDs then agreed to form the official opposition so that a semblance of democratic government could be established. The new government performed quite efficiently for the following four years with order being restored by the firm action of Kevin O'Higgins as Minister for Justice and General Richard Mulcahy as Minister for Defence.

It was during the term of this government that the problem of Northern Ireland really came to the fore. The 'Government of Ireland Act' which had been passed in 1920 established the principle of a separate parliament for 'Northern Ireland'. The proportion of the province to remain under the control of the Protestant Unionists was not specified but would be decided at a later date. The Irish Civil War sidelined the problem until well into 1923 and in fact the Free State government probably hoped that the problem would go away.

In 1926 de Valera founded the new political party, Fianna Fáil, which had quite a successful debut in the general election the following year. They won 44 seats, while the Cumann na nGaedheal party only did marginally better with 47 seats. Although the number of Fianna Fáil seats was only equal to that of the Republican successes of the 1923 election, it was a good showing, considering that many of their supporters had deserted them because of their abstentionist policy. Many of these voters had voted for the Labour Party purely out of frustration.

De Valera now set about devising some way of taking up seats in the Dáil. Three constitutional lawyers said that Fianna Fáil

———— ◎ ————

On 13 August 1927 the leader of the Labour Party, Tom Johnson, William O'Brien of the Irish Transport and General Workers Union, and RJP Mortished, another trade union activist, held a secret meeting in Powerscourt Arms Hotel in Enniskerry, County Wicklow. During the meeting they discussed who would be the ministers in a coalition government that would not include Fianna Fáil. The list of names was eventually agreed but at the end of the meeting the list was torn up and thrown into the waste paper basket in the room.

As the three men left to make their way back to the city by bus, RM Wylie of *The Irish Times* noticed them standing at the bus stop. He made some enquiries and discovered the venue for the meeting. He then went back to the hotel, searched the room and found the list in the wastepaper basket. The next day he published the list of proposed cabinet members in the paper.

———— ◎ ————

When Deputy Jinks failed to turn up for the Dáil vote on the motion of no confidence there were rumours afterwards that some Cumann na nGaedheal supporters had got Jinks drunk and put him on the train home to Sligo. One newspaper correspondent wrote of 'High Jinks in the Dáil!'

———— ◎ ————

In the general election of 1932 there were widespread accusations of vote-rigging, impersonation and intimidation in connection with the Fianna Fáil victory. Many 'dead' people cast their votes and some people are reputed to have voted fifty times!

———— ◎ ————

deputies could take their seats without the oath before the president was elected. So de Valera and the other successful candidates went to the Dáil building and demanded entrance to the chamber. They were told that they could do so only if they took the oath. When they refused to do this, the doors to the chamber were locked and they walked out on to the street again. There, de Valera addressed the large crowd that had gathered and explained how taking the 'false' oath would be a betrayal of the Irish people.

Next de Valera announced that they would start a campaign to force the government to hold a referendum to abolish the oath. But then on 10 July 1927 Kevin O'Higgins, Minister for Home Affairs, was assassinated as he walked to Mass in Booterstown in the south of the city. He had no bodyguard and was unarmed. De Valera's supporters were suspected as being the perpetrators but he denounced the killers in the strongest language and it later emerged that the attackers were IRA men who were driving to a GAA match in Wexford. They had noticed O'Higgins without a bodyguard and availed of the opportunity to publicise their cause. The IRA command had not ordered the killing.

The government reacted by proposing a new Public Safety Bill and an Electoral Amendment Act, which would require every candidate in subsequent elections to swear an affidavit that he or she would take the Oath of Allegiance. Cosgrave also proposed to hold an election for the seats held by the abstentionists.

The bills were passed on 4 August 1927 after an all-night sitting of the Dáil. A week later the Fianna Fáil members again went to the Dáil. Again they said they would not take the oath but de Valera removed the Bible from the table and signed his name in the book, which contained the names of those who had taken the oath. By this 'sleight of hand' it was deemed that the necessary formalities had been fulfilled.

As soon as the new session began Fianna Fáil proposed a motion of no confidence in the government. The crucial vote was set for 16 August 1927. Before that date Labour, led by Tom Johnson, and the National Progressive Democratic Party, led by William Redmond, son of John, came to an agreement to support a coalition government which did not include Fianna Fáil.

On 16 August 1927 there was high drama in the Dáil chamber when the motion of no confidence was debated for four hours.

———— ◎ ————

When the Northern Prime Minister Andrews was accused in the early 1940s of employing twenty-eight Catholic porters in government buildings he answered that he had checked on the matter and found that 'there are thirty Protestants and only one Roman Catholic there temporarily'.

In 1926 as Minister for Labour when he discovered two 'Free Staters' in his ministry he ordered that they be disqualified on the spot.

———— ◎ ————

One Northern minister did not want to have even the most junior Catholic clerk or typist in his ministry. When he was surprised to learn that there was one such telephonist appointed he refused to use the telephone until the employee was moved.

———— ◎ ————

When Lord Craigavon opened a new session of the Ulster parliament on Friday 30 September 1932 without making reference to a motion from a Labour MP, Jack Beattie, regarding the plight of the unemployed, Beattie jumped up and seized the mace. There was uproar in the house and another Labour member, Tommy Henderson, joined in to support Beattie. When the Speaker called for order, Beattie shouted 'I am going to put this out of action. The House indulges in hypocrisy while there are starving thousands outside.' He then threw the mace on the floor and walked out of the chamber. Again there was bedlam and Henderson shouted 'What about the 78,000 unemployed who are starving?' When the government benches shouted 'God save the King', he shouted 'God save the People' and followed Beattie outside.

———— ◎ ————

The Eucharistic Congress of June 1932 was enthusiastically celebrated by Northern Ireland Catholics with thousands travelling to Dublin and the Catholic areas of towns such as Belfast, Derry, Newry and others being gaily decorated for the occasion. James Craig, now Lord Craigavon, responded at the following month's Twelfth of July celebration by stating 'Ours is a Protestant government and I am an Orangeman.'

———— ◎ ————

When the vote was taken there was a tie at 71 votes each for the government and opposition. (One Labour deputy was in Canada and his leader, Johnson, had forgotten to request his return home, and another deputy, John Jinks from Sligo, was not in the House). The Ceann Comhairle (Speaker) gave his casting vote to the government.

In the general election of 1932 Fianna Fáil was more successful but still ended up some seats short of an overall majority. After consultations with Labour, and an agreement to introduce some social legislation, Fianna Fáil and Labour agreed to form a coalition government. On 9 March 1932 Fianna Fáil took office for the first time, with the support of Labour. They had a combined overall majority of 13.

There were various 'scares' at the time that Cumann na nGaedheal would try to prevent Fianna Fáil taking power. When the Fianna Fáil deputies entered the Dáil for the first time after the election they were carrying revolvers which had been issued to them beforehand. However, there was certainly no threat from William Cosgrave – he had too much respect for the institutions of the state. Once in office de Valera proceeded to remove some of the old restrictions and one of his first acts was to abolish the Oath of Allegiance to the British Crown. He also accepted the presidency of the council of the League of Nations, thereby emphasising that Ireland was an independent state.

In February 1932, one month before Fianna Fáil had taken office, the Army Comrades Association was formed with Dr TF O'Higgins (brother of the murdered Kevin) as its elected leader. Irish army ex-servicemen flocked to join and in a few months it had about 3,000 members.

The growth of the association was seen as a threat by the IRA, which had begun to exhibit left-wing tendencies at the time and who now wholeheartedly supported Fianna Fáil. The tough attitude of the previous Cumann na nGaedheal government to the IRA had provoked bitter enmity. They had celebrated the Fianna Fáil victory with reference to 'the downfall of the Cosgrave murder gang' also stating that 'the IRA stood firm and defeated Cosgrave and coercianism'. The Army Comrades and the IRA had clashed frequently, particularly when the Comrades were acting as guards during Cumann na nGaedheal meetings. The IRA tried to prevent

The distribution of housing and employment throughout the Northern province was blatantly biased in favour of the Protestants and was to be a source of bitter resentment for many years. In July 1933 Sir Basil Brooke made a speech at Newtownbutler where he declared 'There are a great number of Protestants and Orangemen who employ Roman Catholics. I feel I can speak freely on the subject as I have not a Roman Catholic about my place . . . I would appeal to Loyalists, therefore, whenever possible, to employ Protestant lads and lassies.' When the Nationalist MP, Cahir Healy, protested in Stormont later, Lord Craigavon replied 'There is not one of my colleagues who does not entirely agree with him and I would not ask him to withdraw one word.'

Basil Brooke (Lord Brookeborough) became Prime Minister
of Northern Ireland in 1943 and held office until 1963.
He was succeeded by Captain Terence O'Neill.

the meetings taking place, using the slogan 'No free speech for traitors' as justification.

The growth of fascism in Catholic countries like Italy and Spain inspired many in Ireland to follow the same path. When Eoin O'Duffy was sacked as Garda Commissioner by de Valera on 22 February 1933 he was free to devote his energies to the Army Comrades Association and in July of the same year he was elected leader. The association was then renamed the National Guard. The members chose a blue shirt as their uniform and the flag of St Patrick as their banner. O'Duffy saw himself as an Irish Mussolini but at the same time he did not aspire to be a dictator nor did he have the necessary qualities to become one.

Nevertheless he threatened to lead a march on the Dáil on 13 August 1933 – the day of commemoration for Arthur Griffith and Michael Collins. In reply, the government banned the march, placed an armed guard on Leinster House and raided homes of known 'Blueshirts' in the search for arms. In August the National Guard was banned. Military tribunals were set up and the full force of the Offences against the State Act was brought to bear on all offenders.

The three opposition parties, Cumann na nGaedheal, the National Centre Party and the National Guard, then came together to form a single party on 8 September 1933. The United Ireland Party (or Fine Gael) appointed Eoin O'Duffy as leader but since he was not a member of parliament, William Cosgrave was elected leader of the parliamentary party.

For several months after the formation of Fine Gael there were violent clashes between Blueshirts and IRA supporters. Then on 30 November 1933 police raided the party headquarters and also the homes of hundreds of Fine Gael supporters. Next the government introduced a bill making it illegal to wear military uniforms and badges or use military titles in support of a political party. The carrying of weapons, even sticks, was forbidden at public meetings. The bill was passed in the Dáil but the Seanad (Senate) rejected it. A week later the government introduced a bill to abolish the Seanad itself. In September O'Duffy was manoeuvered into resigning and although he later tried (unsuccessfully) to regain power, it effectively ended his role in Irish politics.

With the ending of the Blueshirt threat de Valera was able to

———— ◎ ————

In 1934 Lord Brookeborough urged loyalists not to employ Catholics, 'ninety-nine per cent of whom are disloyal'. The same year, Prime Minister Craig declared 'All I boast is that we are a Protestant parliament and a Protestant state.'

———— ◎ ————

With the outbreak of World War Two in September 1939 a blackout was imposed all over the Six Counties of Northern Ireland but not in the remaining three counties of Donegal, Cavan and Monaghan. This led to the bizarre situation of towns, such as Strabane and Belcoo, on one side of the border being in complete darkness while those, such as Lifford and Blacklion, just across on the other side still had lights showing.

———— ◎ ————

turn his attention to the IRA. He was becoming increasingly annoyed with their activities. When he was giving a radio broadcast after an army march-past in Dublin on St Patrick's Day 1936 the IRA managed to jam the broadcast. Most of the speech could not be heard and at one time a voice was heard to say, 'Hello comrades. For the last half-hour we have just witnessed a very fine display of English militarism.'

In June that year de Valera declared the IRA to be an illegal organisation and Maurice Twomey, a leading IRA figure, was arrested and jailed for membership of an illegal organisation.

In 1937 de Valera succeeded in getting a new constitution passed for 'a sovereign, independent, democratic' Ireland. He also instituted the office of President of Ireland in place of that of Governor-General and Dr Douglas Hyde, founder of the Gaelic League, was elected as first holder of the office. The counties of Ireland, minus the six counties of 'Northern Ireland' (Derry, Antrim, Down, Tyrone, Fermanagh and Armagh), were to be known henceforth as Éire 'or in the English language, Ireland'. The fact that Éire only consisted of twenty-six counties was looked upon as a temporary measure and de Valera insisted that 'the national territory consists of the whole island of Ireland'.

When World War Two began in September 1939 the Dáil passed a bill declaring Ireland's neutrality and the period known as 'The Emergency' began. There were those who felt that Éire should have sided with the Axis powers against England but de Valera in fact pursued a 'pro-Allies neutrality' during the conflict. About 50,000 Irish men and women served in the British forces, and Allied personnel from aircraft or ships who ended up in neutral Éire were quietly returned across the border. Axis prisoners, on the other hand, were interned for the duration of the war.

Nor did his government ease up on suppression of the activities of the IRA. The rift between Fianna Fáil and the organisation became complete when a government ammunition dump, the Magazine Fort in Dublin's Phoenix Park, was raided by the IRA on 23 December 1939 and thirteen lorry-loads of ammunition (almost the entire Irish army's stock) were stolen.

These and other acts forced de Valera to crack down hard on the IRA. Many were arrested and sent to detention camps, and some were executed by firing squad.

———— ◎ ————

On Monday 3 October 1932 over 60,000 unemployed workers from all over Belfast gathered to march in a torch-lit procession to the Custom House. A further 7,000 marched the following day and prevented the trams from running by lying on the tramlines. On Wednesday another huge demonstration took place in spite of a police ban and the crowds were baton-charged repeatedly and eventually beaten back to Sandy Row.

A final demonstration for the unemployed was banned by the government but the Unemployed Workers' Committee decided to go ahead anyway. The five assembly points were raided by baton-wielding police and a furious battle ensued between the police and stone-throwing crowds. The worst violence took place in the lower Falls where the police opened fire on the crowds who had erected barricades. A Protestant flower seller was shot dead and a Catholic was mortally wounded. The Northern Ireland Labour Party noted that the police only opened fire in Catholic areas. The imposition of a curfew brought that day's disturbances to an end but the next day another death occurred in the York Street area when police opened fire on looters.

———— ◎ ————

All during the 1920s there were sectarian incidents in Belfast but 1935 saw a new level of violence. The celebration of the jubilee of George V led to vicious attacks on Catholics where twenty-six people were injured and forty homes destroyed in May and June. On the evening of 12 July rioting broke out as Orangemen returning home went on the rampage in Catholic areas. One of the worst ever nights of rioting followed by the end of which two civilians were dead and thirty-five injured, three policemen were wounded, fourteen homes were set on fire and forty-seven others wrecked. The rioting and mayhem continued night after night and did not stop until near the end of August, leaving eight Protestants and five Catholics dead, with over 2,000 Catholics and a small number of Protestants driven from their homes.

———— ◎ ————

The fact that most employers in the new state of Northern Ireland were Protestant inevitably led to discrimination against Catholics. As an example of this, the huge ship-building firm of Harland and Wolff, situated close to a Catholic area, only employed 400 Catholics in a workforce of 10,000. Two other firms, Mackie's Foundry and the Sirocco Works, although situated in Catholic areas, had very few Catholic employees. Even though Catholics were denied employment many ordinary working-class Protestants regarded them as work-shy. One popular Loyalist ballad had the verse

> And when their babies learn to talk
> They shout 'discrimination',
> Their dad just lies in bed all day
> And lives upon the nation.

Edward Carson had a very low opinion of the Celtic race. 'The Celts have done nothing for Ireland but create trouble and disorder. Irishmen who have turned out successful have not, in any case that I know of, been of true Celtic origin'

Edward Carson was born in Dublin and became a leading barrister. He was the relentless prosecuting council at the trial of Oscar Wilde. He is widely regarded as the father of Northern Ireland.

22

◎

FROM THE 'EMERGENCY' TO THE PRESENT DAY

Even though the Irish Free State was neutral in World War Two it did not escape entirely the horrors of war. In 1940 three people were killed in an accidental bombing by German aircraft at Campile, County Wexford. In January 1941 German bombs fell in Terenure and Harold's Cross in Dublin but there were no casualties and little damage was caused.

Soon after the outbreak of war Lady Londonderry, wife of the Northern Ireland Minister for Education, complained to her husband 'All sorts of rot going on here. Air raid warnings and blackouts! As if anyone cared or wished to bomb Belfast.' The German High Command thought otherwise and launched massive bombing raids on Belfast on 15 April 1941. Terrible devastation was caused and hundreds of fires burned out of control. The situation was beyond the capacity of the city's fire services and Prime Minister Basil Brooke gave permission for a request to Dublin for help. De Valera agreed immediately and thirteen fire engines from Dublin, Dun Laoghaire, Drogheda and Dundalk rushed northwards. Over nine hundred people were killed in the raids and about six thousand refugees fled to Dublin, while many more thousands moved out of the city to the countryside.

During those same raids two parachute bombs were dropped near the Buncrana Road in Derry. One of these caused some damage to houses and railway carriages but the other fell on ex-servicemen's homes in Messine Park and killed fifteen people, destroyed five houses and left over 100 people homeless.

Another raid took place on Belfast on 4–5 May 1941 in which 96,000 incendiary bombs and 257 tons of high-explosive bombs were dropped. Again thirteen fire brigades rushed up from the Free State but there was little they could do. Once more there was an exodus from the city to small towns and villages in the province, so that 220,000 people had left by the end of May.

On the night of 31 May 1941 the last German bombing raid on the country took place, not on Northern Ireland, but on Dublin. A bomb which fell in the Phoenix Park near the zoo only caused minor damage, including the windows of Áras an Uachtaráin, but it created consternation and panic among the zoo animals. Other bombs fell on the North Strand area and on the North Circular Road, Ballybough, and at Summerhill Parade near the Christian Brothers' O'Connell Schools. Many houses were demolished and the final casualty list including thirty-two dead and over eighty injured. (After the war the British Air Ministry confirmed in 1946 that they had diverted the wireless beam used for navigation purposes by the Germans, who then thought they were over Britain when they released their bombs. The Irish government was in the 1950s paid £327,000 in compensation by the Germans.)

In February 1942 the government announced that, due to grain shortages, bread would be made from 100% wheaten flour. This produced a much darker loaf than before, in other words, the famous 'black' bread of the war years. Rationing was introduced in May of that year. Every household was issued with ration books containing different-coloured numbered coupons. At first the clothing allowance for a year was fifty-two coupons but forty coupons were needed for a man's suit and there were such strong protests that the allowance was increased to seventy-eight for the year. Other items rationed were tea (about fifteen grams) per person per week, footwear, sugar and butter.

During the war the fuel situation in cities and towns became acute. Coal supplies were extremely low and while at first the allowance of coal per household for the months of February and March 1942 was two bags, by April this was cut to zero – all coal was needed for industry. More and more the citizens had to rely on turf. In October that year the Turf Controller (there was such an official!) announced that there were 500,000 to 600,000 tons of turf available but that there was no place to store it. The solution was simple. Dublin's Phoenix Park provided ample space and soon huge stacks of turf along the roads through the park became a familiar sight. In fact they remained there long after the war had ended.

During John A Costello's first term as Taoiseach he visited
Canada in 1948 to attend the Ottawa Conference. During a
reception in his honour the Governor-General of Canada,
Earl Alexander, chose as a centrepiece for the table a silver
replica of the 'Roaring Meg' cannon of Siege of Derry fame.
Costello was so annoyed at the blatant use of such a
Unionist symbol that he declared that the Twenty-six
Counties would withdraw from the Commonwealth and
become a Republic.

John A Costello passed the Republic of Ireland Act in 1949
which declared the state to be a republic.

Eamon de Valera became President of Ireland in 1959 and
served for two terms. Prior to his retirement in 1973 he was
the world's oldest head of state at 91 years of age.

De Valera was Taoiseach in seven governments, Seán
Lemass and Jack Lynch were Taoiseach in three, and
Charlie Haughey in four.

At the end of the war, on 13 May 1945, Winston Churchill made a victory speech in which he paid tribute to Northern Ireland for its part in the World War just ended but he bitterly criticised Éire's neutrality:

> . . . had it not been for the loyalty and friendship of Northern Ireland we should have been forced to come to close quarters with Mr de Valera. However . . . his Majesty's government never laid a violent hand upon them though at times it would have been quite easy and quite natural, and we left the Dublin government to frolic with the Germans and later with Japanese representatives to their hearts' content.

De Valera replied on 17 May.

> Mr Churchill makes it clear that in certain circumstances he would have violated our neutrality and that he would justify his action by Britain's necessity. It seems strange to me that Mr Churchill does not see that this, if accepted, would mean that Britain's necessity would become a moral code that, when this necessity became sufficiently great, other people's rights were not to count . . . this same code is precisely why we have the disastrous succession of wars . . .

De Valera's dignified and restrained reply won the universal approval of the Irish people. (He could have pointed out that over 50,000 Irish men and women served in the Allied forces, that he allowed British aircraft to fly over Donegal to attack German U-boats in the North Atlantic, had returned rescued Allied servicemen across the border to rejoin their units, and many other incidents in his 'pro-Allied neutrality'. Also, had Churchill launched an attack on the Twenty-six Counties who knows what effect that would have had on Irish Americans and the Irish members of the Allied forces.)

The de Valera government, after sixteen years in office, was defeated in 1948 and was replaced by a coalition of parties under the leadership of John A Costello of Fine Gael. On a visit to Canada in September that year he announced that Ireland would become a republic and in 1949 the Coalition government declared that Ireland was a republic outside the British Commonwealth – all of Ireland in theory but in reality only the twenty-six counties under Dublin rule. The British government responded by passing the Ireland Act of June 1949, which declared that 'in no event will Northern Ireland or any part thereof cease to be a part of His Majesty's dominions and of the United Kingdom without the consent of the parliament of Northern Ireland.'

One of the most dynamic members of Costello's Coalition government was the Minister for Health, Dr Noel Browne of Clann na Poblachta. He immediately set about eradicating the terrible scourge of tuberculosis from the country. About one person in every 800 of the population was being killed by it and Browne had lost both his parents and his eldest sister from the disease. Browne attacked the problem with such speed and vigour that the death rate fell dramatically but his unorthodox methods and disregard for red tape had offended some members of the powerful medical profession. They reacted angrily to the 'Mother and Child' scheme proposed by Browne to provide free maternity care to mothers and free medical attention for all children up to sixteen years of age. The doctors were actively supported by the Catholic authorities who said the scheme was an infringement of the rights of the family and could lead to abuse. They were particularly against proposals to provide sex education to women because they thought it would lead to contraception and even abortion.

The pressure grew so great that Dr Browne was forced to resign, thus causing a general election in 1951, which was won by Fianna Fáil. De Valera retired from the Dáil and was elected President of Ireland in 1959. He was succeeded as Taoiseach by Seán Lemass. Together with a brilliant civil servant named TK Whitaker, Lemass produced Ireland's first real plan to expand the country's economy on every front. The plan was very successful with a sustained growth rate of 4% per annum for the years 1959 to 1964 – unemployment and emigration was cut, investment increased and

Seán Lemass took part in the War of Independence and became
Taoiseach in 1959. He is largely credited with the great expansion
of the country's economy in the years 1959–64.

national output soared.

Attempts to repeat the performance in the following years were
not so successful, however, due mainly to outside events and, in
particular, the imposition of import levies by Britain in the mid-
1960s.

The political situation in Northern Ireland had begun to intrude
more and more into life in the Republic in the 1960s. During the
previous decade the IRA had become more active, attacking
border posts and assassinating policemen. Between 1956 and 1961
Belfast became the centre of a bitter sectarian war between the
IRA and two Protestant organisations, the Ulster Volunteer Force
and the Ulster Freedom Movement. The authorities in the North
cracked down particularly heavily on the IRA, imprisoning over
100 members and supporters without trial. The Catholic areas
exploded with resentment and large parts of Belfast became no-go
areas to the police. The Unionist government continued its policy
of discrimination in its usual insensitive way by creating a new
town, called Craigavon, in County Armagh and by choosing the
Protestant town of Coleraine to be the centre for the new
University of Ulster. The aim was, no doubt, to restrict the
education of Catholics and so diminish their employment
possibilities.

The possibility of a change for the better arose with the election of Terence O'Neill as Prime Minister of Northern Ireland in 1963. He did not share the almost pathological hatred of Catholics of his predecessors and set about improving relations with the minority population. He visited Catholic towns, schools and institutions and actually met the Taoiseach, Seán Lemass, in 1965, an action that was regarded by some Unionists as akin to treason.

This more enlightened policy towards the Catholic minority raised the ire of the more rabid hardline Unionists as exemplified by the Reverend Ian Paisley of the Free Presbyterian Church. He denounced O'Neill as an 'arch traitor' and when the Ulster Volunteer Force was proscribed by O'Neill in 1966, Paisley organised violent opposition to a legal Catholic march. He was arrested, tried and jailed for three months as a consequence.

Ian Paisley vehemently denounces any rapprochement
between the two parts of the island.

By this time Catholic tolerance of the status quo was wearing thin and in 1967 the Northern Ireland Civil Rights Movement, based on the civil rights campaign of America's Black population, was established.

Matters came to the boil in 1968 when in June that year a Miss Emily Beattie, a nineteen-year-old Protestant, unmarried and without children, secretary to a local council's solicitor, was allocated a council house in the small village of Caledon, County Tyrone. A Catholic family who were squatting in the house was evicted but then Austin Currie, a young Nationalist MP for the area, began squatting in the house himself. He was removed, in the full glare of the television cameras, by a policeman who happened to be the brother of Miss Beattie.

The outrage which followed resulted in various protest meetings and on 24 August 1968 over 2,500 protesters gathered in Coalisland before marching to Dungannon. Before the march began the organisers were warned that they would not be allowed to march into the town. The march proceeded peacefully along the eight kilometres between the towns but as it approached Dungannon the way was blocked by 400 RUC men with dogs. An ugly confrontation was narrowly averted by appeals from the leaders, such as Austin Currie, Gerry Fitt, Erskine Holmes and Betty Sinclair. The latter told the marchers 'what we have done today will go down in history and in this way we will be more effective in showing the world that we are a peaceful people asking for our civil rights in an orderly manner.'

The next civil rights demonstration took place in Derry City on 5 October 1968 when over 400 marchers assembled at the Waterside railway station. Among them were John Hume, Gerry Fitt (with three Westminster MPs), Eddie McAteer, Austin Currie, Eamon McCann, Betty Sinclair, Michael Farrell, Bernadette Devlin, and other prominent activists. Before the march began RUC County Inspector, William Meharg, warned them that they would not be allowed to march 'in this part of the Maiden City'. As the marchers headed the short distance along Duke Street to Craigavon Bridge across the Foyle they were brutally stopped by police with batons and several of the march leaders were injured. This was followed by an indiscriminate attack on any demonstrators who came within reach of police batons.

The violence then spread to the City side of the river and furious battles between police and Catholic youths from the Bogside continued into that night and the following day.

It so happened that Gay O'Brien, a cameraman from the Irish national television station, Raidió Teilefís Éireann (RTÉ), had managed to record the unprovoked attacks by the police on the marchers and the terrible scenes were flashed around the world. So it was that a few hundred feet of television film changed the course of the history of the Six Counties.

Two weeks after the march in Derry a group of Queen's University students led by Bernadette Devlin and Eamon McCann formed a non-sectarian organisation called the People's Democracy. It had six objectives: one person one vote, an end to gerrymandering, free speech, an end to job discrimination, a fair allocation of housing, and the repeal of the Special Powers Act.

Towards the end of 1970 Taoiseach Jack Lynch, said he was shocked when told that arms had reached Northern Nationalists through the activities of some of his ministers. (On 13 December 2001 *Prime Time*, a programme on RTÉ, claimed that, far from being unaware of what was happening, he had actually ordered that arms and ammunition be sent to the border for use by the Nationalists if they were being massacred.)

In the subsequent Arms Trial all of the accused, including Charles Haughey, were found not guilty. The result was greeted ecstatically by Haughey's supporters who gathered outside the courthouse and inside the Four Courts Hotel on the Dublin quays. They shouted 'We want Charlie' and 'Lynch must go'. Haughey himself called for Lynch's resignation. But Jack Lynch was made of stern stuff. He called for a vote of confidence in the Dáil in November. Haughey and Kevin Boland had threatened to vote against the government but in the end neither of them did so.

Jack Lynch, 'Honest Jack', succeeded Seán Lemass as Taoiseach.
His exchange of visits with the Northern premier, Terence O'Neill,
helped greatly to improve relations between the two parts of the island.

Charles Haughey was dismissed from Jack Lynch's government along with Neil Blaney for alleged involvement in arms smuggling.

The next civil rights march to hit the headlines started on New Year's Day 1969 when a group of young people organised by the People's Democracy set out to march the 112 kilometres from Belfast to Derry. The marchers were harassed and beset all along the route by Loyalists led by Major Ronald Bunting, one of Paisley's lieutenants. It emerged later that there was much police collusion with the Paisleyites.

Nevertheless the marchers struggled on but encountered an elaborate ambush at Burntollet Bridge on the Derry-Claudy road. A fierce attack with bottles, stones, crowbars and sticks wreaked havoc on the marchers and those who tried to escape across the fields were batoned back onto the road by police. (Many of the attackers were later identified as being members of the B-specials.) When those marchers who were capable of doing so finally struggled into Derry they were again attacked by Protestant mobs. The police did not stand idly by – in fact they quickly disappeared from the scene. Later that night the police actually ran amok, wrecking the local Wellworths' store and invading the Bogside and causing general mayhem.

Attempts at reform by the Northern Prime Minister, Terence O'Neill, led to calls by some of his backbenchers for his resignation. Stormont elections were held in February 1969 and

Bernadette Devlin was the youngest ever woman to be elected to Westminster and the youngest MP for 200 years.

Bernadette Devlin was a prominent activist in the
Northern Ireland Civil Rights movement.

In the general election of 1974 Bernadette Devlin lost her seat and she never again held elected office. She did, however, continue to articulate her radical views and in January 1981 a Protestant paramilitary gang attacked herself and her husband in their home and left them severely wounded.

even though the pro-O'Neill side won twice as many seats as their opponents Terence O'Neill resigned on 28 April and was succeeded by Major James Chichester-Clark. (Before O'Neill resigned he had granted the principle of 'one person, one vote' on 22 April.) That same April Bernadette Devlin was elected to the British House of Commons for the constituency of Mid-Ulster.

Violence continued, particularly in Belfast, all during the following months and the tension mounted as the time for the traditional Apprentice Boys' March in Derry approached.

On the morning of 12 July 1969 15,000 Orangemen gathered in Derry for their march. For the most of the day events passed off peacefully but then as the parade passed along the city walls overlooking the Bogside several of the marchers threw pennies down to the Catholic areas below. Some youths from the Bogside replied by throwing stones at the marchers and within minutes a full-scale riot had developed. Police in riot gear then charged and efforts by John Hume, Ivan Cooper and Eddie McAteer to restrain the crowd resulted in their being swept aside; Cooper was knocked unconscious by a stone but Bernadette Devlin, on the other hand, took an active part in manning the barricades. Absolute chaos then ensued, involving Bogsiders, police and Loyalists. The violence raged all day and all night with volleys of 'riot-control' CS gas being fired into the crowd by the police. Taoiseach Jack Lynch went on air to say that the Republic 'can no longer stand by and see innocent people injured, and perhaps worse'. This further enraged the Loyalists who took it as a threat to use the Irish army to defend the Derry Catholics. British soldiers were then dispatched to Derry and on 14 August 1969 eighty members of the Prince of Wales Own Regiment took over from the police in Waterloo Place and an uneasy calm descended on the Bogside. The 'Battle of the Bogside' was over.

Events might have calmed down in Derry but the happenings there had led to widespread rioting in other parts of the province, with attacks on police barracks in Strabane, Newry, Coalisland, Dungannon, Armagh and Dungiven. Belfast soon caught the fever and crowds of Loyalists and Nationalists began to assemble in the flashpoints of the Shankill Road and the Falls Road.

Police raced to the area in armoured cars which were immediately attacked with stones, bottles and petrol bombs. That

———— ◎ ————

The findings of an investigation by the Cameron Commission in 1966 illustrated how the gerrymandering system worked in Derry. The adult population of the city consisted of 20,102 Catholics and 10,272 Protestants but, because only ratepayers had the vote, the electorate was 14,429 Catholics and 8,781 Protestants. The South Ward containing 10,047 Catholics and 1,138 Protestants elected 8 Nationalists, the North Ward with 3,946 Protestants and 2,530 Catholics elected 8 Unionists, while the Waterside ward with 3,697 Protestants and 1,852 Catholics elected 4 Unionists. Consequently less than 9,000 Protestants elected 12 Unionists while more than 14,000 Catholics elected 8 Nationalists.

———— ◎ ————

The worst winter of the twentieth century hit the country in 1947. The previous summer had been one of the wettest for decades with the result that huge quantities of oats, wheat, barley and potatoes lay rotting in the fields by autumn. Thousands of volunteers from towns and cities went to the aid of desperate farmers in an attempt to save what they could. Then to add to the misery, on 24 January there came a violent snowstorm which was followed by more arctic conditions until the middle of March. It snowed on nearly thirty days during that period, with some snowfalls lasting for twenty hours. All parts of the country were affected and many were cut off for weeks. Several people died in the blizzards and the farmers lost thousands of sheep and cattle. Public transport was severely disrupted and very many homes were without fuel as coal and turf supplies were exhausted.

———— ◎ ————

night police and B-specials entered the area on foot with large crowds of Loyalists following behind. Very soon someone started shooting and the police armoured cars opened fire with their Browning machine guns – one of the bullets killing a nine-year-old boy in Divis Street Flats. The Loyalist mobs set fire to many homes with petrol bombs and soon fighting between Nationalists and Loyalists erupted in Divis Street and the Ardoyne. By dawn of 15 August six people had been fatally wounded, twelve factories destroyed and more than one hundred houses destroyed by petrol bombs, with a further three hundred badly damaged.

Later that day soldiers from the Queen's Regiment moved into the area and were welcomed by the people of the Falls with cups of tea. Even so there was further violence that night, with nearly every house in Bombay Street being destroyed and others in Brookfield Street being damaged by fire.

The Cameron Commission was set up by the British government to enquire into the causes of the riots and its report published in September 1969 highlighted the discrimination suffered by Catholics in housing, political gerrymandering, the Special Powers Act and the absence of 'one person, one vote'. The following month the Hunt Report recommended the abolition of the B-specials and the complete reform of the RUC. Loyalist riots followed, which included attacks on British soldiers during which twenty-two soldiers were injured and two attackers were killed.

The British government stood firm, however, and forced through the reforms recommended by Cameron and Hunt but it did not abolish the Stormont government as demanded by the Catholic population.

In 1970 the IRA split into the 'Official IRA', which had left-wing tendencies, and the traditional wing which called themselves the 'Provisional IRA', which had the single aim of getting the British out of Northern Ireland and uniting the country.

Inevitably the British army became more and more involved over the succeeding months and in the early hours of Monday, 9 August 1971, squads of soldiers, accompanied by RUC Special Branch officers, swept through Nationalist parts of Belfast seizing suspects. Altogether 342 men were taken into custody and brought to various holding centres. Some 104 were later released and the rest were brought to Crumlin Road jail or the prison ship, the

Maidstone, in Belfast docks. The arrests and internments were entirely one-sided – every single one of the men on the army's 452 arrest list was a Nationalist.

Nationalist Belfast erupted when the news spread and two soldiers and eight civilians were killed. Two days later eleven people were killed in Belfast and over 240 houses were destroyed by fire. Many Protestant families fled from Nationalist Ardoyne, some setting fire to their homes as they left, while Catholics fled from Protestant areas. The rioting and shooting spread across the province to Armagh, Strabane, Newry and Derry, where barricades were erected in the Nationalist Creggan and Bogside. Overall there were thirty-five people killed and more than a hundred bombings. Large-scale evacuations occurred that month, with over 7,000 Catholics fleeing to Irish Army camps across the border and to Dublin, while many Protestants fled to Liverpool.

Naturally enough, internment, instead of ending the violence during the following months, only served to increase it. Bombings, shootings and burnings continued unabated for the rest of the year – but worse was to follow.

On Saturday, 22 January 1972, British troops from the Parachute Regiment attacked a Nationalist demonstration outside the internment camp at Magilligan on the shores of Lough Foyle with batons and CS gas. The following week on 30 January a march organised by the Civil Rights Association in Derry set out from the Creggan on their way to Guildhall Square. They marched down the hill towards the Bogside and by the time they reached William Street they numbered over 15,000. The army then sealed off entrances to the Guildhall Square and the crowd turned towards 'Free Derry Corner' in the Bogside. As they turned towards the new assembly point youths in the march pelted the soldiers with stones and other missiles. The initial response of the British soldiers was relatively restrained but then the Paras of the First Parachute Regiment opened fire and killed thirteen men and wounded twelve others and one woman. Many of the dead and injured had been shot in the back, prompting the Derry coroner, Hubert O'Neill, to declare, 'It was sheer, unadulterated murder.'

Three days later, on 2 February, a large crowd of about 30,000 people marched on the British Embassy in Merrion Square in Dublin with sections of the crowd chanting 'Burn, Burn, Burn'.

The embassy windows were first of all smashed by a man wielding a hammer, and fire bombs were then hurled in through the smashed windows, setting the building on fire.

The IRA had gained control of the march and although it was supposedly organised by the Dublin Trade Unions, they were not sufficiently strong to maintain control. It was quite evident that the IRA had planned the whole thing.

Because of the increasing IRA activity the Lynch government introduced an Offences Against the State (Amendment) Bill in the Dáil. It gave sweeping powers to the police against the IRA. Both Fine Gael and Labour opposed the bill and when the final debate began on Friday 1 December 1972, the government side was facing defeat.

That same day two bombs exploded in Dublin, killing two people and injuring 127. Immediately Fine Gael announced that they would no longer oppose the bill and it was carried by 69 votes to 22. The following month another Loyalist bomb killed a bus conductor just off O'Connell Street in the city.

That same year (1972) the British government finally decided to get directly involved in Northern Ireland affairs by abolishing the government at Stormont and initiating direct rule from Westminster. In December 1973 the Sunningdale Agreement was agreed between the UK, the Republic of Ireland, and representatives of the Ulster Unionist Party and the Nationalist SDLP. It established an eleven-member power-sharing executive in Northern Ireland involving Unionists, Nationalists and the Alliance Party. There would also be a Council of Ireland representing both parts of the island.

The Republic made two concessions – the right of Northern Ireland to exist (contrary to Articles 2 and 3 of the Constitution of 1937) and that there would be no change in the status of Northern Ireland without the approval of the majority of its citizens. Unfortunately the agreement did not last very long – Brian Faulkner, the Unionist leader lost the support of his party, the IRA continued its bombing campaign and Ian Paisley, the extremist Protestant leader, opposed every part of it. The Loyalists then organised a workers' strike which paralysed the province, Faulkner resigned and the agreement collapsed.

On Friday 27 May 1974 the whole country was shocked when

twenty-three people (fifteen women, six men and two baby girls) were killed and over 100 injured in three car-bomb explosions in Dublin and five people were killed and twenty-eight injured in Monaghan. Two of the three cars had been hijacked in Belfast the day before.

For a short while in 1976 it appeared that the strength of public opinion might force the paramilitaries to desist. The catalyst was a horrible incident in Belfast where two IRA men were in a car being pursued by British soldiers. When the driver was shot dead the car plunged into Annie Maguire and her four children. Three of the children were killed and Annie was severely injured. Thousands of Catholic and Protestant women took to the streets in protest and their organisation became known as the 'Peace People'. The two founding members, Betty Williams and Mairead Corrigan, the latter an aunt of the Maguire children, were awarded the Nobel Peace Prize in 1976 for their work.

The destruction continued, however. In July the British Ambassador, Christopher Ewart-Biggs was killed when his car was blown up just outside his residence near Stepaside in south Dublin. In September a pub and a cinema in Dublin's Lower Abbey Street were bombed in protest against the government's introduction of legislation which would allow suspects to be detained for seven days without trial.

Another horrific assassination occurred on 27 August 1979 when Lord Mountbatten and two fifteen-year-old companions were killed when a bomb exploded on their fishing boat at Mullaghmore in County Sligo. The following month Pope John Paul II arrived in Ireland for a three-day visit and celebrated Mass in Dublin's Phoenix Park before a crowd of one million people. He later travelled north to Killineer just outside Drogheda and again celebrated Mass before a huge crowd and called for peace.

The British government had decided in 1976 to end the special category status of paramilitary prisoners and in protest the IRA prisoners in the 'H Blocks' in Long Kesh refused to wear prison-issue uniforms. The prison authorities then confined the prisoners to their cells and they in turn went on a 'dirty protest' where they refused to wash and smeared the cell walls with their excrement. By 1980 over 1,300 prisoners, including some Loyalists, were 'on the blanket'.

On 1 March 1981 Republican prisoners in the Maze prison in Northern Ireland began a hunger strike in an effort to win five concessions, including the right of political prisoners to wear their own clothes. The strike continued without the authorities yielding and on 9 April one of the strikers' leaders, Bobby Sands, was elected as MP for Fermanagh and South Tyrone. Sixty-six days after he began his hunger strike Sands died on 5 May. Others joined the hunger strike at various times and nine of them had died before the strike ended on 3 October, with the prisoners being more or less again granted political status.

The Irish general election of 1981 was won by a coalition led by Dr Garrett Fitzgerald of Fine Gael but in the Budget for that year he proposed a tax on shoes and resisted pleas that children's shoes should be exempt. The Coalition then collapsed when the socialist Independent TD for Limerick, Jim Kenny, withdrew his support.

After the subsequent general election of February 1982 Charles Haughey, now leader of Fianna Fáil, succeeded in wooing the Independents who held the balance of power. One of them was Tony Gregory, who represented a North Dublin inner city constituency. Haughey offered him an £80 million deal, including the building of 440 new houses in his constituency and the development of a 27 acre site at Dublin Port. The wheeling and dealing to gain the support of the fringe deputies led to a bizarre scene in Leinster House when the division bell for the crucial vote was sounded on 9 March 1982. Three Workers' Party deputies, Joe Sherlock, Paddy Gallagher and Proinsias de Rossa, had promised to vote for Haughey but found themselves outside the chamber of the House when the vital vote was to be taken. Undeterred, they burst into the press gallery, climbed into the distinguished visitors' gallery and then jumped down to the floor of the house just in time to vote!

A new coalition government of Fine Gael and Labour took office in 1983 and although it provided honest and competent government it was powerless against the rising tide of unemployment which engulfed the country.

In 1984 the then Taoiseach Garret Fitzgerald travelled to London to meet the British Prime Minister Margaret Thatcher to persuade her that some gesture must be made to assist nationalist SDLP in the North, because otherwise they would be overtaken by

On 29 September 1979 Pope John Paul II addressed a huge crowd at Killineer, Drogheda and speaking to 'all men and women engaged in violence' said 'On my knees I beg you to turn away from the paths of violence and return to the ways of peace.' Unfortunately his words were not heeded by the men of violence although his plea was supported by most Irish people.

———— ◎ ————

In July 1982 an extraordinary sequence of events began to unfold. First a young nurse named Bridie Gargan was attacked in Dublin's Phoenix Park as she was sunbathing beside her car. She later died in hospital from the horrendous wounds inflicted. Some days later an Offaly farmer named Donal Dunne was callously shot dead with his own shotgun by a man who pretended to buy the gun from him. An intensive police hunt for the killer finally ended in the south Dublin seaside village of Dalkey at the flat of the Attorney General, Patrick Connolly, where the killer, Malcolm MacArthur, was staying while Mr Connolly was in America on holiday. The whole affair was later described by Taoiseach Haughey as 'Grotesque, Unbelievable, Bizarre and Unprecedented'. The Labour TD, Conor Cruise O'Brien seized on the initials GUBU and so the 'GUBU factor' entered the lexicon of Irish political life.

———— ◎ ————

Dr Garrett Fitzgerald became leader of Fine Gael in 1977 and Taoiseach in 1981. The imposition of VAT on children's shoes in the budget of 1982 led to a Fianna Fáil government.

the more extreme Sinn Féin. Thatcher seemed to agree but later at a press conference, with Fitzgerald beside her, she made her famous 'Out! Out! Out!' statement, declaring that a united Ireland, a confederation of the two states, or a joint authority, were all 'out'.

After a suitable length of time, things began to move again and the culmination was the signing of the Anglo-Irish Agreement in November 1985. The Dublin government was given a say in Northern Ireland affairs through the Anglo-Irish Conference, and in return it recognised the status of the Northern state and that any change would have to be at the will of the majority of its citizens.

The Unionists were outraged but Thatcher was 'not for turning' and instructed the security forces to deal with any resistance with a firm hand.

In 1983 Gerry Adams took over the leadership of Sinn Féin at a time when the fortunes of the party were at a low ebb with the SDLP successfully winning the support of Nationalists and the IRA being increasingly isolated by a series of dreadful blunders in the late 1980s. On 8 November 1987 an IRA bomb went off in Enniskillen during a ceremony honouring the dead of the First World War. Eleven Protestants were killed, including a twenty-year-old girl called Marie Wilson. She and her father, Gordon Wilson, were buried under rubble by the blast and as she awaited rescue she held her father's hand and said, 'Daddy, I love you very much.' She died later in hospital and her father gave a remarkable display of Christian charity and forgiveness by saying that he bore no ill will or no grudge against her killers. 'God is good and we shall meet again,' he said.

The general election in 1989 resulted in Charles Haughey again becoming Taoiseach with the assistance of the Progressive Democrats party, which was mostly composed of ex-Fianna Fáil people, and led by Desmond O'Malley and Mary Harney. In the following year the British government made secret contacts with Sinn Féin and these culminated in a speech by Peter Brooke, the Secretary of State for Northern Ireland, on 9 November 1990, in which he said, 'An Irish Republicanism seen to have finally renounced violence would be able, like other parties, to seek a role in the peaceful political life of the community.' He added that the British government had 'no selfish or strategic or economic interest in Northern Ireland: our role is to help, enable and encourage'. The IRA responded by calling a three-day ceasefire over the Christmas period.

In 1991 Margaret Thatcher was succeeded as British Prime Minister by John Major and a year later Albert Reynolds became Taoiseach when Charles Haughey resigned over allegations that he knew of the tapping of journalists' phones in 1982.

Albert Reynolds became Taoiseach in 1992. He set out as his two principal aims the achievement of peace in Northern Ireland and prosperity in the Republic.

John Major succeeded Margaret Thatcher as Prime Minister
of England in 1991. Two years later he signed the
Downing Street Declaration with Albert Reynolds.

Reynolds then announced that his two top priorities were to achieve peace in Northern Ireland and prosperity in the Republic. He had become friendly with Major when they both held the Finance portfolio in their respective governments over the previous years and shortly afterwards Reynolds started talks about Northern Ireland with his friend. After some tough negotiations the two leaders signed the Downing Street Declaration in December 1993. It declared that Britain had 'no selfish, strategic or economic interest' in Northern Ireland and that it was 'for the people of the island of Ireland alone' to decide their future. The Irish side again recognised that unity would only come about with the consent of the majority and agreed to support moves to remove clauses in the Irish constitution that claimed sovereignty over the whole island.

In the North Ian Paisley reacted with fury, declaring that Major had 'sold Ulster to buy off the fiendish Republican scum'. The Loyalist paramilitary organisation, the UVF, however, said that the Downing Street Declaration posed no threat to the Unionist population.

The following year (1994) saw a ceasefire being declared by the IRA and this was followed six weeks later by a similar action by the Loyalist paramilitaries. These events were hailed by Albert Reynolds as 'the end of twenty-five years of violence, and the closure of a tragic chapter in our history'. Post-ceasefire talks in which all sides participated led to an agreement on Good Friday 1998 to set up a Northern Ireland Assembly that would share power with all parties who renounced violence. The principles of the Downing Street Declaration were re-affirmed and institutions were set up to end discrimination against Catholics. It was again agreed that Northern Ireland would remain within the United Kingdom as long as a majority wished it so.

The agreement was approved on 22 May 1998 by more than 70% of the North's voters, while in the Republic, more than 95% approved of changes in the Irish constitution which ended claims to sovereignty over Northern Ireland. Later that year both John Hume and David Trimble were awarded the Nobel Peace Prize for their good work but others, such as Taoiseach Albert Reynolds, British Prime Minister John Major, the US president Bill Clinton and the US Ambassador to Ireland, Jean Kennedy Smith, also deserve a lot of the credit.

Unfortunately the killing and bombing in Northern Ireland did not end on 22 May 1998. In August of that year a dissident Republican group set off a bomb which caused the deaths of twenty-nine people and injured many more in Omagh, County Tyrone. Other atrocities have followed in the intervening years but

John Hume was one of the founders of the Northern Ireland Civil Rights movement. His work to set up the Good Friday Agreement of 1998 was rewarded with the Nobel Peace Prize.

David Trimble, the Northern Ireland Prime MInister, shared the Nobel Peace Prize with John Hume in 1998 for their work towards peace in the province.

in 1999 a North-South Ministerial Council and other cross-border institutions were created in accordance with the British-Irish agreement. Early in 2000 the Northern Ireland Assembly was suspended because of deadlock over the decommissioning of weapons held by terrorist organisations and direct rule was again imposed but in June of that year the assembly resumed its functions.

At the time of writing (2002) the all-party assembly still functions in Stormont, the very symbol of monolithic Unionist rule, and with David Trimble of the Unionist party as Prime Minister, Mark Durkan of the SDLP as Deputy Prime Minister and Gerry Adams and Martin McGuinness of Sinn Féin as ministers, no one can deny that all has changed in the Northern state.

Another notable change in modern-day Ireland is the attitude of Irish people to the Catholic Church. The far more open and questioning society that is Ireland today has seen a greatly lessened power of the Church over people's lives. Subjects such as contraception, divorce and abortion that were once taboo prior to the advent of television began to be openly debated on programmes such as Gay Byrne's *Late, Late Show* on RTÉ and other radio and television shows hosted by, among others, Pat Kenny and Gerry Ryan.

Gerry Adams became leader of Sinn Féin in 1983 and was elected to
Westminster the same year. He refused to take his seat because
of the compulsory Oath of Allegiance to the queen.

In February 1991 the Irish Family Planning Association lost an
appeal against a prosecution for selling condoms in a Dublin store.
The government promised a review but the Catholic archbishops
of Dublin and Armagh warned of the 'dire consequences' which
would follow any lifting of the ban. Eventually anyone over
seventeen years was allowed to purchase them and today they are
freely available and no one passes the slightest heed.

The Irish Catholic Church's resistance to change was not helped
by a number of scandals involving some very well-known priests –
the most famous example being that of Bishop Eamonn Casey, who
was discovered to have had an affair and had fathered a child, and
Father Brendan Smyth who was imprisoned for sexually molesting
children.

Scandals such as these notwithstanding, Ireland is still one of the
most steadfast Catholic countries in Europe. Mass attendance,
while not as great as in earlier centuries, is still greater than that of
other Catholic countries such as Spain, France and Italy.

Over the last four decades Ireland has steadily evolved as a go-
ahead, self-confident and prosperous nation. An important
building block in this growth in prosperity was the white paper *A
Programme for Economic Expansion* compiled by TK Whitaker in
November 1958 which recommended a five-year programme

during which every effort should be made to attract foreign investment to the country, that protective tariffs should be removed to make Irish industry more competitive and that a target growth of 2% per annum should be set. The programme was enthusiastically supported by the energetic, efficient and pragmatic Taoiseach at the time, Seán Lemass

In 1962 Ireland's application to join the European Economic Community was refused, principally due to objections by the French led by Charles de Gaulle but with his retirement in 1969 the way was clear for both Ireland and Great Britain to join. In May 1972 over 83% of the Irish people voted 'yes' to membership and on 1 January 1973 Ireland was formally admitted to membership of the EEC.

In the succeeding years, planning, foreign investment and great work by the Irish Development Authority in attracting companies from the USA, Germany, the UK and other countries to set up in Ireland transformed the industrial scene. Generous grants along with the educated and skilled workforce prepared to work for relatively low wages all contributed. For the first time in its history Ireland was able to break free from the economic stranglehold of the UK. (Before entering the EU over 70% of exports went to the UK while by 1987 only about 34% did so.)

Ireland today looks with confidence to the future with its young, well-educated and forward-looking population. It can be said with truth that Ireland has indeed 'taken its place among the nations of the world'.

Index